Building and Maintaining a Data Warehouse

OTHER NEW BOOKS FROM AUERBACH

The Business Value of IT: Managing Risks, Optimizing Performance and Measuring Results
Michael D. S. Harris, David Herron, and Stasia Iwanicki
ISBN: 1-4200-6474-6

CISO Leadership: Essential Principles for Success
Todd Fitzgerald and Micki Krause
ISBN: 0-8493-7943-1

The Debugger's Handbook
J.F. DiMarzio
ISBN: 0-8493-8034-0

Effective Software Maintenance and Evolution: A Reuse-Based Approach
Stanislaw Jarzabek
ISBN: 0-8493-3592-2

The Ethical Hack: A Framework for Business Value Penetration Testing
James S. Tiller
ISBN: 084931609X

Implementing Electronic Document and Record Management Systems
Azad Adam
ISBN: 0-8493-8059-6

Implementing the IT Balanced Scorecard: Aligning IT with Corporate Strategy
Jessica Keyes
ISBN: 0-8493-2621-4

Information Security Cost Management
Ioana V. Bazavan and Ian Lim
ISBN: 0-8493-9275-6

The Insider's Guide to Outsourcing Risks and Rewards
Johann Rost
ISBN: 0-8493-7017-5

Interpreting the CMMI (R): A Process Improvement Approach, Second Edition
Margaret K. Kulpa and Kent A. Johnson
ISBN: 1-4200-6052-X

Knowledge Management, Business Intelligence, and Content Management: The IT Practitioner's Guide
Jessica Keyes
ISBN: 0-8493-9385-X

Manage Software Testing
Peter Farrell-Vinay
ISBN: 0-8493-9383-3

Managing Global Development Risk
James M. Hussey and Steven E. Hall
ISBN: 1-4200-5520-8

Patterns for Performance and Operability: Building and Testing Enterprise Software
Chris Ford, Ido Gileadi, Sanjiv Purba, and Mike Moerman
ISBN: 1-4200-5334-5

A Practical Guide to Information Systems Strategic Planning, Second Edition
Anita Cassidy
ISBN: 0-8493-5073-5

Service-Oriented Architecture: SOA Strategy, Methodology, and Technology
James P. Lawler and H. Howell-Barber
ISBN: 1-4200-4500-8

Six Sigma Software Development, Second Edition
Christine B. Tayntor
ISBN: 1-4200-4426-5

Successful Packaged Software Implementation
Christine B. Tayntor
ISBN: 0-8493-3410-1

AUERBACH PUBLICATIONS

www.auerbach-publications.com
To Order Call: 1-800-272-7737 • Fax: 1-800-374-3401
E-mail: orders@crcpress.com

Building and Maintaining a Data Warehouse

Fon Silvers

CRC Press
Taylor & Francis Group
Boca Raton London New York

CRC Press is an imprint of the
Taylor & Francis Group, an **informa** business

AN AUERBACH BOOK

CRC Press
Taylor & Francis Group
6000 Broken Sound Parkway NW, Suite 300
Boca Raton, FL 33487-2742

First issued in paperback 2019

© 2009 by Taylor & Francis Group, LLC
CRC Press is an imprint of Taylor & Francis Group, an Informa business

No claim to original U.S. Government works

ISBN-13: 978-1-4200-6462-9 (hbk)
ISBN-13: 978-0-367-38764-8 (pbk)

Library of Congress Cataloging-in-Publication Data

Silvers, Fon.
    Building and Maintaining a Data Warehouse / Fon Silvers.
        p. cm.
    Includes bibliographical references and index.
    ISBN 978-1-4200-6462-9 (alk. paper)
    1. Data warehousing--Handbooks, manuals, etc. I. Title.

QA76.9.D37S53 2008
005.74--dc22   2007048792

Visit the Taylor & Francis Web site at
http://www.taylorandfrancis.com

and the CRC Press Web site at
http://www.crcpress.com

CV 10.04.2019 1351

Dedication

This book is dedicated to my three lovely ladies

Deborah,

Emelie,

Cara

Contents

Preface

This book began years ago when I joined the Data Warehousing Team. We read the books and articles by Ralph Kimball and Bill Inmon. We spent years understanding the full meanings and ramifications of Data Warehousing concepts and methods. We lived with our successes and we lived with our failures. That is what sets this book apart from other Data Warehouse literature—the perspective of a data warehouse analyst who has created data warehouses and then lived with them.

When I began in Data Warehousing in 2000, I understood the concepts and principles easily enough. They made sense. Making those Data Warehouse concepts and principles happen in a data warehouse was an entirely different matter. I searched the Data Warehousing literature and found many pockets of very helpful information. Over the years, I have collected and assimilated those pockets of information. Colleagues have given me opportunities to share and refine those pockets of knowledge. Eventually, they melded together to form a single cohesive and holistic approach to Data Warehousing. That single approach is the subject and content of this book.

I invite you to agree or disagree, accept or modify the methods presented in this book as you apply them to your data warehouse. If you agree and accept the methods in this book, they will serve you well. If, however, you disagree and modify the concepts and methods in this book, you will find concepts and methods that more closely fit your data warehouse. Either way, you will find a set of concepts and methods, either from this book or in response to this book, which will serve you well in your data warehouse. After all, that is the purpose of this book— to answer the question: "How do I build a data warehouse?"

Thank you for reading *Building and Maintaining a Data Warehouse.* I enjoyed writing this book. Writing it was an opportunity to capture in one document the concepts, principles, and methods that are common throughout Data Warehousing. Writing such a book, without the normal pressures and deadlines of a data warehouse development project, has also given me the opportunity to reflect on and consider all aspects of Data Warehousing. My intention is that, as you read this book, you will also gain insights into Data Warehousing beyond the obvious databases and tables, and that reading this book will be as much or more of a learning and understanding experience for you as writing it was for me.

Acknowledgments

I thank my family for their patience and understanding as I wrote this book, especially my wife, Deborah, who reviewed and edited the manuscript as well as encouraged me throughout this entire journey. Many thanks go to Jack Rader for giving me my first opportunity in Information Systems, and mentoring me through my rookie years. I thank Kevin Lewis for inviting me to join the Data Warehousing Team, and, yes, I would like to join the team.

A lot of appreciation and gratitude goes to my colleagues who have mentored and inspired me through many Data Warehouse development efforts, including Kevin Lewis, Michael Feist, Naresh Agarwal, Brian Christjohn, Mark Beyer, Dan Koller, Carla Aber, Brian Terrell, Mike Steeves, Dennis Fortier, and Anthony Jones. I thank J.D. and Sue Anderson for allowing the children to spend the summer with them, so I could have the peace and quiet necessary to write this book. I thank God for making this book possible in so many ways. And, I thank Steve Olive, who years ago recognized a rookie who was in over his head and helped me succeed. Finally, I thank Auerbach Publishing for this opportunity.

The Author

Fon Silvers began his career in Information Systems as a one-person IS shop, doing everything from hardware, software, application development, and data entry. After completing his MBA with a concentration in Information Systems from the University of South Florida (Tampa), he moved to a position with a Fortune 500 company, which is where Silvers was introduced to Data Warehousing. While there, he participated in the creation of Data Warehouse solutions that included retail sales transactions, Online Analytical Process (OLAP) analytics, and real-time logistics transactions.

Introduction

Purpose

The purpose of this book is answer the question: "How?" How can a data warehouse team build a data warehouse, a data warehouse that actually works? It's very easy to build a data warehouse that incorporates all the Data Warehousing concepts and principles, and, yet, is useless. But, how to build a data warehouse that provides the answers needed by all the data warehouse customers, when they need it? That's difficult.

Building and Maintaining a Data Warehouse provides a cohesive and holistic approach to building a data warehouse. Written from the perspective of having created a successful data warehouse as well as a failed data warehouse, *Building and Maintaining a Data Warehouse* presents the success factors that should be achieved along with the failure factors that should be avoided. The Data Warehouse Philosophy presents, in Chapter 2, the concepts and principles that are the foundation of every data warehouse. In the chapters following, as data warehousing methods are presented and explained, these methods are presented within the context of the concepts and principles in the Data Warehouse Philosophy. By doing so, the Data Warehouse Philosophy provides a consistent focus.

Audience

Building and Maintaining a Data Warehouse is intended for four groups of people. First, those considering the creation of a data warehouse will find this book very helpful in scoping the work and magnitude of a data warehouse. Building a data warehouse is like building a house. Most of the work necessary to build a house, and a data warehouse, is neither visible nor obvious when looking at the completed product. Thus, an enterprise considering their first data warehouse will not perceive all the work necessary to create one by visiting existing data warehouses.

Building and Maintaining a Data Warehouse opens the hood and exposes the bits of work necessary to build a data warehouse.

The second are those who are currently building a data warehouse. Having jumped into Data Warehousing without the help of *Building and Maintaining a Data Warehouse*, a data warehouse team can become quickly overwhelmed. The areas of a data warehouse are presented individually and in sequence. By understanding how each piece of a data warehouse fits in the entire data warehouse, a data warehouse team is able to focus on each piece, making each piece fit correctly in its data warehouse.

The third are those who have a data warehouse. Having moved to the maintenance and support stage of a data warehouse, a data warehouse team begins to understand the relevance and impact of gaps in their data warehouse. *Building and Maintaining a Data Warehouse* identifies the pieces of the puzzle that fill those gaps, and how those pieces fill their gaps. Recognizing that a gap exists is the first step. Understanding where that gap exists is the second step. *Building and Maintaining a Data Warehouse* can guide a data warehouse team through these two steps to the third step: filling the gap.

Finally, the managers and planners who define the scope of a data warehouse are the fourth group of people. The success of a data warehouse begins in the planning stages, where the scope and boundaries of a data warehouse are defined. *Building and Maintaining a Data Warehouse* provides the big picture perspective necessary to understand the work inside the scope and boundaries.

Organization

The organization of *Building and Maintaining a Data Warehouse* is from general to specific, and left to right. Chapter 1 presents, in summary, an entire data warehouse. For those new to Data Warehousing, this provides a general outline and context for all the detailed elements of a data warehouse. Chapter 2 presents Data Warehousing concepts and principles that are the foundation of every data warehouse. These two chapters present the general information necessary to understand the detailed information presented in the subsequent chapters.

Chapters 3 through 10 present the detailed elements of a data warehouse and the work necessary to create a data warehouse, from left to right. Beginning with source data, *Building and Maintaining a Data Warehouse* follows the flow of data from its source to its home in a data warehouse to its use and consumption by data warehouse customers. These chapters present the nuts and bolts of a data warehouse. The methods presented in each subject area are presented so that they can be assimilated and incorporated individually as well as within the context of a holistic approach. These chapters serve as instructions, advice, examples, and reference material.

Time to Build a Data Warehouse

The best way to begin any endeavor, including a data warehouse, is to learn from those who have gone before. That is the approach of *Building and Maintaining a Data Warehouse*. Beginning with the foundation laid by Data Warehousing pioneers and visionaries Ralph Kimball and Bill Inmon, *Building and Maintaining a Data Warehouse* presents the knowledge, insights, and lessons learned of Data Warehousing. Having learned the concepts, principles, and methods from two decades of Data Warehousing, it's time to build a data warehouse.

Chapter 1

The Big Picture:
An Introduction to
Data Warehousing

Introduction

In 1977, Jimmy Carter was President of the United States, *Star Wars* hit the big screen, and Apple Computer, Inc. introduced the world to the first personal computer. Four years later, Ronald Reagan was president, Prince Charles and Lady Diana married, and IBM began selling its IBM PC. From that beginning, computing power started moving from the mainframe to the desktop. Soon thereafter, spreadsheets and word processing applications began their journey to replace clipboards and typewriters. By 1985, Mikhail Gorbachev was the leader of the Soviet Union, New Coke hit the shelves, and data was going everywhere. Even inside the mainframe computers, data was finding its own home. Supervisors, managers, and executives alike were no longer able to look at a single clipboard to find out how the business was performing. The data was hopelessly entrenched in applications and nooks and crannies that would never again see the light of day. Such was the origin of Decision Support Systems.

Decision Support Systems

Decision Support Systems allowed managers, supervisors, and executives to once again see the clipboard with all its information. The information, which previously had been on a clipboard, had become a report, either printed on paper or displayed on a screen. One report revealed one single business area. Another report revealed a different business area. By 1992, Windows® 3.1 was in the stores and Ralph Kimball and Bill Inmon were figuring out how to gather data from two business areas and figuring out how to warehouse the data of an enterprise (Figure 1.1).

> Ralph Kimball was a co-creator of the Xerox Star Workstation, the world's first commercially viable GUI application. Ralph was the founder and CEO of Red Brick Systems, the group which created an extremely fast RDBMS targeted specifically for data warehousing. When he authored *The Data Warehouse Lifecycle Toolkit*, Ralph introduced the Dimensional Data Model (discussed in Chapter 5, Database Design).

Kimball and Inmon, working separately, arrived at a common set of guidelines (or principles). These principles are:

> Bill Inmon was the creator of the Corporate Information Factory and Government Information Factory. In so doing, Bill also established many of the principles of Data Warehousing.

- **Subject Orientation**: Data will be grouped by subject, rather than author, department, or physical location. So, all manufacturing data goes together, and the sales data, and the promotions data, etc., regardless of where it came from.
- **Data Integration**: Even though data comes from separate applications, departments, etc., differences should be smoothed out so they have the same look and feel.
  - Form: When two data elements (e.g., phone numbers) have different layouts (e.g., 123-123-1234 and (123) 123-1234), one layout will be superimposed on both of them.
  - Function: When two data elements identify the same thing (e.g., a hammer) with two different names (e.g., part 32G and part B49), these two names will be replaced with one name.
  - Grain: When two data elements apply different hierarchies (e.g., region and district) to the same thing, or different levels of detail (e.g., miles and feet), the two data elements will be resolved to the same level of hierarchy or detail.
- **Nonvolatility**: Unlike the data in operational applications, which is discarded once the company is finished using it, the data in a data warehouse will remain in the warehouse.

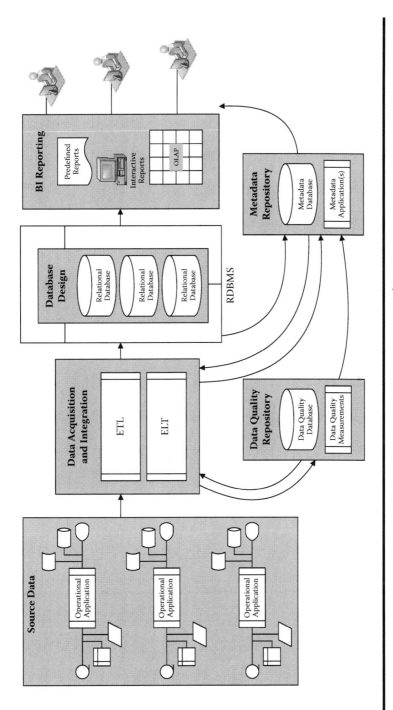

Figure 1.1   The big picture.

- **Time Variant**: All data has a context at a moment in time. A data warehouse will keep that context. So, all data from 1995 will retain its context within 1995.
- **One Version of the Truth**: The proliferation of data in the 1980s and 1990s yielded many copies of the same data. Only the one, true gold, standard copy of each data element would be included in a data warehouse.
- **Long-Term Investment**: A data warehouse should be flexible enough to absorb changes in the company and the world, and scalable enough to grow with the company. By doing so, a data warehouse can add value to the company for a long time.

Dimensional and Third Normal Form Data Models

Kimball and Inmon arrived at the same set of principles, yet each used completely different designs. Kimball created the Dimensional Data Model (Figure 1.2).

Also known as the Star Schema (because it resembles a star), a Dimensional Data Model has a distinct shape. In the middle is a Fact table (a Fact is an event, transaction, or something that happens at a single moment in time). Surrounding the Fact table are Dimension tables. Each Dimension table holds all the permutations of a single hierarchy of the company (e.g., geography: city, county, state, region, district, etc.; or time: second, minute, hour, day, fiscal week, payroll week, fiscal quarter, etc.).

Bill Inmon preferred the Third Normal Form Data Model (Figure 1.3). Rather than capture hierarchies and relationships in Dimension tables, the Third Normal Form allowed the data to have the same flexibility as the company.

Within the data warehousing community, a debate emerged. Which was better, the Dimensional Data Model or the Third Normal Form data model? By the twenty-first century, the answer was clear — both. Both designs had their strengths and their weaknesses. Rather than apply a "one size fits all" mindset, data warehouse designers learned to apply the strengths and avoid the weaknesses of both in each situation.

Storing the Data

While the debate between Dimensional Data Model and Third Normal Form Data Model was still going on, the data warehousing community was also deciding how to physically store the data. Three methods were found: a central Enterprise Data Warehouse (EDW), several distributed Data Marts, and an Operational Data Store (ODS).

The central EDW held all the data from all the business subjects in one database (Figure 1.4). The Data Mart held one subject area only (Figure 1.5). If another subject area were needed, then that would be another Data Mart. The best method of feeding data to a Data Mart was to integrate that data into an Enterprise Data Warehouse first and then send the data on to its Data Mart.

The Operational Data Store (Figure 1.6) lives on the other side of the EDW and retrieves operational data from the business, integrates the data, and stores the data in its own database. Unlike the EDW, the data in an ODS is volatile. Volatile means the ODS only stores the value for a data element (e.g., balance on hand) that is true at real-time (e.g., balance on hand as of right now). This is different from the non-volatile data in an EDW (e.g., balance on hand for every day for the past two years). When an ODS is present, the EDW can gather its data from the ODS rather than from the business. There's no need to ask the business the same question twice.

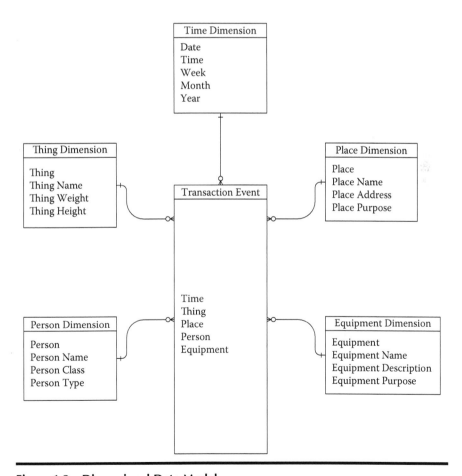

Figure 1.2   Dimensional Data Model.

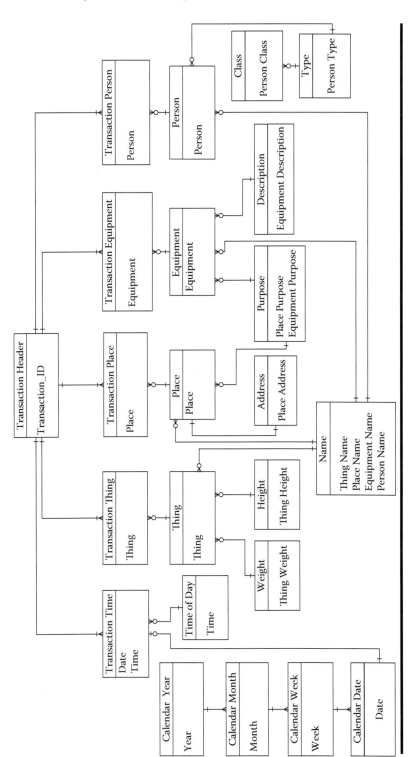

Figure 1.3   Third Normal Form Data Model.

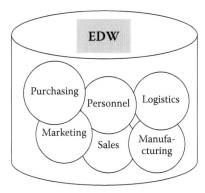

Figure 1.4 Enterprise Data Warehouse (EDW).

The set of applications that gather data from the business and bring that data into the data warehouse are called extract, transform, and load (ETL) applications. The ETL analyst is responsible for making the data warehouse philosophy happen.

- **Data Integration**: ETL applications integrate the data from the business, regardless of its origin, form, function, or grain.
- **Nonvolatility**: ETL applications introduce new data without destroying old data.
- **Time Variant**: ETL applications store the data with a key structure that points to a timeframe.
- **One Version of the Truth**: ETL applications reference only the one gold standard for every data element.
- **Long-Term Investment**: Populate data into a data warehouse, realizing the long-term flexibility of the data warehouse design.

Data Availability

The data inside a data warehouse is of no use to a business without a way to use that data. Business Intelligence Reporting, also known as BI Reporting, is a set of applications by which a business can harness data and information in a data warehouse. Data is individual bits of facts and figures. By itself, data tells the business very little. Information is the compilation of individual bits of data into an observation or conclusion, which adds value to the business.

BI Reporting includes various methods by which data and information can be available to the business. Predefined reports, a staple of all information systems, can disseminate answers to the same questions (e.g., who, how many, where) on a daily basis. Interactive reports allow the business to ask a new question, or revise an existing question, and then receive the answer. OLAP (online analytical processing)

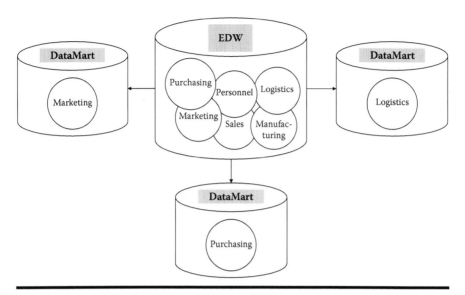

Figure 1.5   EDW and Data Marts.

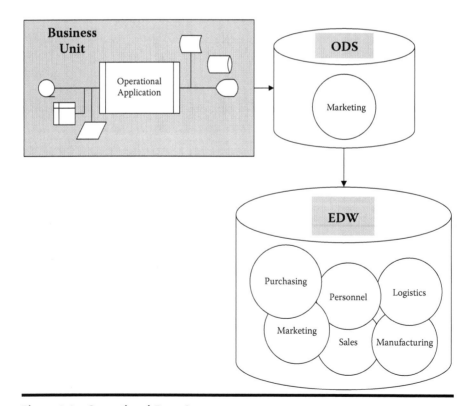

Figure 1.6   Operational Data Store.

reporting allows business analysts to drill up and down, left and right in stream of consciousness analysis. Using the Internet, all of these reporting options are available online. The next frontier of BI Reporting is data mining, the search for correlations in the business, which cannot be seen.

Metadata provides the background and context, which gives concrete meaning to the facts and figures in a data warehouse. Every four years, on the first Tuesday of November, all Americans use the same metadata — the number of voting precincts reporting. With 50 percent of the precincts reporting, no one believes the result. With 75 percent of the precincts reporting, we begin to take the result seriously. When 90 percent of the precincts have reported their numbers, we turn the TV off and go to bed; the election is over. Metadata in a data warehouse works the same way.

- How complete is the data?
- What is the formula for that number?
- When did the new numbers come in?

Like the number of precincts reporting, metadata in a data warehouse gives meaning and context to data.

Monitoring Data Quality

Finally, data quality is the continuous effort to monitor the accuracy, completeness, and confidence of the data in a data warehouse. The world is full of surprises, and some of them affect the data in a data warehouse. Only the naïve assume the business and its data warehouse live in a perfect world where nothing goes wrong. Diligently monitoring data before it enters the data warehouse, the goal is to deliver data and information from which a business can derive its strategic and tactical decisions with confidence.

The explosion of data and information truly was an explosion. The facts and figures of business found their own homes in accounting systems, inventory databases, and a myriad of home-grown applications, all of which help run the business. Data warehousing gathers and integrates that disparate data so the business, through its data, can be seen in one place.

Chapter 2

Data Warehouse Philosophy

Introduction

A data warehouse is an asset of an enterprise and exists for the benefit of an entire enterprise. It does not exist for the benefit of a single entity (e.g., business unit, individual customer, etc.) to the exclusion of all others in the enterprise. As such, data in a data warehouse does not conform specifically to the preferences of any single enterprise entity. Instead, a data warehouse is intended to provide data to the entire enterprise in such a way that all members can use the data in the warehouse throughout its lifespan.

Traditionally, an information system succeeds by satisfying specific requirements of a specific customer. A data warehouse, however, succeeds by satisfying the data needs of an entire enterprise, not just one entity. The "one size fits all" approach to data positions a data warehouse to fail in its mission to provide data to the whole enterprise. All data warehouses would fail in this mission were it not for the foundational principles created by the data warehousing pioneers and visionaries Ralph Kimball and Bill Inmon.

In the 1990s, Kimball and Inmon created and documented the concepts and principles of data warehouses, which today are the foundation of all data warehouses. These concepts and principles will not immediately equip a reader to design and develop a data warehouse; however, they will equip a reader to understand the reasons and intentions underlying data warehouse design. For that reason, these concepts and principles are collectively known as the *data warehouse philosophy*. The concepts and principles within the data warehouse philosophy guide the design and development of a data warehouse.

Inclusion of all elements of the data warehouse philosophy is not mandatory for the success of a data warehouse. Awareness of the elements of this philosophy, however, increases its success and value. A data warehouse designer may choose to include or exclude elements of the data warehouse philosophy. Such decisions should be made from the context of cognitive understanding of the philosophy.

The elements of the data warehouse philosophy are explained in the following sections. Those elements are:

- Enterprise Data
- Subject Orientation
- Integration
- Nonvolatility
- Time Variant
- Single Version of the Truth
- Long-Term Investment and Return on Investment (ROI)

Enterprise Data

A data warehouse should include data that is applicable to the enterprise. The value and relevance of a data warehouse is rooted in that data. If members of the enterprise perceive as superfluous or irrelevant the data in a data warehouse, those same members will cast that perception onto the data warehouse. This principle is not as restrictive as it seems. Frequently, data that is acted on by a single business unit is also relevant to the remainder of the enterprise. For example:

- The Accounting Department uses tax codes; members of other departments understand the relevance of tax codes to the enterprise.
- The Manufacturing Department uses part numbers; members of other departments understand the relevance of part numbers to the enterprise.

Tax codes are not directly applicable to the Manufacturing Department; however, they understand tax codes are relevant to the enterprise. Part numbers may not be directly applicable to the Accounting Department; however, they understand that part numbers are relevant to the enterprise.

Data that is not relevant to the enterprise is localized in its relevance. Localized relevance renders data irrelevant to the enterprise. For example:

- The Accounting Department maintains a list of notary publics in its office.

■ The Manufacturing Department keeps a list of machinists who own and use their own tools, including a designation for United States and metric tools.

The names and availability of notary publics are handy in the Accounting Department, but irrelevant to the rest of the enterprise. Likewise, a list of machinists and their tools helps the shop foreman assign individual tasks, but has little relevance to the rest of the enterprise.

Subject Orientation

Data in a data warehouse is organized around the business subjects of the enterprise.[1] Operational data is organized by its physical manifestations, including file names, job schedules, and application dependencies. A data warehouse does not present data, which reflects the physical manipulation of operational data. Instead, a data warehouse presents data, which reflects major subject areas within the enterprise.[2] For example:

■ **Business Entities**
  - Customers
  - Vendors
  - Agents
■ **Business Processes**
  - Sales
  - Receiving
  - Manufacturing
  - Distribution

Subject orientation of data allows a data warehouse to maintain its overall architecture throughout its lifespan. Individual data elements may change in the enterprise and in the data warehouse. The subject orientation of a data warehouse enables a data warehouse to absorb inevitable changes without drastic changes to its architecture.[3]

Data Integration

The data in a data warehouse is presented in a uniform manner. Uniformity allows data warehouse customers to query data across subject areas without traversing through data translations or look-ups from other data sources.[4] By integrating its data, a data warehouse presents a consistent and seamless statement of the enterprise, which relieves data warehouse customers of the need to reconcile differences and inconsistencies within data from disparate business areas. Data integration occurs in multiple ways, which can be combined into the following three groups:

- **Form**
- **Function**
- **Grain**

Form

Data form includes the types and layouts of data.[5] These are the way data is expressed. Disparate business units may express similar data elements in different ways. For example:

- Money can be expressed as currency or integer data types.
- Phone numbers can be expressed as (123) 123-1234 or 123-123-1234 or 123.123.1234.
- Names can be expressed as First Last or Last, First.

In a data warehouse, the disparate expressions of similar data elements (e.g., money, phone number, names, etc.) are integrated into a single form, which creates consistency within a data warehouse. This helps data warehouse customers query across business subjects.

Function

Function includes the substance and meaning of the data within the data element. Codes and cryptic values often differ between business units and must be reconciled so the entire organization can leverage these codes and values. For example:

- Part Status = 32B: In the Manufacturing Department, 32B means the manufacturing part is on back-order. This translation needs to be provided to others in the enterprise.
- Closing Code = 32B: In the Accounting Department, 32B means the financial statement is out of balance and cannot be closed. This translation needs to be provided to others in the enterprise.

Business units may use the same code or value with two distinct and separate meanings. For example, in the Accounting Department, 32B means "Out of Balance," while in the Manufacturing Department, 32B is a jacket size. Business units may use different codes or values with the same meaning. For example, the Marketing Department refers to a 30-second TV spot as a promotion, while the Distribution and Logistics Department refers to the same 30-second TV spot as an advertisement. In such cases, disparate data from business units must be integrated into one data element, which expresses the function of both.

Grain

Grain refers to the unit of measurement at which data is expressed.[6] Business units may store data using different units of measurement:

- Purchasing measures product by the barrel.
- Transportation measures product by the shipload.
- Sales measures product by the gallon.

In this scenario, a data warehouse will reconcile these different units of measurement, which will allow the integration of data from the Purchasing, Transportation, and Sales business units.

Grain can also refer to a hierarchical level. Individual people, objects, and events are organized into hierarchical groups. Business units may store data using different hierarchical groupings of people, objects, and events:

- A captain commands a vessel in the Third Fleet.
- Captain Roy P. Jones commands a vessel in the Third Fleet.
- A captain commands the USS Hawkins.
- Captain Roy P. Jones commands the USS Hawkins.

In this scenario, a data warehouse will reconcile these different levels of hierarchical grouping, which will allow the integration of data from the Personnel Department and the Third Fleet.

Grain of data has two physical implications for a data warehouse. First, fine grain data expresses more detailed information, but at a cost. The increased detail consumes increased resources to capture, store, and retrieve. Second, a data warehouse cannot provide data to customers at a grain lower than the grain at which it is stored.[7]

A data warehouse must integrate the Form, Function, and Grain of data from disparate business units. Once integrated, data warehouse customers can traverse data within business subjects from across the enterprise.

Nonvolatility

Data, once written to a data warehouse, is never deleted or updated.[8] Operational applications manipulate data to reflect only the current state of a business unit. A data warehouse reflects both the historical and current state of the enterprise by inserting new rows.[9] A data warehouse retains historical rows as well as the most recent rows, which allows a data warehouse to present data in the context of the past and the present. Nonvolatility allows a data warehouse to express the enterprise across time, by retaining that data.[10]

Time Variant

A data warehouse expresses the events of the enterprise across time.[11] Nonvolatile historical data allows a data warehouse to express historical enterprise events in their historical context. For example:

- During the month of January, Fred was the manager of store #1024. January net profit for the store totaled $140,000.
- During the month of February, Alice was the manager of store #1024. February net profit for the store totaled $70,000.
- During the present month, George is the manager of store #1024.

The presence of historical data allows analysis and comparison of these three store managers, even though they occurred at different times. An analyst can ask such questions as:

- What was the profitability of store #1024 when Fred was the manager?
- What was the profitability of store #1024 when Alice was the manager?
- What is the profitability of store #1024 now that George is the manager?

These questions can be answered by translating these questions into a surrogate question based on a simultaneous and coincidental event (e.g., the month).

- What was the profitability of store #1024 in January?
- What was the profitability of store #1024 in February?
- What is the profitability of store #1024 in the current month of March?

Stores will not normally (in fact, rarely) change store managers on a schedule that coincides with the change of the month. So, a business analyst cannot expect to track the performance of store managers by tracking months, expecting each month to represent a different store manager. A data warehouse facilitates the answers to the real questions (e.g., How profitable was each manager?) by allowing a business analyst to track the performance of the managers, regardless of the historical context. The historical data in a data warehouse provides answers to questions of historical events and conditions in this context, based on the events or conditions. A data warehouse does not require its customers to translate historical questions into their historical context because the data in a data warehouse has already framed its data in its historical context.

Time variant data allows a data warehouse to express the enterprise as of a moment in time.[12] That moment in time has a grain. A moment in time can be expressed as a millisecond, minute, hour, day, week, month, year, etc. In the context of digital versus analog, Time is analog. Information systems, however, can only capture Time digitally. Every expression of Time, therefore, is a digital representation of analog Time; hence, Time expressed as a millisecond, minute, hour, day, week, month, year, etc.[13]

Historical data allows a data warehouse to express the enterprise from three different historical contexts:[15]

- **As It Was**: In this context, a data warehouse can express states of the enterprise at the moment they occurred, including the moment the state began and ended. For example:
  - Fred was the manager of store #1024 during the month of January.
  - Alice was the manager of store #1024 during the month of February.
  - George is the manager of store #1024 now.
- **As It Is**: In this context, a data warehouse can superimpose the current (i.e., now) state of the enterprise over the entire history of the enterprise. All historical data is still present in the data warehouse, but not used in the result set returned to the data warehouse customer. For example:
  - George (the current manager) has always been the manager of store #1024.
- **As If Nothing Changed**: In this context, a data warehouse can superimpose a historical state of the enterprise over subsequent periods of the enterprise. All current (i.e., now) data is still present in the data warehouse, but not used in the result set returned to the data warehouse customer. For example:
  - Fred was the manager of store #1024 during the month of January.
  - Alice was the manager of store #1024 during the month of February.
  - Alice (not George) is the manager of store #1024 now.

Ralph Kimball authored these three variations of Time Variance. He named them Type 1, Type 2, and Type 3.[15] These three names have since become part of the data warehousing lexicon.

- **Type 1 (As it is)**: Cast all of history so the enterprise looks as it does now.
- **Type 2 (As it was)**: Express historical data as it was, with each data value as of its moment in history, retaining its context in time.
- **Type 3 (As if nothing changed)**: Cast the enterprise to look as if a change had not occurred.

The retention of nonvolatile historical data allows a data warehouse to express the enterprise within a historical context. This Time Variant principle is a significant difference from operational applications, which function in the now, rather than the past.

One Version of the Truth

For every question that can be answered by data, an enterprise will derive a myriad answers. For example:

> **Q**: How many widgets were assembled?
> **A**: Total number of widgets assembled — 32,000
> **A**: Total widgets net of scrap — 31,195
> **A**: Total widgets adjusted by Activity Costing — 32,120
> **A**: Total widgets approved by Quality Control — 31,148

These different answers illustrate the confusion that occurs when business units look at a question (How many widgets were assembled?) and actually see more than just that one question.

> **Q**: How many widgets were physically assembled?
> **Q**: How many widgets were successfully assembled?
> **Q**: How much assembly activity occurred in conjunction with the widgets?
> **Q**: How many widgets were assembled and approved by Quality Control?

A data element stores the answer to a question. The question is the definition of that data element. A data warehouse must define every data element so that all members of the enterprise will associate one and only one question with that data element. Having narrowed a data element down to one and only one question, a data warehouse must also provide one and only one answer to the question posed by that data element. By doing so, a data warehouse provides the truth (i.e., the true answer to the question posed by a data element) and only one version of that truth.[16]

The One Version of the Truth principle allows a data warehouse to express the entire enterprise. When all members of an enterprise look at a data element with a single understanding of its meaning, then members of the enterprise can use a data warehouse as a shared point of communication across the enterprise.

Long-Term Investment

A data warehouse achieves it greatest ROI through longevity and stability. As the number of subject areas integrated into a data warehouse increases, a data warehouse increases its expression of the enterprise. As time variant history accumulates in a data warehouse, it increases its ability to answer historical questions. A data warehouse must, therefore, be designed and developed as a long-term investment.

A data warehouse team cannot build the entire data warehouse in a single project. The cost would be too high and the delivery schedule would be too slow. Instead, a data warehouse begins with one or two business subjects (e.g., sales, transportation, manufacturing, etc.). Then, each subsequent data warehouse development effort adds another business subject, or a subset of a large or complex subject. Each individual data warehouse project should last only six to nine months. When the duration of an individual data warehouse project exceeds nine months, management typically begins to question the ROI of the project. As multiple individual data warehouse projects integrate multiple business subjects into a single data warehouse, that data warehouse presents a picture of the enterprise, a picture which becomes more complete and comprehensive as each business subject is added to that data warehouse. A data warehouse, therefore, is a long-term investment with a long-term horizon. In fact, a data warehouse may never express the entire enterprise. The success of a data warehouse is not its ability to express the entire enterprise; rather, the success of a data warehouse is its ability to return value to the enterprise using the business subjects included in that data warehouse.

The very first data warehouse project of an enterprise defines the enterprise-level architecture of the data warehouse. The decisions made during the first data warehouse project will lay the foundation for all subsequent data warehouse projects within the enterprise. Physically, these decisions will lay the foundation for the platforms and infrastructures that will be the data warehouse. Logically, these decisions lay the foundation for the subject areas, entities, attributes, and processes as they are captured in a data warehouse. These architectural and foundational decisions will enable, or prevent, the data warehouse and its customers as they include new and additional subject areas in subsequent development efforts. The long-term nature of a data warehouse means the "return" of a data warehouse exists significantly beyond the "investment." If done correctly, the investment should be of a short duration, and the return should extend for years, if not decades.

References

1. Mark Peco, *TDWI Data Warehousing Concepts and Principles: An Introduction to the Field of Data Warehousing*, TDWI World Conference (The Data Warehousing Institute: Renton, WA, 2004).

2. William H. Inmon and Richard D. Hackathorn, *Using the Data Warehouse* (New York: John Wiley & Sons, 1994).
3. William H. Inmon, Claudia Imhoff, and Ryan Sousa, *Corporate Information Factory* (New York: John Wiley & Sons, 1998).
4. Inmon and Hackathorn, *Using the Data Warehouse*.
5. Inmon, Imhoff, and Sousa, *Corporate Information Factory*.
6. Inmon and Hackathorn, *Using the Data Warehouse*.
7. William H. Inmon, *Building the Data Warehouse*, 2nd ed. (New York: John Wiley & Sons, 1996).
8. Peco, *TDWI Data Warehousing Concepts and Principles*.
9. Inmon and Hackathorn, *Using the Data Warehouse*.
10. Inmon, Imhoff, and Sousa, *Corporate Information Factory*.
11. Peco, *TDWI Data Warehousing Concepts and Principles*.
12. Inmon and Hackathorn, *Using the Data Warehouse*.
13. Inmon, Imhoff, and Sousa, *Corporate Information Factory*.
14. Ralph Kimball, *The Data Warehouse Lifecycle Toolkit: Expert Methods for Designing, Developing, and Deploying Data Warehouses* (New York: John Wiley & Sons, 1998).
15. Ibid.
16. Louis Agosta, *The Essential Guide to Data Warehousing* (Upper Saddle River, NJ: Prentice Hall PTR, 2000).

Chapter 3

Source System Analysis

Introduction

A data warehouse expresses the enterprise through its data. An enterprise can be any organization capable of funding, owning and operating a data warehouse, including a corporation, educational institution, department or extremely solvent individual. A data warehouse expresses an enterprise, much like a mirror expresses a reflection, by reflecting the subject areas, entities, attributes and processes of that enterprise by the data structures in the data warehouse and the data which is integrated into those data structures. Applications retrieve data from the enterprise and load this data into a data warehouse. That expression of the enterprise, therefore, begins within the enterprise; begins with the data within the enterprise. To express the enterprise via a data warehouse, a data warehouse designer must understand the enterprise, its environment, processes, and the data within the enterprise as well as the data surrounding the enterprise.

Source system analysis (Figure 3.1) is thought by some to be strictly a tool dedicated to the design of data acquisition and integration applications.[1] To the contrary, source system analysis provides significant insight and understanding of the enterprise and its data, which is vital to the success of all phases of data warehouse design and development. A data warehouse cannot express the enterprise at any level (data model, data acquisition and integration, or business intelligence reporting) without a thorough and insightful understanding of the enterprise and its data.

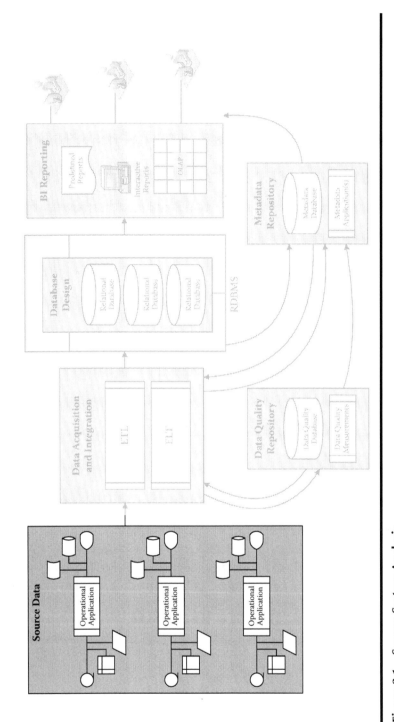

Figure 3.1   Source System Analysis.

Source system analysis is exactly that: an analysis of the enterprise via an analysis of its data. During source system analysis, a data warehouse designer focuses solely on the enterprise, with no thought whatsoever of how it will be expressed in a data warehouse. The Source System Analysis methods, which are discussed in the following sections, are intuitively easy to understand and perform. These analysis methods remove preconceptions about enterprise data that are the result of familiarity with that data. At the end of Source System Analysis, a data warehouse designer should understand the agents, entities, and processes of the enterprise, yet be no closer to the design of a data warehouse.

An early and common mistake in data warehouse design is the use of Source System Analysis to search for source data within the enterprise. When a data warehouse designer is confident that he or she possesses sufficient knowledge of the enterprise to create a data model, which captures and expresses the enterprise, Source System Analysis is then used to search for data that fits the definition of the data warehouse. This backward approach results in a data warehouse that expresses the data warehouse designer's preconceptions rather than the enterprise's. Having put the cart before the horse, the data warehouse designer has designed a square hole and uses Source System Analysis to search for a square peg to fill it. Invariably, this misuse of Source System Analysis results in an abbreviated and erroneous understanding of the enterprise and a misstatement of the enterprise in a data warehouse,[1] and possibly rework that is significant. The discrepancies created by this backward approach may eventually require the data warehouse team go back to Source System Analysis to revisit the data within the enterprise.

The source system itself may be an obstacle to Source System Analysis. No human endeavor ever results in perfection. This truth applies to architecture, medicine, and information systems. The subject matter expert (SME) who is in charge of, and responsible for, a source system may prefer to simply tell about the source system, rather than expose the source system to the scrutiny of a Source System Analysis. There may be a valid reason for this hesitation— or there may not. Either way, the data warehouse designer performing the Source System Analysis will need to employ comforting and reassuring social skills, possibly political skills, or some other tactic. But, the bottom line is the data warehouse designer must be allowed to query and survey the enterprise data, not just a summary or description of the enterprise data.[2] Without the information provided by a survey of the enterprise data, the design of a data warehouse cannot continue and cannot be considered complete.

Source System Analysis examines enterprise data for its informational content—the meaning of the data and how it captures and expresses that meaning. This examination is discussed in the following sections: Source System Analysis Principles and Source System Analysis Methods. The Principles explain what the data warehouse designer is looking for. The Methods explain how the data warehouse designer examines the source system.

- ■ **Source System Analysis Principles**
  - System of Record
  - Entity Data
  - Transaction Data
  - Snapshot Data

- ■ **Source System Analysis Methods**
  - Data Profile
  - Data Flow
  - Data State
  - System of Record

Source System Analysis Principles

Source System Analysis principles identify what the data warehouse designer is looking for when examining enterprise data. These are the questions that guide the examination of a source system. Enterprise data is observed for its operational content as well as for its nature and interaction within the enterprise.

System of Record

Frequently, separate business units and applications within an enterprise will maintain their own copy of a set of data. A data element central to the core function of an enterprise may be copied within every business unit. In this maze of copies, the Source System Analysis is looking for the point of origin,[3] the one dataset, application, etc., that is recognized by the enterprise as the authoritative expression of that data element.[4]

An enterprise may divide a data element among multiple systems of record. This may happen for operational or political reasons. For example:

- ■ The enterprise manufactures replacement automobile parts. The search for an authoritative expression of those automobile parts yields multiple systems of record:
  - Drivetrain parts (domestic)
  - Drivetrain parts (import)
  - Chassis parts (domestic)
  - Chassis parts (import)
  - Body parts (domestic)
  - Body parts (import)
- ■ The enterprise sells home improvement products through a series of retail outlets. A search for an authoritative expression of those retail outlets yields multiple systems of record:

- Retail outlets (West Division)
- Retail outlets (East Division)
- Retail outlets (recently merged, but not yet integrated)

■ These examples of multiple Systems of Record should lead the data warehouse designer to ask two questions: Do the multiple Systems of Record indicate that the single data element (e.g., product, retail outlet) is actually multiple data elements? If so, then the single data element (e.g., product, retail outlet) is actually a bit of language shorthand, which combines separate data elements to make discussing them easier. Members of the enterprise will use shorthand language to render their documentation and discussions cleaner and easier (for those in the enterprise) to understand. This is similar to the common practice of referring to a dog as a dog. Within the word *dog* is a myriad individual species. But, rather than name all the species, we simply use the word dog.

■ Do the multiple Systems of Record indicate that a single data element is fragmented within the enterprise and must be recombined into a complete and cohesive data element in the data warehouse? If so, then Source System Analysis has identified an early requirement for the data acquisition and integration phase of data warehouse design and a risk to the quality of data in the data warehouse.

Source System Analysis includes a search for those datasets, applications, etc. that are the original and authoritative expression of the data within the enterprise. This search will provide insights into enterprise data elements and their point of origin.

Entity Data

Source System Analysis includes a search for the data that defines, describes, and qualifies the entities of the enterprise.[5] Enterprise entities include the physical and logical members, agents, facilities, and resources within an enterprise. An excellent way to identify entities within the enterprise is to document all the business processes of the enterprise using only simple sentences with no pronouns. Using this method, the nouns (names and proper titles) are most likely the entities of the enterprise. The difficulty of this method is understanding the business processes of the enterprise well enough to document them with simple sentences. This method will yield two classes of entities: physical and logical.

■ Physical entities can be touched and include machines, buildings, people, and hardware. These are the people and facilities that are the material manifestation of the enterprise. Physical entities can be uniquely identified (e.g., part number, employee number, facility number, etc.). Instances of physical entities can also be identified (e.g., lot number, vehicle identification number, serial number, etc.). Physical entities can also be described and qualified (e.g., color, region, size, etc.).

■ Logical entities cannot be touched and include calendar, class, type, and status. Although they cannot be touched, logical entities are equally real and relevant to the enterprise. These are the concepts, constructs, and hierarchies that organize and enhance the meaning of enterprise events and entities. Logical entities can be uniquely identified (e.g., regulatory statutes, organizational hierarchy, etc.); however, instances of logical entities cannot exist and, therefore, cannot be uniquely identified. Logical entities can be described and qualified, the same as physical entities.

  – Without a logical "weekday" entity, all days would be the same day.
  – Without a logical "geography" entity, all places would be here, and none there.

We use logical entities on a daily basis with a tangible perception of their reality. So, it may seem a bit odd to think of a day or job title as a logical construct. But, they are. While one company defines Sunday as the first day of the week, another defines Sunday as the last day of the week. While one job title imbues specific authority, another job title does not. By these logical constructs (e.g., business week and chain of authority) a company is able to organize itself.

Entities, both physical and logical, can identify themselves. Also, entities can describe and qualify each other by their association. For example:

■ Building #10 can identify itself as a unique physical facility as well as identify the location of employee #AB-132.
■ Employee #AB-132 can identify himself or herself as a unique person as well as identify the manager of the Parts Department.
■ The Parts Department can identify itself as a unique enterprise department as well as identify the retail distributor of all products within the class "Replacement Parts."
■ The class "Replacement Parts" can identify itself … and so on.

Entity data manifests itself in multiple forms. The form may mislead the data warehouse designer. The function and form of entity data must be considered together. Later, during data warehouse design, this information will be vital to an accurate data warehouse design. The permutations of function and form discussed below are:

■ Arithmetic Data
■ Absolute Arithmetic Data

- Relative Arithmetic Data
- Numeric Data That Isn't Arithmetic
- Alphanumeric Data

This list of function and form permutations is not exhaustive. It does, however, demonstrate that you can't judge a book by its cover and you can't assume an entity's function from its form.

Arithmetic Data

Arithmetic data applies a measurement to an entity. Such measurements include miles per hour, units of work, length, etc. Arithmetic data is applied to an entity and, therefore, is not an entity or entity identifier. An arithmetic description of an entity must be accompanied by a unit of measurement, otherwise, the measurement has no meaning. The unit of measure identifies the rate of movement (speed), activity (work), or existence (physical dimensions) identified by the arithmetic data.[6]

The unit of measurement can be either explicit or implicit. An explicit unit of measurement is expressed by an accompanying unit of measure data element (e.g., liters, dollars, units, etc.). A unit of measurement is implicit when arithmetic data is accompanied by a unit of measure, which is assumed, implied, or expressed by alternative means. For example:

- **Assumed unit of measure**
  - Age (in years)
  - Distance (in miles)
- **Implied unit of measure**
  - 2 × 4 piece of wood (in inches)
  - 24 × 7 (in hours and days)
- **Unit of measure by alternative means**
  - The name of a data element is the unit of measure—a field named "Miles" indicates the unit of measure is Miles.
  - The meaning of a data element is a formula—miles/hour = a field named "Miles Per Hour" indicates the unit of measure is miles per hour.

The data type of arithmetic data can be misleading. Enterprise applications may use large numeric data types to store small numbers. A large data type will allow large numbers, regardless of its intended use. During Source System Analysis, a data warehouse designer will look for discrepancies between each data type and its use. Eventually, when least expected, an enterprise application will write a large number into a large numeric data type. If the data warehouse is not aware of, and prepared for, this circumstance, the large number will become a problem for a data warehouse.

Absolute Arithmetic Data

Absolute arithmetic measurements are arithmetic measurements that are complete within themselves. They express completely an arithmetic measurement within a transaction event. For example:

- The amount of currency consumed in a transaction.
- The quantity of products purchased in a transaction.

In these cases, the amount and quantity express completely the currency and quantity in a transaction and, therefore, are absolute.

Relative Arithmetic Data

Relative arithmetic measurements are arithmetic measurements that are incomplete within themselves. They are incremental and require a context arithmetic value. Without a context, Relative Arithmetic Data has no meaning. For example:

- Balance on Hand was increased by two units. This does not tell the new BoH.
- Federal Reserve increased prime interest rates by 0.25 percent. This does not tell the new prime interest rate.

In these cases, the amount and quantity are relative to a previous arithmetic value, which is the context. Given that context, and only in that context, Relative Arithmetic Data has meaning.

Numeric Data That Isn't Arithmetic

Data written in a numeric data type may not necessarily apply a measurement to an enterprise entity. Such cases can include codes (e.g., zip code), flags (e.g., 1 = on), or unique identifiers (e.g., version number, sequence number, etc.). Nonarithmetic data does not require an accompanying unit of measure (explicit or implicit). In the context of nonarithmetic data, the inclusion of a unit of measure would be nonsense (e.g., part number 321145 liters).

Nonarithmetic numeric data usually occurs when the enterprise needs to uniquely identify multiple instances of an entity. Common examples include building number, part number, and employee number. The numbers used to identify such enterprise entities do not have arithmetic properties.

This information will be useful in data warehouse design. If these numbers are brought into the data warehouse as numeric data, data warehouse customers will be tempted to perform arithmetic operations on them. Also, if a source system uses a large numeric data value (e.g., a 32-digit unique identifier), the data warehouse Relational Database Management System (RDBMS) will consume unnecessary space if it tries to store this data value as a 32-digit number. Since the 32-digit unique identifier has no arithmetic properties, the data warehouse RDBMS can conserve its resources by storing the data value as a 32-character text value.

Alphanumeric Data

Data written as alphanumeric data type provides names, codes, and text descriptions, which identify, describe, and qualify enterprise entities. Alphanumeric data has no arithmetic or measurement properties. The meaning of alphanumeric data corresponds to the meaning of the text inside the data element.

An enterprise application may choose to write only numbers into an alphanumeric data element. During Source System Analysis, a data warehouse designer will look for discrepancies between each data type and its use. Eventually, when least expected, an enterprise application will write an alphanumeric character into an alphanumeric data type, which had previously stored only numbers. If the data warehouse trusts the enterprise to write only numbers into an alphanumeric data type, without preparing for the possibility of alphanumeric data, the alphanumeric data will become a problem for that data warehouse.

Granularity

The grain of data is determined by its level of detail,[7] hierarchical depth,[8] or measurement precision.

- The level of detail refers to the specificity and uniqueness by which data identifies an enterprise entity, or instance of an enterprise entity. Data that identifies the exact person involved in a transaction is more granular than data that identifies the job class of that person.
- Hierarchical depth refers specificity and uniqueness within the context of an enterprise organizational structure. The top of the hierarchy is least granular. The bottom of the hierarchy is most granular and closest to uniquely identifying a specific instance of an enterprise entity.
- A measurement that uses a small unit of measure (e.g., millimeter) is more precise and granular than a measurement that uses a larger unit of measure (e.g., meter).

A data warehouse designer must be aware of the grain of all source data elements. Grain is relevant to the design of a data warehouse because separate business units may use the same entity at different grains. When a data warehouse juxtaposes entities from across the enterprise, the least granular entity or measurement is the grain of that juxtaposition. Data warehouse customers, from those business units as well as others, will have an expectation of the grain of data with which they work. The grain of data in a data warehouse, therefore, must be a designed decision, which can be understood by the enterprise.

Latency

Latency refers to the time gap between an enterprise event (e.g., a new entity is created, an existing entity changes state, a transaction occurs, etc.) and its expression in enterprise data. Latency is built into the business and operating cycles of an enterprise. For example:

■ Transactions occur throughout the day, but are uploaded once each night.
■ Payroll updates are accumulated throughout the week and applied prior to generating payroll checks.
■ Purchase orders are placed online in a real-time user interface.

Latency determines the earliest moment data will be available to the data warehouse. Data cannot appear in a data warehouse until it first appears in the enterprise. The latency built into enterprise data is an important consideration, as it directly affects the earliest moment data will be available in a data warehouse.

Transaction Data

Transaction data is also known as Event data. Transaction and Event data identify the moment when an enterprise performs its primary functions. Again, a good way to identify Transactions or Events within the enterprise is to document all the business processes of the enterprise, using only simple sentences with no pronouns. Using this method, the verbs are most likely the transactions of the enterprise. The difficulty of this method is understanding the business processes of the enterprise well enough to document them with simple sentences. For example:

■ **Sales**: The moment when a retail enterprise sells something.
■ **Manufacturing**: The moment when an assembly plant builds something.
■ **Service**: The moment when a consulting firm provides a service.

Transaction and Event data also identify the moment when an enterprise performs those secondary functions, which enable it to perform its primary functions.

■ **Sales**
  – Primary: The moment when a retail enterprise sells something.

- Secondary: The moment when product is ordered.
- Secondary: The moment when product is delivered.
- Secondary: The moment when product is invoiced.
- Secondary: The moment when the invoice is paid.
- Secondary: The moment when product is received.
- Secondary: The moment when product is placed on the shelf.

■ **Manufacturing**
  - Primary: The moment when an assembly plant builds something.
    - Secondary: The moment when an order is received.
    - Secondary: The moment when parts are ordered.
    - Secondary: The moment when parts are delivered.
    - Secondary: The moment when parts are invoiced.
    - Secondary: The moment when the invoice is paid.
    - Secondary: The moment when product is assembled.
    - Secondary: The moment when product is inspected by Quality Control.
    - Secondary: The moment when product is certified by Quality Control.

■ **Service**
  - Primary: The moment when a consulting firm provides a service.
    - Secondary: The moment when a customer is identified.
    - Secondary: The moment when a customer requests a service.
    - Secondary: The moment when a consultant is identified.
    - Secondary: The moment when a consultant signs a contract.
    - Secondary: The moment when a customer interviews a consultant.
    - Secondary: The moment when a customer accepts a consultant.
    - Secondary: The moment when a customer signs a contract.
    - Secondary: The moment when a consultant begins work for a customer.
    - Secondary: The moment when a consultant ends work for a customer.

Typically, Transaction data includes the following elements:

- **Who**: The entities that are active during the enterprise event. In an enterprise event, the active entities may be people, corporations, governments, or government agencies. Typically, active entities have the free will (unless acting by proxy) to participate or not participate in the event.
- **Action**: The function (primary or secondary) that was performed. The Action is the activity (e.g., buy, sell, deliver, etc.) that was performed by the active entities in the event.
- **What**: The entities that are passive during the enterprise event. In an enterprise event, the passive entities may be product, property, or logical entities.

Passive entities have no free will and cannot choose to participate or not participate in the event.
- **Where**: The geographic place of the Action.
- **When**: The temporal time of the Action.
- **Why**: The meaning or motivation for the event. Of all the elements of Transaction data, Why is most optional. Enterprise entities may not be required to reveal a reason or motivation. Sometimes a reason is included for management oversight. In such cases, the reason is probably a fabrication.

Snapshot Data

Snapshot data expresses the cumulative effect of a series of transactions or events over a range of time. For example:

- Web site hits per hour
- Ball bearings assembled per hour

Snapshot data may be used when the individual events (e.g., Web site hits per hour) are simultaneously too insignificant individually and numerous collectively to justify the capture and storage of each individual event. If the operational system is not able to uniquely identify each individual instance of a Transaction or Event, a data warehouse will also be unable to uniquely identify each individual instance of a Transaction or Event. Snapshot data may also be used when the enterprise specifically requires cumulative data (e.g., ball bearings assembled per hour).

Snapshot data is less granular than individual Transaction data. During Source System Analysis, no judgments should be made regarding which data (Snapshot or Transaction) will be included in a data warehouse. Instead, Source System Analysis should only document the presence of either data (Snapshot or Transaction). The decision to include either or both will be made during data warehouse design, not Source System Analysis.

Source System Analysis Methods

The methods and activities of Source System Analysis are a search to understand how the enterprise and its data interact. System documentation provides information about how an enterprise system is intended and expected to behave. This is a good start. But, it is only a start. Source System Analysis should document this information. The intended and expected behavior and interaction of enterprise data is a good baseline from which to start. Source System Analysis, however, should also document how an enterprise system misbehaves, creating unexpected data and results.[9]

Source System Analysis is a data warehouse designer's opportunity to find those pockets of the enterprise system that are fraught with anomalies. The reason is simple. Most members of an enterprise do not know about the anomalies that already exist in enterprise applications and data. If anomalous enterprise data is integrated into a data warehouse, data warehouse customers will perceive the data warehouse to be the source and cause of the anomalous data. They never saw the anomalous data in their enterprise data, but, now they see the anomalous data in a data warehouse. The data warehouse, therefore, must be the cause of the anomalous data and should not be trusted or used. Source System Analysis is, therefore, the first opportunity to protect the quality of the data in a data warehouse, which also protects the data warehouse.

Data Profile

A Data Profile provides multiple cross sections of enterprise data. These cross sections fall into four basic groups: Data Stores, Data Elements, Data Entities, and Data Model. Each group is intended to provide a cross section description of enterprise data in terms of where data is stored (inventory of Data Stores), what is stored in the data (inventory of Data Elements), how the data is grouped (inventory of Data Entities), and how the data elements relate to each other (Data Model).

■ **Inventory of Data Stores**: This is a list of the physical hardware on which the enterprise places its applications and data. This will provide information about the availability, nature, interface, and security requirements of enterprise data.
  – Servers: The physical platforms that do the work of the enterprise. The inventory should indicate the physical location of servers, operating systems, applications, and interface requirements.
  – Databases: The physical storage of enterprise data. The inventory should include the operating system, database system, and version, and a list of physical databases, tables, views, macros, etc. For each data structure, the inventory of databases should provide the Data Definition Language (DDL), including constraints and relationships.
  – Directories: The physical placement of data in directories. The inventory should include a list of network locations, directories and subdirectories, and the files they contain.
  – Files: The physical placement of data in datasets. The inventory should include a list of files, including file name, path, and layout.
  – Physical and logical partitions: The physical work of the enterprise is divided among various servers. Sometimes this division of work is physical and sometimes the division is logical. The inventory should indicate the physical location of the work of the enterprise.

- Caveat: Any published discussion of the physical manifestations of hardware and software is obsolete before it hits the shelf because hardware and software technology changes constantly. So, if at the reading of this book, the physical manifestations in this chapter (e.g., servers, databases, files, etc.) are no longer in common use, then please apply the goal of an Inventory of Data Stores (identify the physical objects and geographic locations on which source system data resides) to the physical hardware or software in use.

■ **Inventory of Data Elements**
  - Name: The name by which applications reference a data element. Members of the enterprise may have shorthand names for a data element (e.g., the Item file, the list of Items, etc.). Source System Analysis should reconcile all the shorthand names for each physical data element.
  - Format: The layout or DDL for each data element. A single data element may have multiple layouts (e.g., COBOL Redefines, Structured Query Language (SQL) Substring, etc.). The layout should indicate all of the layouts for each data element.
  - Domain of values: When a data element has a known set of values (e.g., Yes or No, Male or Female, provinces of Canada, etc.), the inventory should provide a list of those values.[10]
  - Range of values: When a data element has an infinite and bounded set of values (e.g., Product cost, Assembly throughput, etc.), the inventory should provide the upper and lower boundary values.
  - Frequency of distinct values: A list of distinct values and the number of occurrences of each. In SQL, Select Field_1, count(*) as Freq from Table 1 group by Field_1. The results of a list of distinct values and their frequency are often surprising to both the data warehouse designer and the SME. This method has the potential to reveal unexpected data and data anomalies.
    ■ Most frequent distinct values: The distinct values that occur most often. These are typically the expected and accepted values. In SQL, Select Field_1, count(*) as Freq from Table 1 Group by Field_1 Order by Freq Desc.
    ■ Least frequent distinct values: The distinct values that occur least often. These are typically the unexpected and anomalous values. In SQL, Select Field_1, count(*) as Freq from Table 1 Group by Field_1 Order by Freq Asc.
      - Histogram of enterprise activity: The data in enterprise systems chronicles the activity (e.g., manufacturing, sales, contracts, etc.) of the enterprise. This activity occurred through time, across geographic locations, and within hierarchical levels of the enterprise. A histogram of this activity will reveal trends and patterns within the enterprise. Time, geography, and hierarchy are not

the only possible histograms, just the most universally helpful. Another histogram may prove to be equally or more revealing and helpful.

■ Activity by time (e.g., years, months, days): A histogram of enterprise activity by calendar years, months, and days will reveal the cardinality of enterprise activity as represented in time by the data of the enterprise. Invariably, some data will predate the enterprise because some operational application will not prevent someone from inputting a date value in the 1800s, or some data will show future activity because another operational application will not prevent someone from inputting a date in the 2900s. A histogram of enterprise activity in time will highlight such aberrations in enterprise data.

■ Activity by geography (e.g., region, large municipality, small municipality): A histogram of enterprise activity by physical geographic locations will reveal the cardinality of enterprise activity as represented geographically by the data of the enterprise. Invariably, some data will show states, provinces, and countries that do not exist because some operational application does not validate input geographic values, and the multiple permutations and abbreviations of states, provinces, and countries are nearly infinite and can be found somewhere in enterprise data. A histogram of enterprise activity by physical geographic locations will highlight such aberrations in enterprise data.

■ Activity by hierarchy (e.g., corporation, division, department, subdepartment): A histogram of enterprise activity by the hierarchical level of the enterprise entities (e.g., people, buildings, products) involved in the activity will reveal the cardinality of enterprise activity as represented hierarchically by the data of the enterprise. Invariably, some data will reference unknown or nonsense hierarchies or no hierarchy at all because some operational application does not validate input hierarchical values. Typically, corporate reports based on key performance indicators (KPIs) will identify to management hierarchical data that is incorrect. Underneath the radar of KPI reports, however, often lurks another set of data with incorrect hierarchical values. A histogram of enterprise activity by hierarchy will highlight such aberrations in enterprise data.

■ **Inventory of Data Entities**: Enterprise entities (e.g., people, building, property) are recorded in enterprise systems as data. The inventory of data elements will identify the methods by which enterprise data identifies each entity and records its attributes.

 − Core data element: An individual and unique entity as defined in enterprise data. The inventory should include the unique identifier for a Core entity and an explanation of what makes that identifier unique.

- Combined data elements that define a Logical entity: A logical entity may be an intersection of multiple Core data elements. For example:
  - Project Team: Multiple people from disparate departments brought together to achieve a single goal. The Core entities are the individual people.
  - Product Offering: Multiple individual products merchandised as one logical unit. The Core entities are the individual products.
  - Facility Groups: Multiple individual facilities from various geographic regions, which are grouped together based on common shared demographic criteria. The Core entities are the individual facilities.
- The inventory should include the unique identifier for a Logical entity, an explanation of what makes that identifier unique, and how Core entities are associated to a Logical entity.
  - Descriptive data elements: The attributes of a Core or Logical data element may be stored in an associated data element. The inventory should include descriptive data and its association with a data element.
  - Associative data elements: The associations between multiple Core or Logical data elements may be stored in an associative data element. The inventory should indicate the associative data element(s) and the method by which it associates data elements to each other.
- **Data Model of the Source System**: Enterprise system documentation will probably include data models. These should be included in the data profile in conjunction with the inventories of data entities and data elements. If, however, an enterprise system does not have a data model (Logical, Physical, or otherwise), the data warehouse designer should create one. The Logical and Physical data models will prove to be beyond value through the design of a data warehouse and data acquisition applications.[11] If a data warehouse designer does not have sufficient knowledge of enterprise systems to model the enterprise data, then the Source System Analysis has not delivered information sufficient to allow the design of a data warehouse. The Source System Data Model should, at a minimum, include a Logical and Physical data model.
  - Logical: A Logical data model typically indicates the business understanding and meaning of the data within the enterprise. The Logical data model will indicate the relationships by which entities are grouped and associated.
  - Physical: A Physical data model indicates the data structures within which enterprise data is physically stored. The Physical data model should indicate the Primary key/Foreign key relationships between data structures.

The purpose of a Data Profile is to provide a cross section of enterprise data. Typically, an enterprise will have too much data for every row to be reviewed and understood within the context of the enterprise. A sufficient number of "slices" of enterprise data will provide more insight into the enterprise and its data than could be garnered by a review of every row or record in the enterprise.

Data Flow Diagram

The Data Flow Diagram method (Figure 3.2) that is used to design a source system is also used during Source System Analysis. After the data profile identifies enterprise data elements, the Data Flow Diagram identifies where the data comes from, goes to, and by what transport mechanism it moves. The Data Flow Diagram should include all the names and descriptions of the physical environment provided by the data profile. In addition to the names and descriptions of the physical environment, a Data Flow Diagram will add the dimensions of time, sequence, and movement to the Source System Analysis.

In a Data Flow Diagram, a data warehouse designer reverse-engineers the movement of data within the enterprise. This is the opportunity to discover the lifespan and location of data as it is used by enterprise systems. For example:

■ A file is deleted by the operational application that reads it.
■ Data is appended to previously existing data, permanently blending the two sets of data together.
■ Data only occurs in the form of asynchronous messages.
■ A file is only available on the other side of a file transfer protocol (FTP) firewall.

A Data Flow Diagram is intended to discover these and other aspects of the physical movement of enterprise data. Typically, the diagram requires many pages of diagrams to document the flow of data in an enterprise. The movement of a data element should ideally be captured in a single page of a Data Flow Diagram.

Data State Diagram

The Data State Diagram (Figure 3.3) is used to capture the various business meanings of a data element as it flows through the Data Flow Diagram. After the Data Flow Diagram identifies where the data comes from, goes to, and by what transport mechanism the data moves, the Data State Diagram identifies the business meaning, the relevance to the enterprise of a data element at each point in its journey through the enterprise.

A Data State Diagram is built from the Data Flow Diagram. In addition to the names and descriptions of the physical environment, a Data State Diagram indicates the relevance of a data element to the enterprise (Table 3.1).

A Data State Diagram also includes any physical indications of each state (Table 3.2).

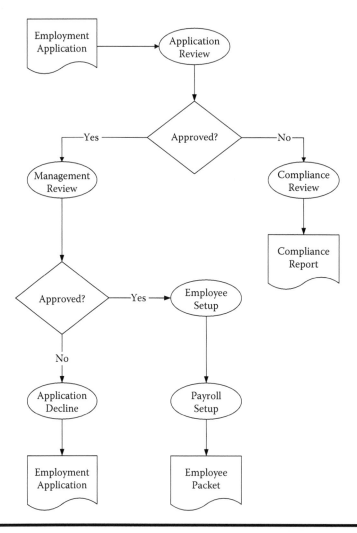

Figure 3.2   Data Flow Diagram.

As data flows through the enterprise, its meaning and relevance change. Throughout the life of a data element, what are all the business meanings (i.e., states) of that data element? When and where do these business meanings occur? A Data State Diagram is the opportunity to discover the answers to these questions. At the conclusion of the Data Profile, Data Flow Diagram, and Data State Diagram, a data warehouse designer is prepared to identify the System of Record for each enterprise entity.

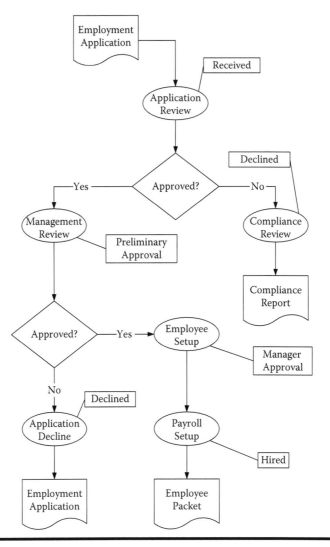

Figure 3.3 Data State Diagram.

System of Record

The identification of the System of Record is the reason Source System Analysis is directly associated with the data acquisition and integration applications, otherwise known as ETL (extract, transfer, and load) applications. ETL applications retrieve data from the enterprise. An ETL design must answer the question: "Where do I get the enterprise data from that will go into the data warehouse?" The answer to this question is the System of Record. These Profiles, Data Flow Diagrams, and

Table 3.1 Data State

Data Element	Data State
Product	Proposed
Manufacturing Design	Finalized
Invoice	Paid in Full

Table 3.2 Physical Indications of Data State

Data Element	Data State	Physical Indications
Product	Proposed	Product approvals are empty
Manufacturing Design	Finalized	Manufacturing design documents were moved to the directory named "Final"
Invoice	Paid in Full	The box marked "Paid in Full" is checked (i.e., set to yes/on)

Data State Diagrams allow a data warehouse designer to discover the authoritative point of origin for each enterprise entity at any given state. That authoritative point of origin is the System of Record.

The Data Profile, Data Flow Diagram, and Data State Diagram are intended to allow significant discovery of the enterprise and its data. This information is significant for the upcoming data warehouse design activities. The Data Model of the data warehouse will derive much of its design from the Data Profile, Data Flow Diagram, and Data State Diagram. The Business Intelligence Reporting will use the information from the Data Profile, Data Flow Diagram, and Data State Diagram to communicate its expression of the enterprise, so that the members of the enterprise can understand it. Data Quality applications will rely heavily on the expectations and anomalies discovered in the Data Profile, Data Flow Diagram, and Data State Diagram. Metadata will be based directly on these three entities.

Business Rules

Finally, the Source System Analysis is the opportunity to document the business rules that govern data in the source system. The Data Profile, Data Flow Diagram, Data State Diagram, and System of Record provide the best opportunity to identify the business rules of the source system. These business rules come in three basic varieties:

■ Intrarecord Business Rules: Column A + Column B = Column C. The business rule exists entirely within each individual record. All the data and information necessary to validate the business rule is present in a single record or row. An Intrarecord business rule can only be validated one record at a time because that business rule applies to only one record at a time.

■ Intradataset Business Rules: Row 1. Column A + Row 2. Column A = Row 3. Column B. The business rule spans across records within a set of data, but still remains within the set of data. All the data and information necessary to validate the business rule is present in a single set of data. An Intradataset business rule can only be validated one dataset at a time because that business rule applies to only one dataset at a time.

■ Cross Dataset Business Rules: File 1. Column A = Table 2. Column B. The business rule spans across sets of data within a source system. The data, therefore, may not be available in the source system. The data may be late arriving, deleted, or renamed. Cross Dataset business rules, therefore, require more effort to define and validate.

Business rules will be used to create the Data Quality validations of inbound data from the source system. So, any data elements from the source system that should maintain a consistent behavior, and can affect the data warehouse, should be included in the list of Business Rules.

Closing Remarks

Thus far, this discussion of Source System Analysis has not addressed the requirements of the data warehouse customer or the preferences of the enterprise. Typically, budget and time constraints restrict the Source System Analysis activities. If, however, a data warehouse designer has been so fortunate as to be allowed to perform most, if not all, of the Source System Analysis activities, that data warehouse designer has the enterprise knowledge and context necessary to effectively discuss customer requirements and preferences.

Rarely does an enterprise create a data warehouse as its initial decision support. Typically, decision support systems evolve and mature along with the enterprise. Eventually, the enterprise is simultaneously ready to invest in, and benefit from, a data warehouse. By that time, an enterprise already has a decision support system of some sort, official or unofficial. Source System Analysis provides the opportunity to locate and identify previous decision support systems. Knowledge of previous decision support systems is important. Individual members of the enterprise will compare the data from a data warehouse to data from a previous decision support system. Any differences between the data from a previous decision support system and the data from a data warehouse will be perceived as errors and flaws in the data warehouse. At the moment a data warehouse is released to the enterprise, the data warehouse team must be prepared to identify and explain all differences between the data warehouse and any previous decision support system. Without a statement of the differences, members of the enterprise will probably perceive the data warehouse to be incorrect, but, with a statement of the differences and explanations, members of the enterprise will probably perceive the differences to be intentional by the design of the data warehouse, and probably accept those differences and the data warehouse.

References

1. Louis Agosta, *The Essential Guide to Data Warehousing* (Upper Saddle River, NJ: Prentice Hall PTR, 2000).
2. Michael Scofield, *Understanding and Reconciling Source Data for ETL and Data Warehousing Design*, TDWI World Conference (The Data Warehouse Institute, Renton, WA, 2002).
3. Ralph Kimball and Joe Caserta, *The Data Warehouse Etl Toolkit: Practical Techniques for Extracting, Cleaning, Conforming, and Delivering Data* (Indianapolis, IN: John Wiley & Sons, 2004).
4. William H. Inmon, Claudia Imhoff, and Ryan Sousa, *Corporate Information Factory* (New York: John Wiley & Sons, 1998).
5. Agosta, *The Essential Guide to Data Warehousing.*
6. William H. Inmon, R. H. Terdeman, and Claudia Imhoff, *Exploration Warehousing: Turning Business Information into Business Opportunity* (New York: John Wiley & Sons, 2000).
7. William H. Inmon, *Building the Data Warehouse*, 2nd ed. (New York: John Wiley & Sons, 1996).
8. Les Barbusinski, Chuck Kelley, and Joe Oates, What does granularity mean in the context of a data warehouse and what are the various levels of granularity? DM Review. Online, June 25, 2002, www.dmreview.com/news/5460-1.html
9. Scofield, *Understanding and Reconciling Source Data for ETL and Data Warehousing Design.*
10. Ibid.
11. *TDWI Data Acquisition: Techniques for Extracting, Transforming and Loading Data,* (The Data Warehouse Institute, Renton, WA, 2001).

Chapter 4

Relational Database Management System (RDBMS)

Introduction

Few things in life are certain—death and taxes are two of them. Another certainty is that a data warehouse has to be stored on a Relational Database Management System (RDBMS)(Figure 4.1). The reason is very simple. A RDBMS allows individual data elements to be combined in an almost infinite set of permutations.[1] Ad hoc reporting, a key advantage of a data warehouse can only be performed by a platform that accommodates an almost infinite set of data permutations, such as a RDBMS. But, we need to go back to the 1970s to understand the value and versatility of the RDBMS.

Relational Set Theory

The patent for the ENIAC (electronic numerical integrator and computer) was filed on June 26, 1947.[2] Since then the volume of data stored and processed on computing platforms has continued to grow. From 1947 onward data was stored in a flat format. Records could not be joined to each other. So, records had to be complete within

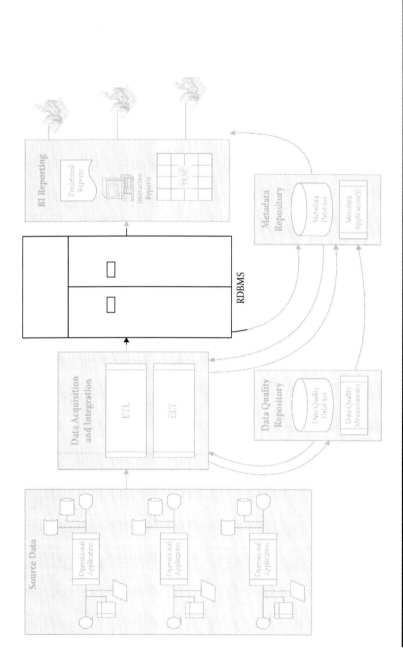

Figure 4.1   Relational Database Management System.

themselves. This flat format architecture resulted in significant data redundancy, as seen in Figure 4.2. For example, every record had to include an item description to provide a text definition of the item number.

Hierarchical databases significantly reduced data redundancy by isolating each data element in its own file. The complete statement of purchase activity, as shown in Figure 4.2, would be reassembled by reading the data from a parent file and then reading related data from a child file (Figure 4.3). The data from each "read" would be stored in internal memory and processed by a procedural computer program. The reduced data redundancy also reduced the data volume. The introduction of Read functions, by which a complete set of data can be assembled, rendered the data accessible only by way of a procedural application (e.g., COBOL). The result was reduced redundancy, reduced volume, and reduced accessibility.

In June 1970, Dr. E. F. Codd proposed a solution to all three problems (redundancy, volume, and accessibility) when he published his groundbreaking article "A Relational Model of Data for Large Shared Data Banks."[3] Dr. Codd's article

Name	Activity	Date	Item Number	Item Description
Sue Smith	Purchase	March 4, 2007	1234-ab	Computer Keyboard
Sue Smith	Purchase	March 4, 2007	2345-cd	Backup Tape
John Jones	Purchase	March 5, 2007	1234-ab	Computer Keyboard
John Jones	Purchase	March 6, 2007	2345-cd	Backup Tape
John Jones	Purchase	March 7, 2007	2345-cd	Backup Tape

Figure 4.2

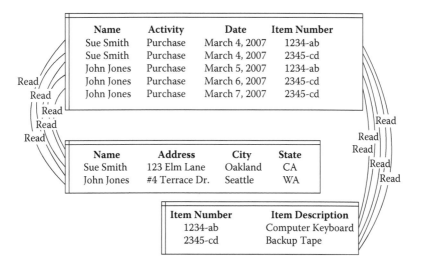

Figure 4.3   Hierarchical Database Architecture.

introduced relations and normalization, which are the basis of all RDBMSs. Relations and normalized data rendered large volumes of data accessible by the use of Structured Query Language (SQL). By 1995, Ralph Kimball had documented and published the direct connection between large volumes of normalized data in a relational database and the almost infinite permutations of data elements, which make the ad hoc reporting of a data warehouse possible.[4] A data warehouse, therefore, must be stored on a RDBMS.

RDBMS Product Offerings

Relational databases offer a wide selection of features and functions. Primarily, these features and functions include some permutation of data volume, throughput, and price (Figure 4.4). Data volume and throughput are inversely related. As data volumes increase, a RDBMS requires more time to process the additional data. Throughput is directly related to price. The processing capacity required to increase throughput also increases costs. Data volume is also directly related to price. The data storage required to increase data volume also increases the costs.

Data volume and throughput are the primary features by which to compare RDBMS product offerings. RDBMS products will typically fit one of the following permutations of features:

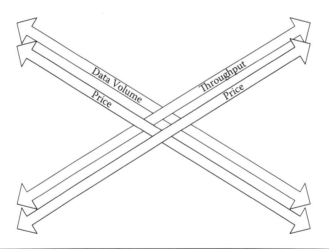

Figure 4.4   RDBMS primary features.

- **High Disk Capacity**
  - Large number of CPUs
    - Result:
      - Able to store and process large data volumes
      - Able to quickly perform functions and operations
  - Moderate number of CPUs
    - Result:
      - Able to store and process large data volumes
      - Able to perform functions and operations with moderate speed
- **Moderate Disk Capacity**
  - Large number of CPUs
    - Result:
      - Able to store and process moderate data volumes
      - Able to quickly perform functions and operations
  - Moderate number of CPUs
    - Result:
      - Able to store and process moderate data volumes
      - Able to perform functions and operations with moderate speed

The decision to purchase a RDBMS should include consideration of expected data volume and throughput. By matching expected data volume and throughput against the accepted price, an enterprise can select the RDBMS that best meets its data warehousing needs, budget, goals, and plans.

This activity of matching volume and throughput to disk capacity and CPUs (central processing units) is a bit tricky. RDBMS vendors need sales revenue to keep their businesses afloat. They will represent the minimum cost for the minimum hardware (i.e., disks and CPUs) necessary to achieve the storage capacity and throughput required by the customer. Then the customer realizes they did indeed purchase the *minimum* hardware, which was within the budget, and which, coincidentally, achieves *minimum* performance. That customer soon has another decision to make—scrap the minimum hardware already purchased and start over with another RDBMS, or purchase the incremental hardware necessary to achieve the desired performance. The money for the previously purchased hardware has already been invested and cannot be considered in any future costs. So, invariably, the least cost option is the purchase of the incremental hardware necessary to achieve the desired performance. Therefore, when matching the hardware required to achieve the desired performance, include all possible extenuating circumstances. For example:

- Many customers simultaneously contending for resources on the RDBMS.

- Load jobs loading tables A, B, and C while many customers are using all the other tables.
- Backup jobs backing up tables A, B, and C while many customers are using all the other tables.
- Applications querying large volumes of data on the RDBMS.

If these answers are not available, then an alternative question is: At what density of processes, operations, and data volume will the RDBMS become pegged at 100 percent capacity? In other words, if the matching of requirements to hardware cannot be achieved by starting from maximum processes, maximum operations, and maximum data volumes, which lead to RDBMS capacity, then go the other way, from maximum RDBMS capacity to the processes, operations, and data volumes, which achieved that maximum RDBMS capacity. If either of these questions can be answered, the RDBMS customer will most likely have the information necessary to make the right selection the first time and not require a second purchase.

RDBMS product offerings often include other features and functions, such as:

- **Security**: Protect the data from unauthorized access.
- **Reliability**: Redundant array of independent disks (RAID)[5] reduce the downtime of the RDBMS and reduce the loss of data.
- **OLAP**: Online analytical process.
- **Procedural Language**: Allow the creation and use of native computer programs.
- **Graphical User Interface (GUI)**: Present a user-friendly interface to the RDBMS.

Features such as these are relevant in varying degrees to the success of a data warehouse. All of these features, however, are secondary to the primary features—data volume and throughput. A RDBMS vendor proposing a product offering that is weak in data volume or throughput will try to sell a RDBMS based on secondary features.

The decision to purchase a RDBMS is an investment decision. The enterprise should expect a Return On Investment (ROI) from the creation of a data warehouse. The best case scenario, therefore, is to purchase the data volume, throughput capacity, and other RDBMS features key to the success of the data warehouse for a price low enough to allow a reasonable ROI.

Residual Costs

RDBMS hardware can be, and often is, purchased. The cost of the hardware, therefore, quickly becomes a "sunk cost." The money and hardware asset trade sides of the balance sheet and the cost of the hardware become irrelevant. The operating system (OS) and RDBMS application, however, are not purchased, they are licensed. Future maintenance and support of the RDBMS is purchased annually. The cost of licensing, support, and maintenance, therefore, are not sunk costs, they are continuing costs. The negotiated purchase of a RDBMS should also include fixed pricing of all costs (e.g., licensing, support, and maintenance) for as long as possible. This will define a significant portion of the cost of ownership of a data warehouse, which will be included in the ROI of a data warehouse.

Licensing

A License Agreement outlines the terms and conditions by which an enterprise is allowed to use the OS and RBMS, and the price that the enterprise will pay for this privilege. Typically, the price of a License Agreement is directly based on one, but not all, of the following:

- The number of physical CPUs in the RDBMS hardware
- The number of individual logon IDs
- The number of concurrent logon IDs active on the RDBMS at one time
- A fixed price for the entire site

The willingness of a RDBMS vendor to negotiate the terms of a License Agreement is inversely proportionate to the size of the RDBMS hardware purchased.

Support and Maintenance

Support typically refers to RDBMS assistance troubleshooting and the solving of problems with the RDBMS. Maintenance typically refers to the resolution of hardware problems, and installation of future code (OS and RDBMS) updates. A RDBMS vendor will offer a menu of options for the support and maintenance, which will be provided by the RDBMS vendor. The rule of thumb for these options is simple:

- Increased involvement by the RDBMS vendor will cost the enterprise increased money.
- Decreased involvement by the RDBMS vendor will cost the enterprise less money.

Extensibility

Extensibility refers to the architected ability to increase the data storage and processing throughput of a RDBMS by adding additional hardware (e.g., disk drives and

CPUs). An OS or RDBMS has a maximum capacity. Until that maximum capacity has been reached, every addition to the RDBMS hardware (e.g., disk drives and CPUs) is expected to improve the performance of the data warehouse.

Knowledge of the maximum capacity or maximum extensibility of a RDBMS is extremely helpful, especially during the negotiation of the purchase of the hardware. A data warehouse team must know the fully extended and maximum capacity of a RDBMS when negotiating the purchase and licensing of a RDBMS.

Over time, the price for license, support, and maintenance will increase. The negotiated license, support, and maintenance agreements should lock down the price of these services for a duration as far into the future as possible.

Connective Capacity

Applications interact with a RDBMS via a connectivity interface. The methods by which a RDBMS allows external applications to interact with the data within that RDBMS is known as Connective Capacity (or Connectivity). The standard method, an open database connectivity (ODBC), is provided to establish a SQL-based connection by which external applications can interact with the data in a RDBMS.

To create a competitive advantage, RDBMS vendors include Connectivity methods in addition to ODBC, with enhanced features and capacity. The decision to purchase a RDBMS must include a match between the Connectivity provided by a RDBMS and the Connectivity required by the applications that will interact with the data in a data warehouse.

Closing Remarks

A data warehouse must reside on a RDBMS. The question is: which RDBMS? A data warehouse designer selects a platform and RDBMS based on many factors, such as:

- How will the customers connect to the RDBMS?
- How will the customers use the RDBMS?
- How will the data acquisition and integration applications connect to the RDBMS?
- How will the data acquisition and integration applications load data into the RDBMS?
- What are the goals and plans of the enterprise regarding the data warehouse?
- What is the current hardware budget?

■ What primary and secondary features of the RDBMS product offerings are within the hardware budget?

These and other similar factors are the considerations taken when selecting a RDBMS. The right answer may not be the biggest, fastest, or most highly rated RDBMS. Like a carpenter looking for a specific tool, a data warehouse designer is looking for the right tool for the right job.

References

1. Louis Agosta, *The Essential Guide to Data Warehousing* (Upper Saddle River, NJ: Prentice Hall PTR, 2000).
2. Martin H. Weik, The ENIAC story — The world's first electronic digital computer was developed by army ordnance to compute World War II ballistic firing tables, (1961). http://ftp.arl.army.mil/~mike/comphist/eniac-story.html
3. Susan Harkins, Relational databases: The untold story, *ZDNet Australia* (2003).
4. Ibid.
5. The use of redundant disk arrays is an accepted best practice. Redundant disks, however, reduce the available data storage. If a megabyte of data is stored using redundant disks, then that megabyte of data consumes two megabytes.

Chapter 5

Database Design

Introduction

Database Design is the first true design activity of a data warehouse (Figure 5.1). In the preceding chapter, Source System Analysis was the primary analysis activity. The information provided by this analysis, describing and defining the entities and processes within the enterprise, is the information on which the Database Design is based. A data warehouse designer organizes the entities and processes of the enterprise, via the principles in the Data Warehouse Philosophy, in the form of databases, tables, and views. Equally important is the usage patterns by which data warehouse customers will use a data warehouse. Discussed in Chapter 10 (Data Warehouse Customers), customers and their usage patterns also influence the design of a data warehouse. These two considerations, Source System Analysis and customer usage patterns, taken together identify the resources (i.e., source data) and requirements (i.e., usage patterns) of a data warehouse.

Database design simultaneously encompasses three architectural decisions. The first decision has been made—the data warehouse will reside on a Relational Database Management System (RDBMS). The remaining questions, in relation to Data Models and Data Architecture, are more difficult to answer.

- Data Model: How will the data be organized within relational tables? What are the subject areas? What are the entities? How will they relate? What will they mean?

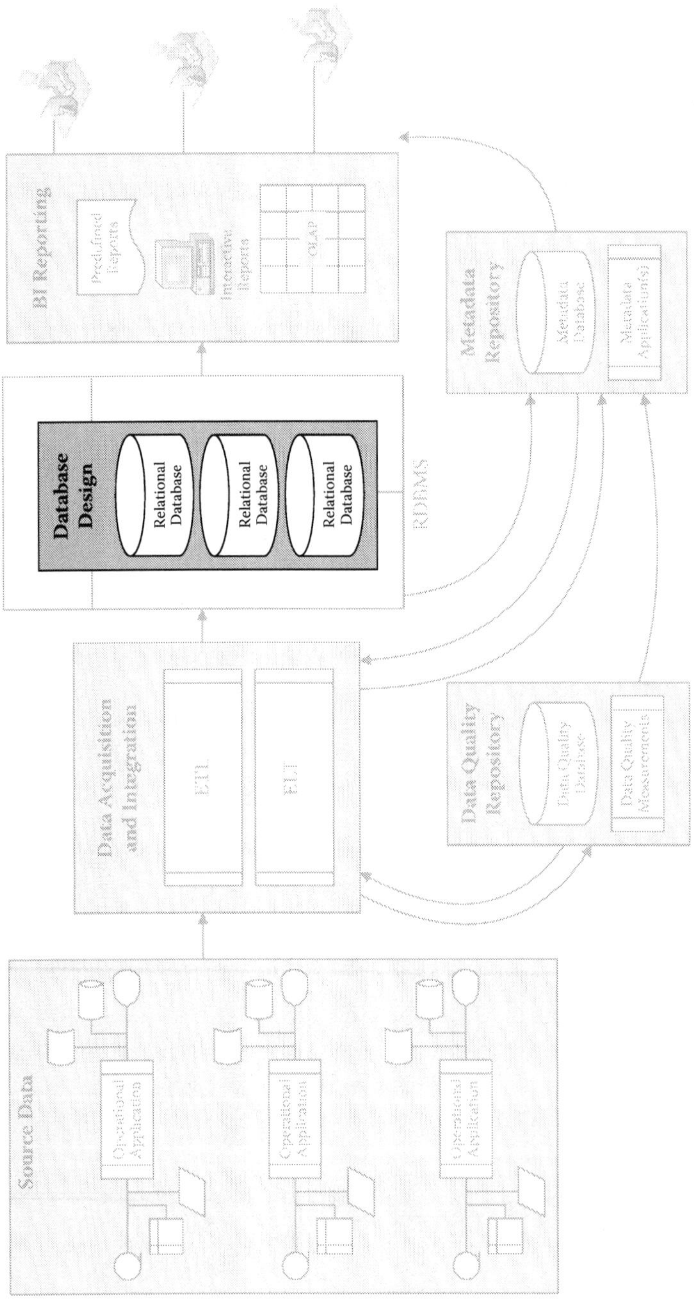

Figure 5.1   Database Design.

■ Data Architecture: How will the relational tables be organized? Will they reside in a single central data warehouse, or will they reside in distributed data marts? Will an Operational Data Store be included?

These design decisions have significant influence on each other. Every permutation of RDBMS platform, data integration volumes and throughput, BI Reporting data volumes and throughput, and data warehouse customer needs will suggest its own optimal combination of Data Architecture and Data Model. Some in the data warehousing community will declare a "best practice" Data Architecture and Data Model. Data warehousing, however, is not a "one size fits all" decision support system. Data warehousing, instead, requires an understanding of the enterprise and the data warehouse customers. In between the enterprise and the customers is data. The big picture question is:" "What should that data look like?"

The following sections will explain the methods used in data warehousing to organize data within tables. Data Architecture will explain how tables are organized within databases. The combined result of a Data Model and Data Architecture is a data warehouse design. The individual deliverables in a data warehouse design include:

■ Conceptual Data Model
■ Logical Data Model
■ Physical Data Model
■ Data Architecture

These are discussed in the following sections.

Data Modeling Methodology

Data modeling methodology includes three phases: Conceptual, Logical, and Physical Data Models. They are created in that sequence. A Conceptual Data Model is a prerequisite for a Logical Data Model, which is a prerequisite for a Physical Data Model. The physical database and table structures are based directly on the data structures outlined in the Physical Data Model.

■ Conceptual Data Model: How will the enterprise be organized within the data warehouse? The Conceptual Data Model defines the subject areas and major entities.
■ Logical Data Model: Which entities exist within each subject area? How will those entities relate to each other? The relationships extend beyond just primary key/foreign key relationships. They include Super Type, Subtype, Attribute, and Associative Entities.[1]

■ Physical Data Model: Databases hold the data of a data warehouse. How will that data be assigned to columns, which are inside tables that are organized into databases that collectively hold the data of a data warehouse? Though not quite the Data Definition Language (DDL) of the tables and databases, the Physical Data Model is very close to the DDL of the tables and databases.

Data modeling can occur in one of two sequences: Top-to-Bottom and Bottom-to-Top. The Top-to-Bottom approach begins with the top level Conceptual Data Model. The Logical Data Model derives from the Conceptual Data Model, and the Physical Data Model derives from the Logical Data Model. The Bottom-to-Top approach begins with the detailed Physical Data Model. The Logical Data Model explains the rationale behind the Physical Data Model, and the Conceptual Data Model explains the context of the Logical Data Model. Both methods can be equally successful. The discussion that follows will use the Top-to-Bottom approach, which begins with the Conceptual Data Model.

Conceptual Data Model

The Conceptual Data Model identifies the main subject areas of a data warehouse.[2] Implicitly, the Conceptual Data Model also identifies the boundary of a data warehouse because any subject area not included in the Conceptual Data Model is not included in the data warehouse. The Conceptual Data Model provides an overall map to a data warehouse. The applicable subject area can identify the location of data within a data warehouse.

The definition of a subject area within the Conceptual Data Model is not a binding statement that the data, tables, and possibly database for that subject area will be created. Data warehouse development best occurs in iterative slices of development, not all at once. Taken all at once the immediate cost of a data warehouse is too high. Without the opportunity to generate return on investment (ROI), a data warehouse development budget will be cut and data will be descoped. The result would be a fully implemented data warehouse, which is missing some of its parts. The better, as well as tried and true, method is iterative development. Iterative development creates one subject area, or a portion of a subject area, at a time. This allows an initial subject area to be created with a reasonable budget, and to generate ROI, which justifies the budget for the development of subsequent subject areas.

Slicing along two axes can slice an enterprise into subject areas: business processes and business entities. These two axes work well because they facilitate the creation of mutually exclusive subject areas, which helps avoid confusion about the subject areas. The importance of these axes is that the Logical and Physical Data Models for each subject area will be based directly on a subject area in the Conceptual Data Model. Information from the source system analysis guides the selection

Table 5.1 Business Processes

Subject Area	Definition	Examples
Subject Areas by Business Process		
Sales	The exchange of a product or service for a fee	Retail transactions Consulting contract
Manufacturing	The value-adding assembly of a product from materials and ingredients	Automotive assembly Furniture carpentry
Billing	Invoicing, collecting, and posting the money owed to the enterprise	Accounts Receivable Collection agency
Receiving	Accepting and storing materials or product from a supplier	Warehouse dockIn-store delivery
Shipping	Delivery of product to retail or wholesale outlets or customers	Delivery trucking Third-party transportation

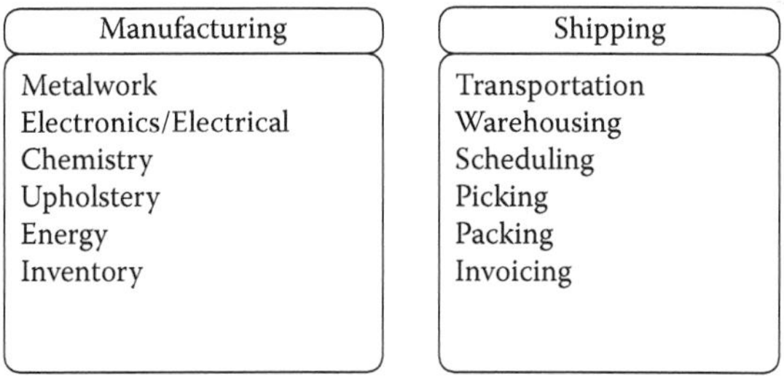

Manufacturing	Shipping
Metalwork	Transportation
Electronics/Electrical	Warehousing
Chemistry	Scheduling
Upholstery	Picking
Energy	Packing
Inventory	Invoicing

Figure 5.2 Conceptual Data Model processes.

of subject areas that best express the structure and nature of the enterprise. Possible subject areas for Business Process subjects are listed in Table 5.1.

An enterprise will typically have more than one major business process. Major business processes are the first addition to a Conceptual Data Model (Figure 5.2). Each major business process is listed with its subordinate areas. The example in Table 5.2 shows the major business processes manufacturing and shipping, and their subordinate areas. Major business processes are not related. The entities, which will relate these business processes, will be added later.

Table 5.2 Subject Areas by Business Entity

Subject Areas by Business Entity		
Subject Area	**Definition**	**Examples**
Facilities	Physical plants that house enterprise operations	Store Warehouse
Capital Equipment	Materials, tools, and hardware that contribute to the functions of the enterprise	Forklift Display cabinet Drill and drill bits
Product	The object of a retail or wholesale sales transaction	Automobile Groceries
Customer	The participant in a sales transaction who receives a product or service	Grocery shopper Corporate buyer
Supplier	The vendor who provides to the enterprise materials and ingredients used in the business of the enterprise	Automobile parts manufacturer Wholesale broker

The selection of major business process subject areas can occur by two methods.

■ One to Multiple: Select one major business process. Add subordinate business processes. As the number of subordinate business processes exceeds the meaning of the major business area, create new major subject areas, which encompass them. Move the subordinate business areas to a new or previously existing major business area. As subordinate business areas accumulate, assign them to a major business process, which naturally groups them.

■ Multiple to Few: Select all possible major business areas. Add subordinate business areas to each major business process. Identify and consolidate redundant subordinate business processes. As major business processes decline in significance by losing subordinate business processes, move all subordinate business processes to remaining major business processes, and remove the unpopulated major business areas.

The selection of major business processes is iterative and multidirectional. Before the selection of all major and subordinate business processes in a Conceptual Data Model is complete, both methods (One to Multiple and Multiple to Few) will be utilized in the selection process.

The subject areas of an enterprise are also sliced by the business entities within, and possibly around, the enterprise. These are the physical and logical objects by which the enterprise achieves its business functions. Possible subject areas for Business Entity subjects are shown in Table 5.2.

Major business entities are the second addition to a Conceptual Data Model and an enterprise will typically have more than one. Each major business entity is listed with its subordinate entities. The example in Figure 5.3 shows the major entity areas: Product, Facilities, and Capital Equipment, and their subordinate entities.

Major business entities relate to each other. Capital Equipment is located in a Facility and used to manufacture a Product. Facilities are used to shelter the manufacture of a Product. Major entities also relate and connect major business processes, as seen in Figure 5.4. Manufacturing and Shipping both handle Product. Manufacturing and Shipping both use Capital Equipment inside Facilities.

A subordinate entity can occur multiple times in a Conceptual Data Model. In the Conceptual Data Model in Figure 5.4, the entity Function occurs three times and the entity Inventory occurs twice. This is normal. As a Conceptual Data Model is expanded into a Logical and then Physical Data Models, this phenomenon will occur many times. Eventually, as the Physical Data Model is normalized, removing redundancy, redundant entities will be consolidated. The consolidated entity will be referenced within each subject area. This highlights the need for consistent entity names. For every instance of business meaning, use the same entity name. You don't want to discover redundant data after a data warehouse has been implemented, and someone remarks, "Hey, did you know these two tables have different names, but the same data?" This situation can be worse: If the two tables do not

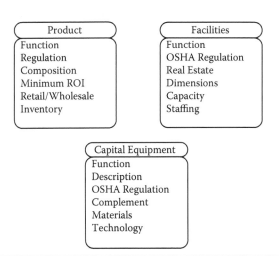

Figure 5.3   Conceptual Data Model entities.

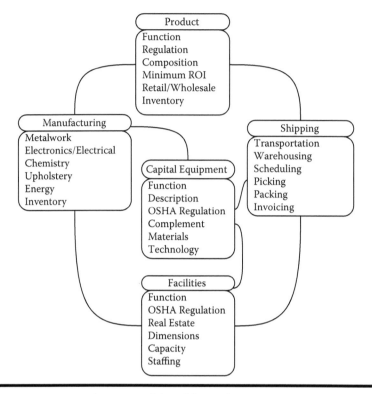

Figure 5.4   Conceptual Data Model entities and processes.

have exactly the same rows. The first defense against such confusion is consistent entity names.

A Conceptual Data Model will require numerous iterations of brainstorming, model, review, model, brainstorming, model, etc. Conceptual Data Modeling is not just an activity that has been perpetuated for no apparent reason from the early days of data warehousing. Rather, a Conceptual Data Model is the first foundation of a data warehouse and provides the roadmap to a data warehouse via the subject areas of the enterprise. Details and enhanced meaning are added to that roadmap as it is transformed into a Logical Data Model.

Logical Data Model

A Logical Data Model presents the entities and relationships of the enterprise. Logical Data Modeling uses Entity Relationship Diagram notation.[3] An Entity Relationship Diagram visually displays the relations between the entities of a enterprise. A Logical Data Model achieves this visual display by focusing on each major subject area from the Conceptual Data Model. Each major subject area of a Conceptual Data Model, therefore, will become a page by itself in a Logical Data Model. Each page will present all entities relevant to the major subject area. Using the Conceptual Data Model in Figure 5.4, a Logical Data Model would include five pages.

- Manufacturing
- Shipping
- Product
- Capital Equipment
- Facilities

A Logical Data Model enhances the information already available in a Conceptual Data Model by including five categories of information.

- Logical (Primary) Key
- Attribute
- Primary Key/Foreign Key Relation
- Cardinality
- Super types and subtypes

Additional information may be included. That additional information, however, should not replace or alter the following five categories of information.

Logical (Primary) Key

What identifies each instance of an entity? Given that piece of information, a person can search the enterprise and always identify the same instance of an entity. The Logical Key does not identify an entity; rather, a Logical Key identifies an instance of an entity. For example:

- Facilities: An individual building
- Capital Equipment: An individual lathe
- Shipping: An individual invoice

The Logical Key is usually referred to as the Primary Key. The term Primary Key is also used in other forms of data modeling, including the upcoming discussion of Physical Data Modeling. The Primary Key of a Logical Data Model is similar to, but not exactly the same as, the Primary Key of a Physical Data Model. During this discussion of Logical Data Modeling, the term Primary Key will refer explicitly to the Logical (Primary) Key.

Attribute

An Attribute is a nonidentifying aspect of an entity. An Attribute describes, but does not define, an individual instance of an entity. Rather, an attribute provides information about an entity, which enhances its meaning and relevance. Common attributes include:

- Color
- Size
- Formula
- Taxing Municipality

Primary Key/Foreign Key Relation

A Logical Data Model includes a representation of the method by which an instance of an individual entity is associated with an instance of another individual entity. The definition of a Logical Key for each instance of each entity is a prerequisite for the definition of an associative relation because each instance of both entities must be identified before they can be associated to each other.

A Primary Key/Foreign Key Relation exists between two and only two entities. A business scenario may require that multiple relations exist simultaneously for that business scenario to be valid. For the purposes of Logical Data Modeling, these multiple relations are seen as individual relations. Constraints, which exist in a business scenario, are business rules that will be enforced by applications and not by the Logical Data Model.

A Primary Key/Foreign Key Relation is achieved by embedding the Primary Key of a subordinate entity as a nonidentifying attribute in a superior entity. For example:

- Real Estate (i.e., a building) has a Function. A Function describes a building. A Function, therefore, is subordinate to Real Estate. The Primary Key of a Function is embedded as a nonidentifying attribute of Real Estate.[4]
- Capital Equipment (i.e., a car) has Features. A Feature describes a car. A Feature, therefore, is subordinate to Capital Equipment. The Primary Key of a Feature is embedded as a nonidentifying attribute of Capital Equipment.

The relation between two entities may not be obvious when defined in terms of a superior and subordinate entity. The superior/subordinate relation between two entities may be more clearly defined in terms of Cardinality.

Cardinality

Cardinality refers to quantity, or the number of instances of something (i.e., marbles in a bag). In a Logical Data Model, Cardinality refers to the number of entity instances involved in a relation. Obviously, in many relations, the number of entity instances can change from one moment to the next. A Logical Data Model, therefore, makes no attempt to capture moment-by-moment the number of entity instances. Instead, a Logical Data Model categorizes the number of entity instances into four groups, which are show in Figure 5.5.

A relation is notated as a line that connects two, and only two, entities. The line represents the relation, and the entities at each end of the line are the only entities included in the relation. The Cardinality of each entity is notated by placing a Cardinality symbol at the end of the relation line. A Cardinality symbol applies to the entity it touches tangentially. Examples of relation lines with Cardinality symbols are shown in Figure 5.6.

Cardinality may help define the superior/subordinate relation between entities. The permutations of Cardinality and the inferences that can be drawn are shown in Table 5.3.

Cardinality refers to the number of instances of an entity included in a relation between two entities. Cardinality is categorized into the following four groups.

- One
- One or Zero
- One or Many
- One, Zero, or Many

If an entity has a higher Cardinality than its related entity, then that higher Cardinality entity is the subordinate entity. The lower Cardinality entity is the

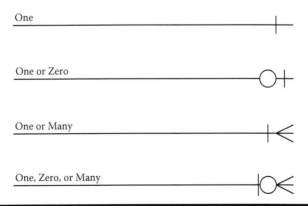

Figure 5.5 Cardinality symbols.

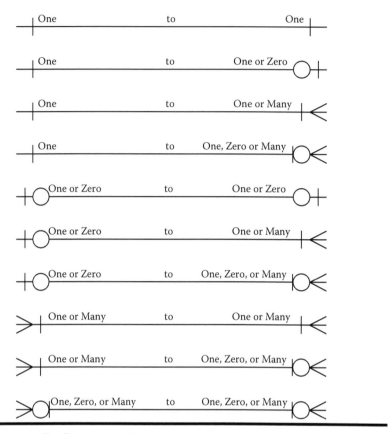

Figure 5.6 Cardinality permutations.

Table 5.3 Cardinality and Superior/Subordinate Relations

Entity A	Entity B	Superior Entity	Subordinate Entity
One	One	n/a	n/a
One	One or Zero	n/a	n/a
One	One or Many	A	B
One	One, Zero, or Many	A	B
One or Zero	One or Many	A	B
One or Zero	One, Zero, or Many	A	B
One or Many	One, Zero, or Many	n/a	n/a
One, Zero, or Many	One, Zero, or Many	n/a	n/a

superior entity. Many-to-Many and One-to-One Cardinalities do not indicate a superior/subordinate relation. Rather, Many-to-Many Cardinalities indicate the need for an associative table (see Physical Data Model below). And, One-to-One Cardinalities indicate a strong positive correlation, which may mean that the two entities joined by a One-to-One relation may actually be a single entity. So, Cardinality cannot be the sole source of information regarding superior/subordinate relations, but may cast the tie-breaking vote when you're not quite sure which entity is superior and which is subordinate.

Super Types and Subtypes

Entities that are extremely similar, but not identical, can be grouped into a Super Type (Figure 5.7). An Entity with a distinct set of mutually exclusive variations can cast those variations as Subtypes of itself, making itself the Super Type. Either path toward a Super Type/Subtype set of entities resolves confusion about similar entities, so they can be included in a Logical Data Model simultaneously as one collective entity (Super Type) and individual entities (Subtypes).

Putting It All Together

Having identified the pieces (Primary Key, Primary Key/Foreign Key Relation, Attribute, Cardinality, and Super Type/Subtype) of a Logical Data Model, we are ready to put the pieces together. For the purpose of this discussion of Logical Data Modeling, we will use the Shipping subject area from the Conceptual Data Model in Figure 5.4. A Logical Data Model expands one subject area, exposing all it entities and relations, e.g., the list of entities shown in Table 5.4.

Notice that all attributes dealing with Date/Time and Price are listed as Event Data. This is showing that these are values derived at the moment of an enterprise event and not modeled as entities.[5]

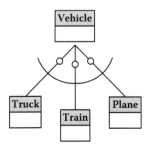

Figure 5.7   Vehicle Super Type.

Table 5.4   Shipping

Shipping — Business Process	
Transportation	Business Process
Product	Business Entity
Warehouse	Business Entity
Vehicle	Business Entity
Destination	Business Entity
Departure Date/Time	Event Data
Arrival Date/Time	Event Data
Warehousing	Business Process
Product	Business Entity
Warehouse	Business Entity
Storage Slot	Business Entity
Storage Pallet	Business Entity
Storage Date/Time	Event Data

Table 5.5   Business Entities

Business Entities	Subject Area
Product	Product
Warehouse	Shipping
Vehicle	Shipping
Destination	Shipping
Storage Slot	Shipping
Storage Pallet	Shipping

This expansion of the Shipping subject area yielded a set of Business Entities, which are listed in Table 5.5. If the entities yielded by expanding a subject area do not have a natural home in the Conceptual Data Model, that probably means the Conceptual Data Model is incomplete or incorrect; either way, the Conceptual Data Model must be updated to provide a natural home for all entities. If the entities yielded by expanding a subject area do have a natural home in the Conceptual Data Model, then probably the Conceptual Data Model is complete and correct.

Finally, the Business Processes (Warehousing and Transportation) and Business Entities (Product, Warehouse, Vehicle, Destination, Storage Slot, and Storage Pallet) are placed into a Logical Data Model of the Shipping subject area using Logical Data Modeling techniques (Primary Key, Primary Key/Foreign Key Relation,

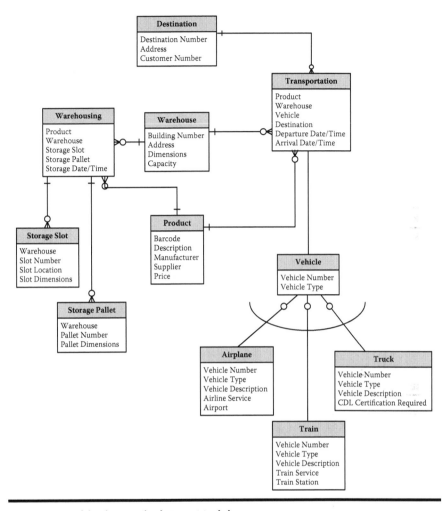

Figure 5.8   Shipping Logical Data Model.

Attribute, Cardinality, and Super Type/Subtype). A possible combined Logical Data Model of the Shipping subject area is shown in Figure 5.8.

A rule of thumb for Logical Data Models is that they don't cross relation lines. If a Logical Data Model does cross relation lines, it probably means one of two things:

- The Conceptual Data Model subject area on which the Logical Data Model is based includes too many entities.
- The entities within the Logical Data Model are defined incorrectly.

While this rule of thumb may seem a bit constraining or arbitrary, Logical Data Models without crossed lines coincidentally tend to avoid confusion about the data and relations within a data warehouse.

The final installment of a Logical Data Model is a Logical Data Model Justification, which is a text explanation by the data modeler of the entities and relations in a Logical Data Model. This is the data modeler's opportunity to document reasons for including and excluding entities and relations as well as provide sample data. A Logical Data Model should address every entity and relation in a Logical Data Model. For example:

- Destination (entity): This is the recipient of a Transportation. Typically, a Destination is a customer. The address must be included, otherwise, we don't know the physical location to which product was transported.
- Destination (one) to Transportation (many): A Destination may have never received a Transportation (i.e., a Product). Alternatively, a Destination may have received many Transportations (i.e., Products). A Transportation can be addressed to one, and only one, Destination.

The source system analysis should be complete before beginning the Logical Data Model. Information from the analysis feeds directly into the Logical Data Model. Specifically, the business subject areas discovered in the analysis are candidates for subject areas in the Conceptual Data Model, which become subject areas in the Logical Data Model. The Logical Data Model may reveal questions and gaps in the information provided by the analysis. That is normal. Rarely does a source system analysis provide all the required information. At that point, the ability to know information is missing is valuable on its own. When the entire Logical Data Model is finished, it should present in symbols and text the enterprise as explained in the analysis. A Logical Data Model should be reviewed against the analysis, which yielded the Conceptual Data Model on which the Logical Data Model is based. Discrepancies between the analysis and Logical Data Model should be resolved at this point.

Finally, Logical Data Modeling is an inexact science, or an art form, or both. From a single source system analysis, multiple Logical Data Models may be created and all of them equally correct. So, there is no single right answer. In Logical Data Modeling, there are many right answers. The best approach to Logical Data Modeling, therefore, is practice. Like other skills, don't wait until you need the skill to develop the skill. Develop the skill, and continue developing the skill, of Logical Data Modeling. That way, when you need it you have it.

Physical Data Model

A Physical Data Model is a representation of the data structures that will hold the data in a data warehouse, and is directly based on a Logical Data Model. The structures of a Physical Data Model are databases, tables, and views. A Physical Data Model indicates the physical data types of all fields, and continues the display of relations that originally appeared in the prerequisite Logical Data Model.

Unfortunately, the notations of a Physical Data Model are very similar to the notations of a Logical Data Model. This similarity tends to cause confusion. The databases, tables, and views of a Physical Data Model are distinctly different from the entities and relations of a Logical Data Model. Whereas the entities and relations of a Logical Data Model represent an enterprise, the databases, tables, and views of a Physical Data Model represent physical data structures. The difference is similar to comparing the real estate listing for a house and the blueprint of the same house. Both provide some similar information, but with different meanings. Fortunately, no one confuses a real estate listing for a blueprint.

A major difference between Logical and Physical Data Models is the incorporation of the Data Warehouse Philosophy. Data elements that facilitate the Data Warehouse Philosophy are included in a Physical Data Model. Subject Orientation is the only part of the Data Warehouse Philosophy that is included in a Logical Data Model, and that happens because a Logical Data Model is based directly on a subject area of the Conceptual Data Model. A review of the elements of the Data Warehouse Philosophy will help incorporate the remaining elements of the Data Warehouse Philosophy into the physical data structures of a data warehouse.

- **Subject Orientation**: The subject orientation was established by the Conceptual Data Model and perpetuated by the Logical Data Model. The Physical Data Model continues the subject orientation of the data warehouse by instantiating one page of the Logical Data Model at a time. The creation of the Physical Data Model does not take three entities and relations from each page of the Logical Data Model to form a single page of the Physical Data Model. Rather, a page of the Physical Data Model addresses the entities and relations in a page of the Logical Data Model.
- **Data Integration**: Thus far, the Conceptual and Logical Data Models have given no thought to the source of any data. The entire enterprise is considered as a whole. The data from the enterprise as displayed in a data warehouse, therefore, should be homogenous, as though the entire enterprise built its data the same way.
  - Form: All the data elements of similar function will look the same, such as,
    - Phone number
    - Employee IDs
    - Currency (i.e., money)

- Dates
- Times
- Timestamps
- Building IDs
- Product IDs

And, will all look the same, regardless of their origin in the enterprise.

- Function: Data elements with similar functions will function the same way.
    - Binary data elements are a common source of disconnect. Applications in the enterprise may use the forms Y/N, Yes/No, 1/0, Y/null, Yes/null. A data warehouse will resolve all such fields to one form, possibly (but, not necessarily) Y/N.
    - Redundant data elements are another common source of disconnect. Applications across the enterprise may communicate the same function different ways. The identifier for a product could be: Prod_ID (Integer), Product_ID (Long Integer), UPC (Long Integer), etc. In the Physical Data Model, all of these disparate data elements will be resolved and consolidated into a single data element with a single data type.
- Grain: Enterprise data encounters granularity primarily in two ways: measurement and hierarchy.
    - The measurement applied to similar data elements will be homogenous. For example, liquids will be measured by the liter, widgets will be counted by units, and gases will be measured by pounds per square inch (PSI).
    - The hierarchy applied to similar data elements will be homogenous. In this sense, hierarchy includes corporate, personnel, product, and calendar hierarchies. For example:
        - Throughput figures for a corporate region cannot be compared to throughput figures for a corporate division.
        - Total hours worked for a single facility cannot be compared to the total hours worked for the entire corporation.
        - The manufacturing figures for a Type A product cannot be compared to the manufacturing figures for a Class 32B product.
        - Sales totals for a calendar week cannot be compared to sales totals for a calendar quarter.
    - For the comparison of measurements within a data warehouse to work correctly, they must be presented at the same hierarchical level of detail.
- Data Integration is most necessary, and most difficult, in merged (or, soon to be merged) enterprises. The possible permutations of data form, function, and grain expand geometrically when organizations merge. In that situation, a data warehouse adds significant value to the enterprise by resolving,

reconciling, and integrating multiple heterogeneous data elements into a homogenous statement of the enterprise.

■ **Nonvolatility**: The Conceptual and Logical Data Models present the enterprise as a single slice or set of slices. The enterprise is not in motion and events happen only once. The Physical Data Model must be prepared for the enterprise to be in motion. Events happen many times in a single second/minute/hour/day. A Physical Data Model must be constructed so that each instance of an Event can be distinctly identified from all the other Event instances, without any randomness (i.e., the data warehouse can find the same distinct Event instance every time it looks for that Event, never finding a different Event instance). Whereas operational applications are volatile in the sense that they retain only the instances of a data element needed to perform its functions (discarding the rest), a data warehouse is nonvolatile in the sense that it retains all instances of a data element.[6]

■ **One Version of the Truth**: A Physical Data Model has only one place for every entity, relation, and measurement in the data warehouse. A Physical Data Model does not allow a second opinion of the same data element. In the case of modified data elements (e.g., Price, Discount Price, Actual Price, etc.), each is considered a different data element. Logically, they answer different questions. The Logical Data Model should have allocated a one-to-one relationship between each individual data question and each individual data entity or relation. The Physical Data Model carries this forward to store the answer to one question, and only one question, in each data element.

■ **Time Variant**: Another aspect of the enterprise in motion is Time. Data Warehouse Philosophy intentionally and explicitly includes Time as a method to express an enterprise in motion. The Conceptual and Logical Data Models, which focus on subject areas, entities, and relations do not focus on the mechanics of Type 1, Type 2, and Type 3 time-variant Dimensions. Regardless, Time was always there, waiting to be included. The Physical Data Model is the point at which Time must become visible in a data warehouse. Time is a measurement and all the preceding elements of Data Warehouse Philosophy must be applied to Time.

  – Form: Time must be expressed in the same form throughout the data warehouse.
  – Function: Time must be applied to similar data elements the same way (absolute, relative, etc.) throughout the data warehouse.
  – Grain: Time must be expressed to similar data elements at the same level of precision throughout the data warehouse.
  – Nonvolatility: A Time measurement applied to a data element must be retained despite the presence of a subsequent Time measurement applied to the same data element.
  – One Version of the Truth: A Time measurement applied to a data element is the only Time measurement applied to that data element. Nowhere in

the data warehouse can be found an alternative Time measurement for an instance of a data element.

■ The purpose of Time Variance in a data warehouse is to allow a data warehouse customer to identify an instance of an entity or an instance of an event at a moment in time in the past. Time was the hidden attribute of every entity and event. A data warehouse increases the granularity of its data by adding the attribute Time and its hierarchy to every entity and event. The attribute Time allows a data warehouse customer to identify the time-variant instance of every entity and event in a data warehouse, which allows that data warehouse customer to see the enterprise as of a moment in time in the past.

■ Time as an attribute can be added to entities and events through three primary methods: Point and Range, Range and Point, and Time Key (a surrogate key).[7]

　－ Point and Range: In this method, a point-in-time data element is included in a row. Then that row can be found by searching on a specific point in time. That row and others from the same period can be found by searching on a Range (i.e., where point-in-time is between Range Begin and Range End). A point-in-time data element works well with event data because an event occurs at a point in time. A point-in-time data element does not work well with an entity because an entity can exist over a long period of time, which would require many points-in-time data elements to represent that Range.

　－ Range and Point: In this method, a Range data element (two inclusive time elements: Begin Time and End Time) is included in a row. Then, that row can be found by searching on any time within that Range (i.e., where Time Value is between Begin Time and End Time). A Range data element works well with entity data because entities exist over a period of time. A Range data element does not work well with Event data because an Event occurs at a single moment, whereas a Range encompasses many moments.

　－ Time Key: In this method, the entity Time is recognized and captured in its own table. Each row is assigned a sequential Time Key. That Time Key is then used in the Point and Range and Range and Point methods listed above. The advantage of this approach is that it promotes the use of corporate, fiscal, government, and foreign calendars within a data warehouse. The Time Key can be based on the number of seconds in a year (31,536,000) or the number of minutes in a year (525,600), depending on the required level of detail and precision in the Time dimension. Each second of the year can have its own Time Key. The first second of the year has the Time Key 1 and the last second of the year has the Time Key 31,536,000. By appending the year to the front of the Time Key, first minute of the year 2007 (2,007,000,001) can be distinguished from the first minute of the year 2006 (2,006,000,001).

– Time is inexact and imprecise. No one can name the exact micro nano second that something happened. So, a data warehouse must agree on a lowest granularity of time. That lowest level of granularity should be the level of granularity used in the methods listed above.

■ **Long-Term Investment**: A data warehouse is an enterprise asset. The purpose of any enterprise asset is to generate a ROI. An asset has two methods by which to increase its ROI. The first method is to increase its Return. A data warehouse increases its Return by improving enterprise decisions, yielding information as a competitive advantage. The second method is to reduce its Investment, which includes the Cost of Ownership. A data warehouse can increase its Cost of Ownership by inflexibility. If every time the enterprise changes its landscape, a data warehouse must modify its representation of the enterprise (at a cost of thousands of dollars each time), that data warehouse reduces its own ROI and viability as an enterprise asset. A Physical Data Model should yield a data warehouse flexible enough to express the enterprise in all its permutations. The primary method by which a Physical Data Model contributes to this flexibility is by normalizing hidden attributes out of an entity. For example, an enterprise uses the entity Truck to deliver product. Will the enterprise always use Truck to deliver product? In the future, the enterprise could use Car to deliver product or Third-Party Delivery or Partner Retail Store (allowing customers to pick up the product themselves). Product can get to the customer by any number of means. The enterprise can use one, none, or all of them. A data warehouse can be prepared for such changes by normalizing out the Type, Purpose, and Role from the entity Truck.[8] Normalized this way, the Truck entity becomes a Capital Equipment with the attributes Type = Truck, Purpose = Transportation, and Role = Deliver. Taken to the next level, the Capital Equipment (Type = Truck, Purpose = Transportation, and Role = Deliver) can be further abstracted.

– Type = Truck could be abstracted further to Type = Vehicle and Subtype = Truck.

– Role = Deliver should be removed from the Capital Equipment entity altogether and moved over to the event which captures the delivery.[9] The reason for this move is that the Role of a Capital Equipment can be different in every event without changing the Capital Equipment. In one event, it could Role = Deliver and in another it could Role = Paperweight, with no modification to the Capital Equipment.

– Purpose = Transportation should remain in the Capital Equipment entity. Purpose expresses the intended use of a piece of equipment, whereas Role expresses the actual use of that equipment. The intended purpose for a piece of equipment is a logical attribute of that equipment, regardless of what actually happens. The Purpose of Capital Equipment can change from Transportation to Training. Such a change would reflect on the Capital Equipment, but not on the event two weeks ago when that truck was used to deliver boxes of product to a customer. Purpose, therefore, is a logical attribute of the entity and not the event.

- This abstraction of Truck is achieved by going up one hierarchical level above Truck and then looking hierarchically down at Truck to find the questions it answers. Based on this example, an entity can have a Type, Subtype, and Purpose, which can be normalized in the Physical Data Model, and that entity can have a Role that can be normalized into its events.
- The goal is flexibility. The process of normalizing out the hidden attributes of entities increases the flexibility of a data warehouse, which reduces its Cost of Ownership and increases its ROI and viability as an asset and long-term investment.

Having considered the infusion of Data Warehouse Philosophy (Subject Orientation, Data Integration, Nonvolatility, Time Variance, One Version of the Truth, and Long-Term Investment) into the information provided by the Logical Data Model, a data warehouse designer is ready to begin creating a Physical Data Model. The question is which kind? Data warehousing has yielded three primary varieties of data warehouse: Dimensional Data Model, Third Normal Form, and Recursive Data Model.

Dimensional Data Model

A Dimensional Data Model casts data into two groups: Facts and Dimensions. Facts are also known as Events or Transactions. A Fact is something that happened. For example, a Fact can be a sales transaction, a manufacture event, or a published written statement. Dimensions are data that qualify or describe enterprise entities involved in a Fact.[10] A dimension might include such attributes of an entity as Color, Brand, Date Placed in Service, Department, etc. When a Fact row is joined with such a Dimension row, we can answer such questions as: "What was the color of the thing involved in the event?" or "To which Department do we apply this event?" In that way, a Dimensional Data Model captures an event in a Fact table, and the attributes of entities involved in an event are captured in Dimension tables.

A Fact table incorporates the entities that were identified in the Logical Data Model. Typically, those entities include:

- Time: An event happens at a moment in time
- Place: An event happens in a place or space
- Person: People are usually involved in events
- Thing: Events are often focused on or around an object
- Equipment: Participants in an event often use a tool or equipment
- How: The action that was performed

■ Why: Sometimes, but not always, a reason for the action is provided

This arrangement of a Fact table surrounded by Dimension tables has become known as a Star Schema because it looks like a star, which is shown in Figure 5.9. At the center is a Fact table surrounded by Dimension tables.

A Fact table joins to the surrounding Dimension tables using Primary Key/Foreign Key relations.[11] The Primary Key of a single row from a Dimension Row is embedded into a row in a Fact table. That way, a Fact row will join to one and only one row within each Dimension table. The relational integrity between a Fact table and its associated Dimension tables must be carefully guarded.

■ If a Fact row joins to multiple Dimension rows for a Primary Key/Foreign Key relation, the Fact rows returned by a query will multiply by a factor equaling the number of Dimension rows in the Primary Key/Foreign Key relation.

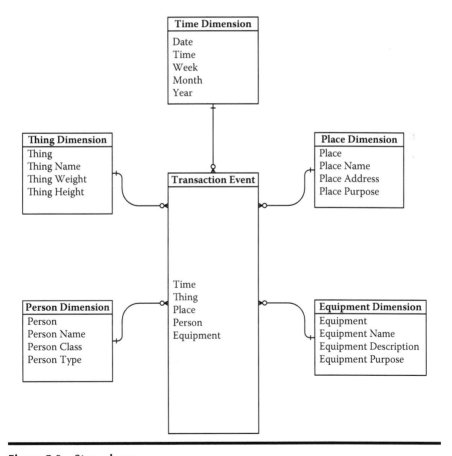

Figure 5.9 Star schema.

■ If a Fact row joins to zero Dimension rows for a Primary Key/Foreign Key relation, a query will return no rows, which include that Primary Key/Foreign Key relation.

The Primary Key/Foreign Key joining between a Fact table and a Dimension table must occur at the same hierarchical grain. For instance, if the Fact table has a Product Key and the primary key of the Product Dimension is a Department Key, they cannot join. They can only join if the foreign key in the Fact table matches the hierarchical grain of the primary key of the Dimension table. If the Fact table has a Product Key and the primary key of the Product Dimension is also a Product Key, they can join.

The hierarchical grain at which a Dimension table joins to a Fact table is the lowest relevant level of that Dimension's hierarchy. No Structured Query Language (SQL) can summarize lower than the hierarchical grain of a Fact table. For instance, if the Fact table has a Product Key and the Dimension table has a Product Key and a Subproduct Key, the Dimension's Subproduct Key will never be used. So, the lowest relevant hierarchical grain of a Dimension table is the hierarchical level at which it joins to a Fact table.

Ideally, a Dimension table contains in each row the entire hierarchy for a given Primary Key. For example, a Date Dimension row for the date August 27, 1993 should include every hierarchical level (e.g., Week, Month, Quarter, Year, etc.) for that Date. A Facility Dimension row for Warehouse #253 should include every hierarchical level (e.g., Warehouse, Warehouse Group, Warehouse Class, Warehouse Type, Warehouse Region, Warehouse District, Warehouse Division, etc.) for that warehouse. By including all hierarchical levels in a single row, a data warehouse customer can summarize data at the Week and Warehouse Region, or Month and Warehouse Type, or Quarter and Warehouse Group without adding any new tables to the SQL. Once a Fact table can join to a Warehouse Dimension and a Date Dimension table, all the hierarchical information necessary to summarize at a higher level is already present.

Dimension tables are very flexible. Attributes, hierarchies, and hierarchical levels can be added, removed, or changed by simply modifying the columns in a Dimension table. Rather than update five normalized tables, a single update to a single table can add a new hierarchy and the Dimension joins to that hierarchy. Immediately, the new hierarchy is available to any Fact table joined with that Dimension table.

Join Strategies

The Primary Key/Foreign Key joining between a Fact table and a Dimension table can occur by various permutations of Source Native Key, Surrogate Key, and Surrogate Key Version. A Source Native Key is the identifier for an entity provided by a source system (i.e., the enterprise). A Surrogate Key is a key generated by and for a data warehouse, and a Surrogate Version Key is a second sequential key, which distinguishes the individual instances of an entity. A Version Key is only applicable when all instances of an entity share the same Surrogate Key.

Source Native Key—The simplest method by which a Fact table can join with a Dimension table is by using the Source Native Key (Figure 5.10), in this example labeled "Thing." Apparently, the enterprise has two unique identifiers: Chair and Table. As long as the Dimension table has only one row for the entity labeled Chair and only one row for the entity labeled Table, this method will work. This achieves only a Type 1 time-variant relation.[12] The SQL WHERE clause joins only on the Thing field:

> Fact.Thing = Dimension.Thing

Source Native Key with Dates—Time Variance can be added to the relation between the Fact and Dimension tables. In this example, each instance of Chair and Table are captured with their Begin and End Dates. The join between the Fact and Dimension tables must include the Source Native Key and Dates (Figure 5.11). This achieves only a Type 2 time-variant relation. The relational integrity of this approach includes the Date fields.

The Dimension table can have only one instance of Chair and Table on a single Date. If the Dimension table has two or more instances of Chair or Table on a single Date, the results from these Dimensional tables will be multiplied by a factor of the number of Dimension rows on a single Date.

A query can select a set of Fact rows across a range of dates. The Fact rows relate to Dimension rows on Source Native Key and dates. The SQL WHERE clause joins on the Thing and Date fields:

Fact Table				
Person	Place	Thing	Date	Equipment
Fred	Seattle, WA	Chair	March 13, 2007	None
Susan	St Paul, MN	Chair	March 15, 2007	Repair Kit
Joe	Tampa, FL	Table	April 2, 2007	Finishing Kit
Alice	Reno, NV	Table	April 4, 2007	None

Dimension Table			
Thing	Description	Begin Date	End Date
Chair	Mahogany Chair	May 1, 2002	December 31, 9999
Table	Victorian Table	August 27, 1993	May 1, 2007

Figure 5.10   Source Native Key.

Fact Table				
Person	Place	Thing	Date	Equipment
Fred	Seattle, WA	Chair	March 13, 2007	None
Susan	St Paul, MN	Chair	March 15, 2007	Repair Kit
Joe	Tampa, FL	Table	April 2, 2007	Finishing Kit
Alice	Reno, NV	Table	April 4, 2007	None

Dimension Table			
Thing	Description	Begin Date	End Date
Chair	Mahogany Chair	May 1, 2002	May 12, 2007
Chair	Pine Chair	May 13, 2005	March 14, 2007
Chair	Oak Chair	March 15, 2007	December 31, 9999
Table	Victorian Table	August 27, 1993	September 5, 2001
Table	Icelandic Table	September 2, 2001	April 15, 2007
Table	Round Table	April 16, 2007	May 1, 2007

Figure 5.11   Source Native Key with Dates.

Fact.Thing = Dimension.Thing
And Fact.Date between Dimension.Begin Date and Dimension.End Date

Data Warehouse Dates—A Dimension table can include multiple Date fields with distinct meanings. The use of multiple Date fields in a data warehouse is different from the multiple fields in an operational database. Typically, in an operational database, one Date field identifies when the data in a row became effective and another field identifies when the data in a row ceased being effective. These dates are basically operational metadata. A data warehouse will typically include additional metadata about each row. The additional Date metadata may include:

- The date or timestamp when the data in a row was extracted from a source system
- The date or timestamp when the data in a row was transformed and ready to load
- The date or timestamp when the data in a row was loaded into the data warehouse
- The date or timestamp on which the data warehouse considers the data in a row to be relevant to the enterprise, i.e., Begin Date
- The date or timestamp on which the data warehouse considers the data in a row to no longer be relevant to the enterprise, i.e., End Date.

Notice that none of these Date fields are the Effective and Not Effective operational metadata Date fields. In the context of a data warehouse, the Effective and

Not Effective operational metadata Date fields are attributes of a row of data; they are not metadata of the data warehouse. In this discussion of Dates in a data warehouse, the Begin Date and End Date fields are not the operational Effective and Not Effective Date fields. Rather, the Begin Date and End Date fields are the dates within which a row of data is/was relevant to the enterprise and, therefore, the data warehouse.

The operational Effective and Not Effective Date fields are relevant to the enterprise. So, why are they not used as the Relevant and Not Relevant Date fields in a data warehouse? The answer is that the operational Effective and Not Effective Date fields are not time variant (that sounds like a contradiction—Date fields are not time variant) and are volatile, whereas a data warehouse is time variant and nonvolatile. For example:

- **Restating the Past:** An operational system can adjust dates in the past to document when something happened. These dates are retroactively relevant to the enterprise; however, they are not a true representation of the data values that were present within the enterprise when information was gathered and decisions made in the past. If a data warehouse wanted to represent restated data values from the past, they should include a date or timestamp showing when the retroactive restated data value was available.
  - Operational System: Fred was the manager of store #1024 from January 1 through March 31.
  - Data Warehouse:
    - As of January, the data warehouse observed that Fred is the manager of store #1024; the Begin Date is January 1.
    - As of March, the data warehouse observed that Fred is no longer the manager of store #1024; the End Date is March 31.
    - As of April, the data warehouse observed that Alice is the manager of store #1024; the Begin Date is April 1.
  - Operational System: On April 14, an operational application adjusted the end of Fred's term as manager of store #1024 to March 29 for payroll adjustment reasons.
  - Data Warehouse: As of April 14, Alice is still the manager of store #1024, and the Begin Date is still April 1.
- **Restating the Future:** Operational applications plan for the future. The Fact tables report events that happened, which implicitly indicates transactions or events that have occurred in the past (not the future). Dimension tables, which join with Fact tables, will, therefore, only join on Dimension data values that correspond to the time variance of the Fact tables that indicate events that occurred in the past. Future events, therefore, are not relevant events to a data warehouse. Future plans, however, can be relevant to a data warehouse. At a moment in the past, a future event (e.g., fire extinguisher inspection, light bulb replacement, employee performance review, etc.) may be planned.

In that scenario, the event in the past is the planning of a future event. That planned future event may be updated multiple times between "now" and the planned future event. Each of those plan updates is a past event.

- – Operational System: As of April 20, an operational application plans to make George the manager of store #1024 beginning June 4.
- – Data Warehouse: As of April 20, Alice is still the manager of store #1024, and the Begin Date is still April 1.

■ **Dates as Attributes**: Operational entities (e.g., software license agreements, planned inspection dates, employee anniversary dates, etc.) are relevant to the enterprise as entity attributes. Date attributes, however, do not describe when something happened in the enterprise such that it will be recorded in a data warehouse. Rather, the appearance or removal of an attribute date is an event, which may be recorded in a data warehouse as either an event in a Fact table or an update to an entity in a Dimension table.

- – Operational System: As of March 11, the lease agreement for store #1024 extends from January 1 through June 30.
- – Data Warehouse: As of March 11
  - ■ The Lease Effective Date is January 1.
  - ■ The Lease Not Effective Date is June 30.
  - ■ The Begin Date is March 11.
- – Operational System: As of May 24, the lease agreement for store #1024 extends from July 1 through December 31.
- – Data Warehouse: As of May 24
  - ■ The Lease Effective Date is July 1.
  - ■ The Lease Not Effective Date is December 31.
  - ■ The Begin Date is May 24.
  - ■ The End Date of the previous Lease row is May 23.

Data warehouse Begin and End Timestamp or Date fields work best as inclusive date fields. Inclusive dates mean the Begin Date is the first date on which a row is relevant, and the End Date is the last date on which a row is relevant. This method facilitates the use of a SQL BETWEEN statement when selecting relevant rows:

Where Event_Date between Begin_Date and End_Date

The ANSI standard for a BETWEEN statement stipulates the rows selected are inclusive of the data values in the BETWEEN statement. Therefore, inclusive Begin and End Date fields fit the ANSI standard.

The Source Native Key method works well when the uniqueness of the keys is enforced by the source system, which implicitly means the data warehouse extracts its dimension data from only one source system. If, however, a data warehouse extracts its dimension data from multiple source systems, the Source Native Key method fails because it cannot integrate the dimension data from multiple disparate source systems. When a data warehouse extracts dimension data from disparate source systems, the disparate Source Native Keys must be integrated into a single set of keys: Surrogate Keys.

Surrogate Key—In a data warehouse that must represent disparate source systems, Surrogate Keys are used to combine and conform entity keys that are not coordinated in the enterprise (Figure 5.12). If so, the Fact table can join the Dimension table using the generated Surrogate Key. This achieves only a Type 1 time-variant relation. This approach requires the Dimension table have only one row for each Surrogate Key, otherwise, the results from these tables will be multiplied by a factor of the number of rows the Dimension table has for a duplicated Surrogate Key. The SQL WHERE clause joins on the Thing Key field:

Fact.Thing Key = Dimension.Thing Key

Surrogate Key with Source Native Key—When the Surrogate Key in the Dimension table identifies the entity, but not the instance of the entity, the Source Native Key can be used to identify an individual instance of an entity (Figure 5.13). This method achieves a Type 2 time-variant relation without actually manipulating the Date fields. In this example:

- The Surrogate Key 123 identifies the entity Chair, but the Source Native Key (Thing ID) must be included to identify the individual instance of Chair.
- The Surrogate Key 234 identifies the entity Table, but the Source Native Key (Thing ID) must be included to identify the individual instance of Table.

The SQL WHERE clause joins on the Thing Key and Thing ID fields:

Fact.Thing Key = Dimension.Thing Key
And Fact.Thing ID = Dimension.Thing ID

Surrogate Key with Surrogate Key Version: Type 2 Join—When the Surrogate Key identifies the entity, but not the individual instance of an entity, a Surrogate

Fact Table				
Person	Place	Thing Key	Date	Equipment
Fred	Seattle, WA	123	March 13, 2007	None
Susan	St Paul, MN	123	March 15, 2007	Repair Kit
Joe	Tampa, FL	234	April 2, 2007	Finishing Kit
Alice	Reno, NV	234	April 4, 2007	None

Dimension Table				
Thing Key	Thing	Description	Begin Date	End Date
123	Chair	Mahogany Chair	May 1, 2002	December 31, 9999
234	Table	Victorian Table	August 27, 1993	May 1, 2007

Figure 5.12   Surrogate Key.

Fact Table

Person	Place	Thing Key	Thing ID	Date	Equipment
Fred	Seattle, WA	123	Chr_B42Z	March 13, 2007	None
Susan	St Paul, MN	123	Chr_B35X	March 15, 2007	Repair Kit
Joe	Tampa, FL	234	Tbl_74CS	April 2, 2007	Finishing Kit
Alice	Reno, NV	234	Tbl_74CS	April 4, 2007	None

Dimension Table

Thing Key	Thing ID	Description	Begin Date	End Date
123	Chr_A23J	Mahogany Chair	May 1, 2002	May 12, 2005
123	Chr_B42Z	Pine Chair	May 13, 2005	March 14, 2007
123	Chr_B35X	Oak Chair	March 15, 2007	December 31, 9999
234	Tbl_89RE	Victorian Table	August 27, 1993	September 5, 2001
234	Tbl_74CS	Icelandic Table	September 2, 2001	April 15, 2007
234	Tbl_35XX	Round Table	April 16, 2007	May 1, 2007

Figure 5.13 Surrogate Key with Source Native Key.

Fact Table

Person	Place	Thing Key	Thing Key Version	Date	Equipment
Fred	Seattle, WA	123	2	March 13, 2007	None
Susan	St Paul, MN	123	3	March 15, 2007	Repair Kit
Joe	Tampa, FL	234	2	April 2, 2007	Finishing Kit
Alice	Reno, NV	234	2	April 4, 2007	None

Dimension Table

Thing Key	Thing Key Version	Thing ID	Description	Begin Date	End Date
123	1	Chr_A23J	Mahogany Chair	May 1, 2002	May 12, 2005
123	2	Chr_A23J	Pine Chair	May 13, 2005	March 14, 2007
123	3	Chr_A23J	Oak Chair	March 15, 2007	December 31, 9999
123	0	Chr_A23J	Oak Chair		
234	1	Tbl_89RE	Victorian Table	August 27, 1993	September 5, 2001
234	2	Tbl_89RE	Icelandic Table	September 2, 2001	April 15, 2007
234	3	Tbl_89RE	Round Table	April 16, 2007	May 1, 2007
234	0	Tbl_89RE	Round Table		

Figure 5.14 Surrogate Key with Surrogate Key Version: Type 2 join.

Key Version can be added (Figure 5.14). The combination of a Surrogate Key and a Surrogate Key Version creates a compound key relation (i.e., a Primary Key/Foreign Key relation based on multiple fields) between the Fact and Dimension tables. This achieves a Type 2 time-variant relation. The SQL WHERE clause joins on the Thing Key and Thing Key Version fields:

> Fact.Thing Key = Dimension.Thing Key
> And Fact.Thing Key Version = Dimension.Thing Key Version

Surrogate Key with Surrogate Key Version: Type 1 Join—Taking the same Fact and Dimension tables, a Type 1 time-variant relation can be achieved if the most recent record in the Dimension table is also written with Thing Key Version = 0 (Figure 5.15). Notice the rows with Thing Key Version = 0 are identical to the rows with Thing Key Version = 3, except for the Begin Date and End Date fields. That is because the third version is the most recent. The Begin Date and End Date fields are irrelevant in the Thing Key Version = 0 rows because those rows create a Type 1 Join, meaning all of history is cast as that Join. Having included the most recent row for each entity with Thing Key Version = 0, the SQL WHERE clause joins on the Thing Key and Thing ID fields:

Fact.Thing Key = Dimension.Thing Key
And 0 = Dimension.Thing Key Version

Surrogate Key with Surrogate Key Version: Type 3 Join—Taking the same Fact and Dimension tables, a Type 3 time-variant relation (Figure 5.16) can be achieved if the historical record that is superimposed over the enterprise is written with Thing Key Version = X.[13] Notice the rows with Thing Key Version = X are identical to the rows with Thing Key Version = 1. That is because the first version is the version that the enterprise wishes to superimpose over other entity values. Having included the superimposed row for each entity with Thing Key Version = X, the SQL WHERE clause joins on the Thing Key and Thing ID fields:

Fact.Thing Key = Dimension.Thing Key
And X = Dimension.Thing Key Version

The advantage of using both a Surrogate Key and Surrogate Key version is that without any table changes, they facilitate Type 1, Type 2, and Type 3 time-variant relations.

Fact Table

Person	Place	Thing Key	Thing Key Version	Date	Equipment
Fred	Seattle, WA	123	2	March 13, 2007	None
Susan	St Paul, MN	123	3	March 15, 2007	Repair Kit
Joe	Tampa, FL	234	2	April 2, 2007	Finishing Kit
Alice	Reno, NV	234	2	April 4, 2007	None

Dimension Table

Thing Key	Thing Key Version	Thing ID	Description	Begin Date	End Date
123	1	Chr_A23J	Mahogany Chair	May 1, 2002	May 12, 2005
123	2	Chr_A23J	Pine Chair	May 13, 2005	March 14, 2007
123	3	Chr_A23J	Oak Chair	March 15, 2007	December 31, 9999
123	0	Chr_A23J	Oak Chair		
234	1	Tbl_89RE	Victorian Table	August 27, 1993	September 5, 2001
234	2	Tbl_89RE	Icelandic Table	September 2, 2001	April 15, 2007
234	3	Tbl_89RE	Round Table	April 16, 2007	May 1, 2007
234	0	Tbl_89RE	Round Table		

Figure 5.15   Surrogate Key with Surrogate Key Version: Type 1 join.

Fact Table					
Person	Place	Thing Key	Thing Key Version	Date	Equipment
Fred	Seattle, WA	123	2	March 13, 2007	None
Susan	St Paul, MN	123	3	March 15, 2007	Repair Kit
Joe	Tampa, FL	234	2	April 2, 2007	Finishing Kit
Alice	Reno, NV	234	2	April 4, 2007	None

Dimension Table					
Thing Key	Thing Key Version	Thing ID	Description	Begin Date	End Date
123	1	Chr_A23J	Mahogany Chair	May 1, 2002	May 12, 2005
123	2	Chr_A23J	Pine Chair	May 13, 2005	March 14, 2007
123	3	Chr_A23J	Oak Chair	March 15, 2007	December 31, 9999
123	0	Chr_A23J	Oak Chair		
123	X	Chr_A23J	Mahogany Chair		
234	1	Tbl_89RE	Victorian Table	August 27, 1993	September 5, 2001
234	2	Tbl_89RE	Icelandic Table	September 2, 2001	April 15, 2007
234	3	Tbl_89RE	Round Table	April 16, 2007	May 1, 2007
234	0	Tbl_89RE	Round Table		
234	X	Tbl_89RE	Victorian Table		

Figure 5.16   Surrogate Key with Surrogate Key Version: Type 3 join.

Conformed Dimensions

Dimensional Data Modeling focuses on the business activities of an enterprise. Each Fact table captures instances of a specific business event. That business event can be a retail sales transaction, consulting contract negotiation, or completion of a manufacturing assembly. An enterprise has many such business events. Fact tables alone are designed to capture all business events.

Ideally, all business events in an enterprise will be able to share the same dimension tables. Consider the example in Figure 5.17 of an enterprise that manufactures and sells a product. This Dimensional Data Model has a Fact table for each of these business events: Manufacture and Sales. In this example, both Fact tables can share the Product, Place, and Date Dimension tables. These shared tables are called Conformed Dimensions.[14] The Manufacture Fact table is not able to share the Store table because the manufacturing plant is not a store.

The hierarchy of Type = Store can be abstracted out of the Store Dimension table, yielding a Facility Dimension table (wherein rows can have Type = Store and Type = Manufacturing Plant). The new Facility Dimension table can now be Conformed (i.e., shared) between the two Sales and Manufacture Fact tables, which are displayed in Figure 5.18.

This practice of conforming dimensions so multiple Fact tables can be shared is relevant to the discussion above of a data warehouse as a long-term investment. A data warehouse can leverage its Dimension tables for multiple Fact tables, which reduces the cost of owning and operating a data warehouse.

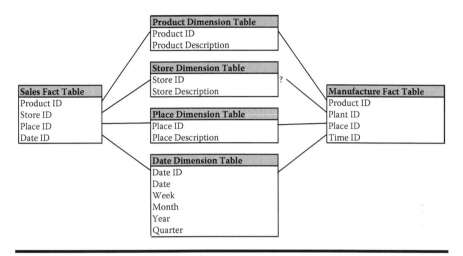

Figure 5.17   Store Dimensions Not Conformed.

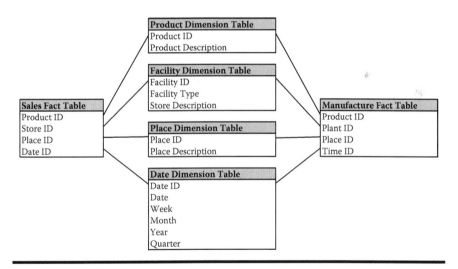

Figure 5.18   Conformed Dimensions.

Junk Dimensions

Every enterprise has its odds and ends data. These are the data that have no hierarchy, specific meaning, and probably no look-up reference data to provide a description or translation. Occasionally, this odds and ends data is needed in a data warehouse. Ralph Kimball created the concept of a Junk Dimension specifically for this circumstance.[15]

A Junk Dimension captures the odds and ends data of an enterprise, while making no attempt to apply a hierarchy or categorization scheme. The method to create a Junk Dimension is simple. Collect all such odds and ends data into a single Dimension table. Derive all permutations of the data values. To each row assign a sequential unique Surrogate Key, as seen in Figure 5.19.

In a Fact table that uses the odds and ends data, apply the Surrogate Key value from the Junk Dimension row that matches the permutation of junk data to each Fact row.

Different Grains

The bane of Dimensional Data Modeling is differing grains. This occurs when grain of a Fact table does not match the grain of an existing Dimension table.[16] The goal is to share Dimension tables as much as possible, which contributes to the consistency and power of a data warehouse. When a Dimension cannot be shared by a specific Fact table, rather than create a Dimension table only for that Fact table, a Bridge or Helper Table can complete the join.

Using the example in Figure 5.20, a Fact table on the left is at the Facility level of granularity, whereas the Fact table on the right is at the Warehouse Group level of granularity. The Facility level Fact table cannot join to Warehouse Group level the Fact table. So, a Warehouse Group Bridge table is constructed to allow the two Fact tables (grained at the Facility and Warehouse Group levels) to relate to each other. Bridge tables, such as the Warehouse Group Bridge table, allow Fact tables of different grains to combine disparate data into a single statement of information.

Multiple Results

A business may generate multiple results for a single event.[17] Such instances include:

■ Multiple Answers: When your mechanic diagnoses three problems with your car.

Surrogate Key	Beagle Code	Buzzer Time	Congo Rule	Doggie Day	Everlong
1	SS	1	Left	Monday	Y
2	ASFG	1	Left	Tuesday	N
3	GFGF	2	Right	Monday	Y
4	F	2	Left	Tuesday	Y
5	RR	1	Left	Wednesday	N
6	GRT	2	Right	Wednesday	N
7	YJ	3	Right	Thursday	N
8	JK	3	Right	Monday	Y
9	DH	4	Left	Monday	Y
10	F	3	Left	Wednesday	N
11	RR	5	Right	Friday	N

Figure 5.19 Junk Dimension.

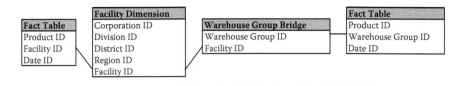

Figure 5.20   Bridge Table.

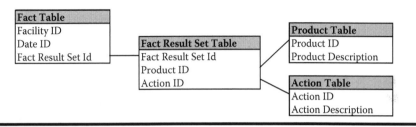

Figure 5.21   Result Set table.

- Multiple Events: When one cell phone customer calls another cell phone customer and both are billed for the same call.

In these situations, a Fact table joins to a Fact Result Set table (Figure 5.21), which is a one-to-many join. The Fact table has its one row. The Fact Result Set table has multiple rows, one for each result of the business event. The Fact Result Set table then joins to Dimension tables.

Factless Fact

A business event may not necessarily transact dollars, move units of product, or return any sort of arithmetic measurement. Business events such as these are known as Factless Facts.[18] Factless Facts do not really lack a fact, rather, they lack a measurement. Business events without a measurement include:

- An airplane lands
- A store opens (and closes) its doors
- A truck arrives at a warehouse

For Facts such as these, a Fact table contains only the Foreign Keys of the entities involved in the business event. No measurements are manufactured or defaulted. Rather, the Factless Fact table is allowed to exist with only Dimension foreign keys and no measurement.

Snowflake Schema

Sometimes a Dimension, or part of a Dimension, is too complex or volatile to work well in a single Dimension row. In such situations, part of the Dimension is normalized out of the Dimension yielding a Dimension of a Dimension, or a Sub-dimension.[19] Splitting a Dimension in a Star Schema yields a Snowflake Schema (Figure 5.22). After enough Dimensions have been split, the schema begins to resemble a snowflake.

A Snowflake Schema is created by normalizing Dimension tables. Figure 5.23 shows the progression from a completely denormalized Facility Dimension table to a fully normalized Facility Hierarchy. In the fully normalized Facility Hierarchy, the Facility Dimension table is no longer necessary and is removed.

Dimensional Data Model Summary

A Dimensional Data Model answers the questions of who, what, when, where, how, and possibly why by combining in a single Fact table row measurements (e.g., units, volume, money, etc.) of a business event and foreign keys to Dimension tables.

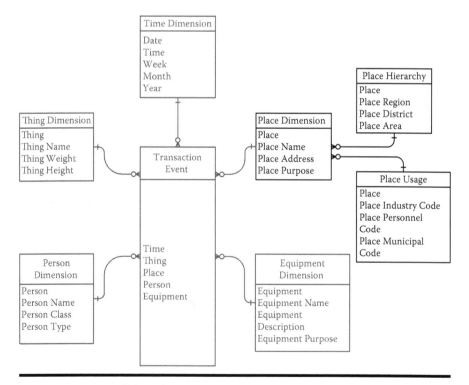

Figure 5.22　Snowflake Schema.

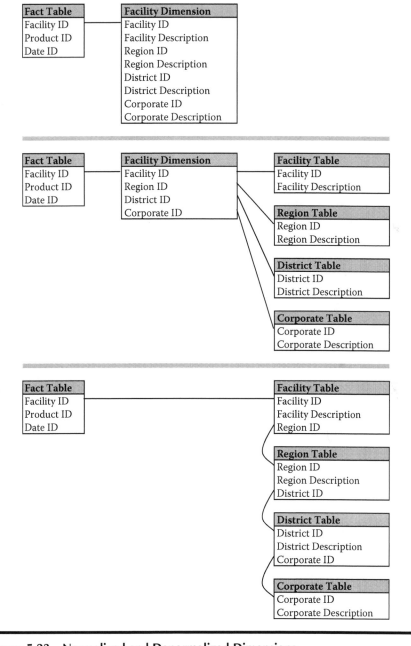

Figure 5.23 Normalized and Denormalized Dimensions.

Dimension tables include in each row enough information about its hierarchy to allow the data warehouse customer to summarize data at a higher level of that hierarchy. Dimension tables can be shared (i.e., Conformed) to multiple Fact tables throughout a data warehouse.

These tools (primarily Fact and Dimension tables) allow a Dimensional Data Model to incorporate the Data Warehouse Philosophy.

- Subject Orientation: A Fact table defines the subject for each section of a data warehouse.
- Data Integration: Conformed Dimension tables express entity information in the same form, function, and grain across the data warehouse.
- Nonvolatility: New rows can be added to Fact and Dimension tables without destroying existing rows.
- Time Variant: Dimension tables allow Fact tables to join to historical Dimension rows in the past.
- One Version of the Truth: A Fact table that captures a business event is the only Fact table to capture that business event. A Dimension table that captures a hierarchy is the only Dimension table to capture that hierarchy.
- Long-Term Investment: The Type and Purpose of an entity can be explicitly expressed in a Dimension. The Role of an entity can be explicitly expressed in a Fact table. The resulting flexibility allows a data warehouse to present enterprise activity over a significant period of time without significant modifications.

Third Normal Form Data Model

In the early days of data warehousing, early developers of decision support systems used the best methods they had available to them. The best, and arguably only, method of modeling data in a RDBMS was the Third Normal Form.[20] The developers' knowledge and methods of Third Normal Form were based on their experience, which occurred in operational relational databases. Their toolset was limited by the RDBMS optimizers that were available. They could only ask an optimizer to perform SQL functions that it could interpret.

During the 1990s, advances in computer science and technology increased the functions available in RDBMS optimizers. Data warehouse developers could ask a RDBMS optimizer to perform logical, mathematical, and statistical functions far more powerful than had been available in 1980. Another event occurred during the 1990s that changed data warehousing: Ralph Kimball introduced the Dimensional Data Model. Kimball used the Dimensional Data Model to solve shortcomings of Third Normal Form data warehouses. Primary among these shortcomings were:

- Third Normal Form data warehouses do not model a business or subject area, they model relationships between data elements instead.
- Third Normal Form data warehouse structures are too erratic and scattered to be easily understood or optimized.[21]

While these complaints were valid, their effect was probably not what Ralph Kimball intended. While some data warehouses incorporated a Dimensional Data Model, others incorporated the Fact and Dimension concepts from the Dimensional Data Model into the Third Normal Form data model. By the end of the 1990s, these two changes (improvements in RDBMS optimizers and Dimensional Data Modeling) made possible Third Normal Form data warehouses, which incorporated the Fact and Dimension concepts, running on optimizers that could perform the required SQL functions.

A Third Normal Form data warehouse uses data structures that are normalized to the Third Normal Form. The result is many small tables rather than a few large tables, and many table joins rather than a few table joins. This is a trade-off between the number of tables and the number of joins. A Third Normal Form physical data model looks like the data model in Figure 5.24. At the top is a Fact table: Transaction Header. Below that table are a series of normalized Fact tables: Transaction Time, Transaction Thing, Transaction Place, and Transaction Person. These tables incorporate the entities that were identified in the Logical Data Model. Typically, those entities include:

- Time: An event happens at a moment in time.
- Place: An event happens in a place or space.
- Person: People are usually involved in an event.
- Thing: An event is often focused on or around an object.
- Equipment: Participants in an event often use a tool or equipment.
- How: The action that was performed.
- Why: Sometimes, but not always, a reason for the action is provided.

Third Normal Form Fact Tables

The rules of normalization remove redundant data elements. Typically, enterprise events generate a fair amount of redundant data. For example, the insurance transaction in Figure 5.25 has four rows and nine columns.

Of these nine columns, the first six are completely redundant because all four rows have the same values in the Facility, Date, Time, Agent, Type, and Transaction # columns. These six columns can be normalized. They are reduced to one column and placed in a Fact Header table.

The remaining fields are placed in a Fact Detail table (Figure 5.26). The Fact Header and Fact Detail table join on the Transaction # and Policy Number fields.

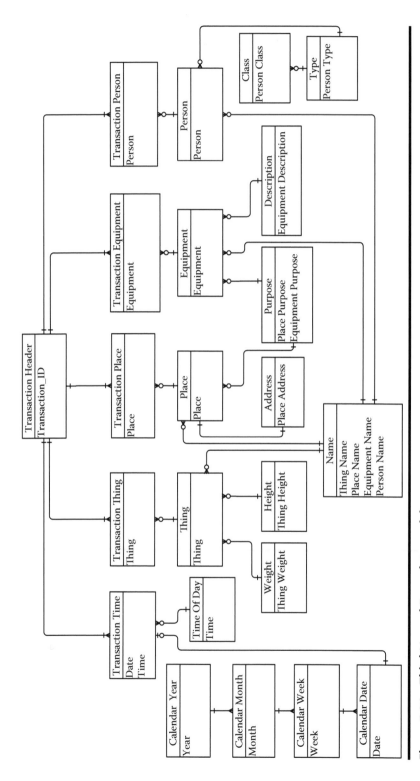

Figure 5.24   Third Normal Form data model.

Fact Table – Insurance Sales Event								
Facility	Date	Time	Agent	Type	Transaction #	Policy Number	Insured	Relation
1357	05/12/1997	13:35	Fred	New	051297-132	AB-2324-01	Jane Doe	Primary
1357	05/12/1997	13:35	Fred	New	051297-132	AB-2324-02	John Doe	Husband
1357	05/12/1997	13:35	Fred	New	051297-132	AB-2324-03	Janice Doe	Daughter
1357	05/12/1997	13:35	Fred	New	051297-132	AB-2324-04	Mark Doe	Son

Figure 5.25   Sales Event.

With this change, each row in the Fact Header table represents an individual transaction and each row in the Fact Detail table represents each individual person who is insured. These Fact Header and Fact Detail tables demonstrate the use of normalization to remove redundancy and expose multiple grains of data within a single enterprise event.

Third Normal Form Fact tables also introduce a level of flexibility. Figure 5.27 shows the addition of another enterprise event: the customer made a payment for the insurance policy. The payment includes a new row in the Fact Header table and a new row in the Fact Payment table. The relational joins from these transactions include:

■ The Fact Header Payment joins to the Fact Header New on Policy Number.
■ The Fact Header Payment joins to the Fact Detail on Policy Number.
■ The Fact Header Payment joins to the Fact Payment on Policy Number and Transaction #.
■ The Fact Payment Amt joins to the Fact Detail on Policy Number.

This example demonstrates the flexibility of Third Normal Form Fact tables to present all the grains of an enterprise event by isolating each individual grain of an enterprise event in its own normalized Fact table. In this example, the grains are:

■ Unique individual transactions
■ Unique individual persons insured
■ Unique individual payments

This example could also include:

■ Claims
■ Claims Details
■ Claims Payments
■ Renewals
■ Changes in persons insured

Fact Table – Sales Event Header

Facility	Date	Time	Agent	Type	Transaction #	Policy Number
1357	05/12/1997	13:35	Fred	New	051297-132	AB-2324

Fact Table – Sales Event Detail

Policy Number	Transaction #	Insured	Relation
AB-2324-01	051297-132	Jane Doe	Primary
AB-2324-02	051297-132	John Doe	Husband
AB-2324-03	051297-132	Janice Doe	Daughter
AB-2324-04	051297-132	Mark Doe	Son

Figure 5.26   Sales Event Detail.

Fact Table – Sales Event Header

Facility	Date	Time	Agent	Type	Transaction #	Policy Number
1357	05/12/1997	13:35	Fred	New	051297-132	AB-2324
1357	06/01/1997	14:21	Fred	Pmt	060197-114	AB-2324

Fact Table – Sales Event Payment

Policy Number	Transaction #	Payment Amt
AB-2324	060197-114	$74.50

Fact Table – Sales Event Detail

Policy Number	Transaction #	Insured	Relation
AB-2324-01	051297-132	Jane Doe	Primary
AB-2324-02	051297-132	John Doe	Husband
AB-2324-03	051297-132	Janice Doe	Daughter
AB-2324-04	051297-132	Mark Doe	Son

Figure 5.27   Sales Event Payment.

In a Dimensional Data Model, Fact tables can never be joined together. The same is true of Third Normal Form Fact tables—individual facts cannot be joined to each other. But, this example looks like we can join multiple Facts to each other. The distinction is that all the rows in Figure 5.27 are one transaction; a transaction that will take a year to complete. Compare an insurance sales transaction to a convenience store sales transaction. In both cases:

- A customer selects a product
  - An insurance policy
  - A soft drink
- An agent of the enterprise records that selection
  - An insurance agent writes a policy
  - A cashier rings up the soft drink
- The customer pays for the product
  - Twelve installment payments of $74.50 each
  - $0.89 (including tax)
- The customer receives the product
  - A term life insurance policy for four people for one year
  - A soft drink

The sales transaction in the convenience store happens much faster than the insurance sales transaction. Regardless, that convenience store sales transaction cannot be joined to any other convenience store sales transaction and the insurance sales transaction cannot be joined to any other insurance sales transaction.

Figure 5.27 demonstrates the ability of Third Normal Form Fact tables to function together as a logical unit. The data in the three tables could be denormalized into Dimensional Data Model Fact tables or remain as normalized Third Normal Form Fact tables. The data in both forms is the same. A cohesive set of Third Normal Form Fact tables function as a logical unit, even though they are individual and separate. In the minds of a data warehouse designer and data warehouse customers, they are a logical unit. They will be queried as a logical unit. They will be joined to Third Normal Form Dimension tables as a logical unit.

Third Normal Form Dimension Tables

Third Normal Form Dimension tables demonstrate the purest form of normalization. The Facility/Region/District/Corporate dimension tables in Figure 5.23 show the normalization of a hierarchy. In the first frame, the entire hierarchy is denormalized into one row. In the last frame, the entire hierarchy is normalized into a Facility table, Region table, District table, and Corporate table.

The individual dimension tables (Facility, Region, District, and Corporate) function together to express the geography of the enterprise. These four tables function as a logical unit, combining to express the Geography dimension. Regardless of whether the Facility, Region, District, and Corporate data elements are captured in a single row or multiple tables, the data is still the same. A cohesive set of Third Normal Form Dimension tables function as a logical unit, even though they are individual and separate. In the minds of a data warehouse designer and data warehouse customers, they are a logical unit. They will be queried as a logical unit.

A Fact table joining to this logical Geography dimension is subject to the same hierarchical constraint that binds Dimensional Data Model dimensions—the lowest relevant hierarchical level is the level at which it joins with the Fact table. If a Fact table joins to the Region table but not the Facility table, then the Facility table (which is hierarchically lowest) is not relevant to that Fact table. The arithmetic data in a Fact table can be summed up (a hierarchy), but not summed down (a hierarchy).

Third Normal Form Conformed Dimension Tables

A cohesive set of Third Normal Form Dimension tables that function as a logical unit can be shared by Fact tables throughout the data warehouse. The concept of Conformed Dimensions, which originated in Dimensional Data Modeling, applies to Third Normal Form data modeling. The benefit is the same: reduced redundancy, storage capacity, cost of ownership, and increased ROI. The limitation is also the same: Fact tables must match the grain of Conformed Dimension tables to leverage them.

Denormalized Third Normal Form Dimension Tables—Occasionally, a set of Third Normal Form dimension tables can be denormalized into one row. This is usually done for one of two reasons:

- Performance: If a RDBMS optimizer has difficulty creating an optimal query path, prejoining a logical set of dimension tables into a single table may give the RDBMS optimizer the help it needs.
- Confusion: If data warehouse customers have difficulty in successfully joining all the tables in a logical set of dimension tables, a view can be created which prejoins those tables.

Neither of these approaches constitutes an abandonment of Third Normal Form. Nor does it mean a data warehouse has just been converted into a data mart. The occasional denormalized dimension is a symptom of a healthy data warehouse. If no one was using the data warehouse, the RDBMS optimizer would be able to join the tables quickly and they would confuse no one.

Third Normal Form Joins Strategies

In a Third Normal Form data warehouse, joining a Fact table to a Dimension includes an additional challenge: Join all the normalized dimension tables in a time-variant data warehouse. A Fact row can join to the hierarchically lowest dimension table. But, after that, the challenge is to join up through normalized dimension tables. A Fact table joins to Table 6,

> which has to join to Table 5,
> > which has to join to Table 4,
> > > which has to join to Table 3,
> > > > which has to join to Table 2,
> > > > > which has to join to Table 1

to allow the aggregation and summary of the Fact data by an attribute of Table 1, without creating the multiplicative effect caused by incorrectly joining tables. Flexibility has a cost. In a Third Normal Form data warehouse, the cost of the Third Normal Form's flexibility is the risk of creating the multiplicative effect caused by incorrectly joining tables and the mitigation of that risk.

Source Native Key—This method, demonstrated in Figure 5.28, uses a key value from the source system. In this example, a Fact table captures seven events. One event references Thing Key VC12, three events reference Thing Key LC32, and three events reference Thing Key AC23. Thing Key VC12 is associated with Comp Key Wd and Type Key Chr. Thing Key LC32 is associated with Comp Key Wd and Type Key Chr_H. Thing Key AC23 is associated with Comp Key FG and Type Key Chr.

These associations are achieved via associative tables. In this example, the entities Thing, Composition, and Type are normalized into their own tables. The associations between these tables are also normalized into their own tables. In some Third Normal Form data models such associations can be embedded in a subordinate table. The subordinate table in Figure 5.28 is the Thing table. The primary keys of the Composition and Type tables can be embedded as foreign keys in the Thing table. While this can be done, it would negate some of the flexibility of a Third Normal Form data model. By normalizing Entities into Dimension tables, Relations into Associative tables, and Attributes into Dimension Attribute tables, a Third Normal Form allows a data warehouse designer to adjust the data warehouse as the enterprise changes.

While this method is simplest and easiest to create, it yields only a Type 1 time-variant relation. If the description of Thing, Composition, or Type changes, all the events in the Fact table will be associated with the updated value. This is the behavior of Type 1 time variant data—all history is restated using data values currently in effect.

The Source Native Key method works well when the uniqueness of the keys is enforced by the source system, which implicitly means the data warehouse extracts

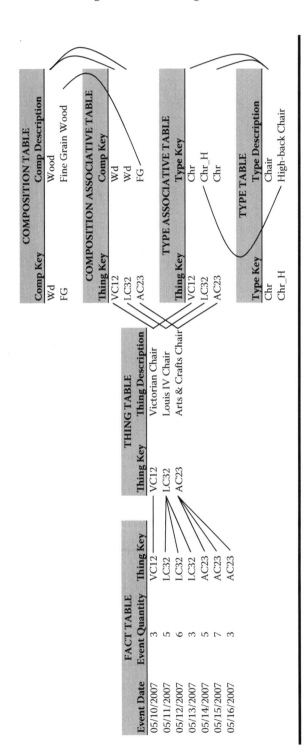

Figure 5.28 Source Native Key.

its dimension data from only one source system. If, however, a data warehouse extracts its dimension data from multiple source systems, the Source Native Key method fails because it does not integrate the dimension data from multiple disparate source systems. When a data warehouse extracts dimension data from disparate source systems, the disparate Source Native Keys must be integrated into a single set of keys : Surrogate Keys.

Surrogate Key—In a data warehouse that must represent disparate source systems, Surrogate Keys are used to combine and conform entity keys, which are not coordinated in the enterprise. For example, the enterprise manufactures furniture. The parent company manufactures Victorian Chairs (Thing Key = ASDSA-2328) and Louis IV Chairs (Thing Key = AGGSD-82732). The newly acquired subsidiary company manufactures Louis IV Chairs (Thing Key = Mom's Favorite Chair) and Arts and Crafts Chairs (Thing Key = Dad Made This Chair). These source native keys simultaneously represent an overlapping entity (Louis IV Chair) and dissimilar keys. Figure 5.29 shows how these overlapping entities and dissimilar keys can be combined and conformed into a single uniform set of keys. The uniform set of Surrogate Keys allows data warehouse customers to query across the data warehouse without encountering the overlapping and dissimilar keys from the parent and subsidiary companies.

Source Native Key with Dates

Having established the Fact (Fact Table), Dimension (Thing Table), Dimension Attribute (Composition Table and Type Table), and Associative (Composition Associative Table and Type Associative Table) tables, the next step is to add Time. Figure 5.30 shows the added Begin Date and End Date fields. Begin Date identifies the first date for which the data in a row is active. End Date identifies the last date for which the data in a row is active.

Figure 5.30 demonstrates the challenge of a time-variant Third Normal Form data model. The Begin Date and End Date fields of associated Dimension and Dimension Attribute tables never all coincide to the same dates. Instead, Begin and End Dates from one table overlap, surround, and bisect the Begin and End Dates from every other table. For example, the Event on May 10 in the Fact Table will join to two rows in the Composition Associative Table, which will join to three rows in the Composition Table. The Event on May 11 in the Fact table will join to one row in the Type Associative Table, which will join to two rows in the Type Table. Left to run amok in this way, this data model will multiply every row in the Fact Table by a factor of at least three, probably four.

The solution to this conundrum is to qualify all tables on one single date. The Fact table provides that one single date for each join. Even though a RDBMS returns data in sets, it actually joins data in rows. Each Fact table row provides the one single date (the Event Date), which will limit all the Dimension, Dimension

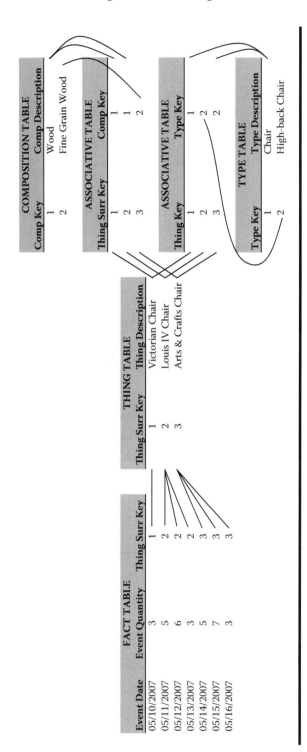

Figure 5.29 Surrogate Key.

COMPOSITION TABLE

Comp Key	Comp Description	Begin Date	End Date
Wd	Wood	04/01/2007	05/11/2007
Wd	Wood (soft)	05/12/2007	12/31/9999
FG	Fine Grain Wood	04/14/2007	05/15/2007
FG	Fine Grain Wood (northern)	05/16/2007	12/31/9999

COMPOSITION ASSOCIATIVE TABLE

Thing Key	Comp Key	Begin Date	End Date
VC12	Wd	04/01/2007	05/13/2007
VC12	FG	05/14/2007	12/31/9999
LC32	Wd	04/01/2007	12/31/9999
AC23	FG	04/01/2007	12/31/9999

TYPE ASSOCIATIVE TABLE

Thing Key	Type Key	Begin Date	End Date
VC12	Chr	03/15/2007	05/12/2007
VC12	Chr_H	05/13/2007	12/31/9999
LC32	Chr	03/01/2007	12/31/9999
AC23	Chr	03/12/2007	05/14/2007
AC23	Chr_H	05/15/2007	12/31/9999

TYPE TABLE

Type Key	Type Description	Begin Date	End Date
Chr	Chair	04/01/2007	05/14/2007
Chr	Chair w/arms	05/15/2007	12/31/9999
Chr_H	High-back Chair	03/16/2007	05/11/2007
Chr_H	High-back Chair w/arms	05/12/2007	12/31/9999

THING TABLE

Thing Key	Thing Description	Begin Date	End Date
VC12	Victorian Chair	01/15/2007	12/31/9999
LC32	Louis IV Chair	02/17/2007	12/31/9999
AC23	Arts & Crafts Chair	02/19/2007	05/15/2007
AC23	New Arts & Crafts Ch	05/16/2007	12/31/9999

FACT TABLE

Event Date	Event Quantity	Thing Key
05/10/2007	3	VC12
05/11/2007	5	LC32
05/12/2007	6	LC32
05/13/2007	3	LC32
05/14/2007	5	AC23
05/15/2007	7	AC23
05/16/2007	3	AC23

Figure 5.30 Source Native Key with Dates.

Attribute, and Associative rows that will join to that Fact row. The following SQL illustrates this method:

```
SELECT
FACT TABLE.EVENT DATE
, FACT TABLE.EVENT QUANTITY
, FACT TABLE.THING KEY
, THING TABLE.THING DESCRIPTION
, COMPOSITION TABLE.COMP KEY
, COMPOSITION TABLE.COMP DESCRIPTION
, TYPE TABLE.TYPE KEY
, TYPE TABLE.TYPE DESCRIPTION
FROM
FACT TABLE A
INNER JOIN THING TABLE B
ON A.THING KEY = B.THING KEY
AND A.EVENT DATE BETWEEN B.BEGIN DATE AND B.END DATE
INNER JOIN COMPOSITION ASSOCIATIVE TABLE C
ON B.THING KEY = C.THING KEY
AND A.EVENT DATE BETWEEN C.BEGIN DATE AND C.END DATE
INNER JOIN COMPOSITION TABLE D
ON C.COMP KEY = D.COMP KEY
AND A.EVENT DATE BETWEEN D.BEGIN DATE AND D.END DATE
INNER JOIN TYPE ASSOCIATIVE TABLE E
ON B.THING KEY = E.THING KEY
AND A.EVENT DATE BETWEEN E.BEGIN DATE AND E.END DATE
INNER JOIN TYPE TABLE F
ON E.TYPE KEY = F.TYPE KEY
AND A.EVENT DATE BETWEEN F.BEGIN DATE AND F.END DATE
```

A Fact table can also be a Summary or Snapshot table. Summary and Snapshot tables represent a multiperiod range of time. For example, a Weekly Summary is a cumulative representation of all Events within a week or a Daily Snapshot is the net effect of all Events within a day. Summary and Snapshot tables remove some of the granular detail, usually Time, from their underlying Event data. By design, therefore, Summary and Snapshot tables usually represent Time with reduced granular detail. To make this time-variant method succeed with Summary and Snapshot tables, a point in time must be chosen when joining with time-variant Dimension, Dimension Attribute, and Associative tables. That point in time may be the initial moment of the time range or the final moment of the time range included in a Summary or Snapshot table. Either way, the choice must be consistent throughout all Summary and Snapshot tables in a data warehouse.

Figure 5.31 demonstrates the time-variant effect of joining with the WHERE clause "Where Event Date between Begin Date and End Date" in the first Event row.

FACT TABLE

Event Date	Event Quantity	Thing Key
05/10/2007	3	VC12
05/11/2007	5	LC32
05/12/2007	6	LC32
05/13/2007	3	LC32
05/14/2007	5	AC23
05/15/2007	7	AC23
05/16/2007	3	AC23

THING TABLE

Thing Key	Thing Description	Begin Date	End Date
VC12	Victorian Chair	01/15/2007	12/31/9999
LC32	Louis IV Chair	02/17/2007	12/31/9999
AC23	Arts & Crafts Chair	02/19/2007	05/15/2007
AC23	New Arts & Crafts Ch	05/16/2007	12/31/9999

COMPOSITION TABLE

Comp Key	Comp Description	Begin Date	End Date
Wd	Wood	04/01/2007	05/11/2007
Wd	Wood (soft)	05/12/2007	12/31/9999
FG	Fine Grain Wood	04/14/2007	05/15/2007
FG	Fine Grain Wood (northern)	05/16/2007	12/31/9999

COMPOSITION ASSOCIATIVE TABLE

Thing Key	Comp Key	Begin Date	End Date
VC12	Wd	04/01/2007	05/13/2007
VC12	FG	05/14/2007	12/31/9999
LC32	Wd	04/01/2007	12/31/9999
AC23	FG	04/01/2007	12/31/9999

TYPE ASSOCIATIVE TABLE

Thing Key	Type Key	Begin Date	End Date
VC12	Chr	03/15/2007	05/12/2007
VC12	Chr_H	05/13/2007	12/31/9999
LC32	Chr_H	03/01/2007	12/31/9999
AC23	Chr	03/12/2007	05/14/2007
AC23	Chr_H	05/15/2007	12/31/9999

TYPE TABLE

Type Key	Type Description	Begin Date	End Date
Chr	Chair	04/01/2007	05/14/2007
Chr	Chair w/arms	05/15/2007	12/31/9999
Chr_H	High-back Chair	03/16/2007	05/11/2007
Chr_H	High-back Chair w/arms	05/12/2007	12/31/9999

Figure 5.31   Transaction One.

■ The Fact Table joins to only one row in the Thing Table (Thing Key = VC12, Begin Date = 1/15/2007, and End Date = 12/31/9999).

■ The Thing Table joins to only one row in the Composition Associative Table (Thing Key = VC12, Comp Key = Wd, Begin Date = 4/1/2007, and End Date = 5/13/2007).

■ The Composition Associative Table joins to only one row in the Composition Table (Comp Key = Wd, Begin Date = 4/1/2007, and End Date = 5/11/2007).

■ The Thing Table joins to only one row in the Type Associative Table (Thing Key = VC12, Type Key = Chr, Begin Date = 3/15/2007, and End Date = 5/12/2007).

■ The Type Associative Table joins to only one row in the Type Table (Type Key = Chr, Begin Date = 4/1/2007, and End Date = 5/14/2007).

Note that all of these dates surround inclusively the Event Date 5/10/2007. That Event Date provides the time-variant orientation for all of these joins to a single day.

Figure 5.32 demonstrates the time-variant effect of joining with the WHERE clause "Where Event Date between Begin Date and End Date" in the second Event row.

■ The Fact Table joins to only one row in the Thing Table (Thing Key = LC32, Begin Date = 2/17/2007 and End Date = 12/31/9999).

■ The Thing Table joins to only one row in the Composition Associative Table (Thing Key = LC32, Comp Key = Wd, Begin Date = 4/1/2007m and End Date = 12/31/9999).

■ The Composition Associative Table joins to only one row in the Composition Table (Comp Key = Wd, Begin Date = 4/1/2007, and End Date = 5/11/2007).

■ The Thing Table joins to only one row in the Type Associative Table (Thing Key = LC32, Type Key = Chr_H, Begin Date = 3/1/2007, and End Date = 12/31/9999).

■ The Type Associative Table joins to only one row in the Type Table (Type Key = Chr_H, Begin Date = 3/16/2007, and End Date = 5/11/2007).

Note that all of these dates surround inclusively the Event Date 5/11/2007. That Event Date provides the time-variant orientation for all of these joins to a single day.

Figure 5.33 demonstrates the time-variant effect of joining with the WHERE clause "Where Event Date between Begin Date and End Date" in the third Event row.

■ The Fact Table joins to only one row in the Thing Table (Thing Key = LC32, Begin Date = 2/17/2007, and End Date = 12/31/9999).

COMPOSITION TABLE

Comp Key	Comp Description	Begin Date	End Date
Wd	Wood	04/01/2007	05/11/2007
Wd	Wood (soft)	05/12/2007	12/31/9999
FG	Fine Grain Wood	04/14/2007	05/15/2007
FG	Fine Grain Wood (northern)	05/16/2007	12/31/9999

COMPOSITION ASSOCIATIVE TABLE

Thing Key	Comp Key	Begin Date	End Date
VC12	Wd	04/01/2007	05/13/2007
VC12	FG	05/14/2007	12/31/9999
LC32	Wd	04/01/2007	12/31/9999
AC23	FG	04/01/2007	12/31/9999

TYPE ASSOCIATIVE TABLE

Thing Key	Type Key	Begin Date	End Date
VC12	Chr	03/15/2007	05/12/2007
VC12	Chr H	05/13/2007	12/31/9999
LC32	Chr H	03/01/2007	12/31/9999
AC23	Chr	03/12/2007	05/14/2007
AC23	Chr H	05/15/2007	12/31/9999

TYPE TABLE

Type Key	Type Description	Begin Date	End Date
Chr	Chair	04/01/2007	05/14/2007
Chr	Chair w/arms	05/15/2007	12/31/9999
Chr H	High-back Chair	03/16/2007	05/11/2007
Chr H	High-back Chair w/arms	05/12/2007	12/31/9999

FACT TABLE

Event Date	Event Quantity	Thing Key
05/10/2007	3	VC12
05/11/2007	5	LC32
05/12/2007	6	LC32
05/13/2007	3	AC23
05/14/2007	5	AC23
05/15/2007	7	AC23
05/16/2007	3	AC23

THING TABLE

Thing Key	Thing Description	Begin Date	End Date
VC12	Victorian Chair	01/15/2007	12/31/9999
LC32	Louis IV Chair	02/17/2007	12/31/9999
AC23	Arts & Crafts Chair	02/19/2007	05/15/2007
AC23	New Arts & Crafts Ch	05/16/2007	12/31/9999

Figure 5.32 Transaction Two.

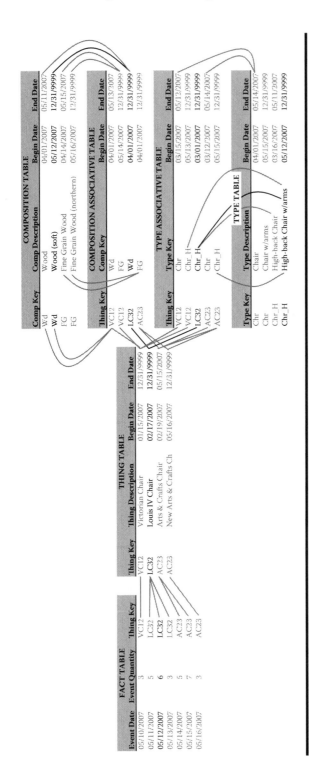

Figure 5.33 Transaction Three.

- The Thing Table joins to only one row in the Composition Associative Table (Thing Key = LC32, Comp Key = Wd, Begin Date = 4/1/2007, and End Date = 12/31/9999).
- The Composition Associative Table joins to only one row in the Composition Table (Comp Key = Wd, Begin Date = 5/12/2007, and End Date = 12/31/9999).
- The Thing Table joins to only one row in the Type Associative Table (Thing Key = LC32, Type Key = Chr_H, Begin Date = 3/1/2007, and End Date = 12/31/9999).
- The Type Associative Table joins to only one row in the Type Table (Type Key = Chr_H, Begin Date = 5/12/2007, and End Date = 12/31/9999).

Note that all of these dates surround inclusively the Event Date 5/12/2007. That Event Date provides the time-variant orientation for all of these joins to a single day.

Figure 5.34 demonstrates the time-variant effect of joining with the WHERE clause "Where Event Date between Begin Date and End Date" in the fourth Event row.

- The Fact Table joins to only one row in the Thing Table (Thing Key = LC32, Begin Date = 2/17/2007, and End Date = 12/31/9999).
- The Thing Table joins to only one row in the Composition Associative Table (Thing Key = LC32, Comp Key = Wd, Begin Date = 4/1/2007, and End Date = 12/31/9999).
- The Composition Associative Table joins to only one row in the Composition Table (Comp Key = Wd, Begin Date = 5/12/2007, and End Date = 12/31/9999).
- The Thing Table joins to only one row in the Type Associative Table (Thing Key = LC32, Type Key = Chr_H, Begin Date = 3/1/2007, and End Date = 12/31/9999).
- The Type Associative Table joins to only one row in the Type Table (Type Key = Chr_H, Begin Date = 5/12/2007, and End Date = 12/31/9999).

Note that all of these dates surround inclusively the Event Date 5/13/2007. That Event Date provides the time-variant orientation for all of these joins to a single day.

Figure 5.35 demonstrates the time-variant effect of joining with the WHERE clause "Where Event Date between Begin Date and End Date" in the fifth Event row.

- The Fact Table joins to only one row in the Thing Table (Thing Key = AC23, Begin Date = 2/19/2007, and End Date = 5/15/2007).

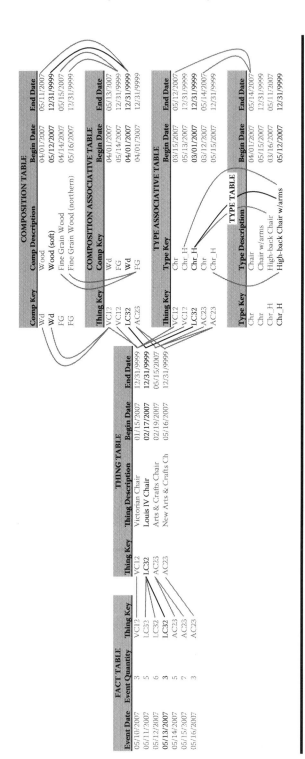

Figure 5.34 Transaction Four.

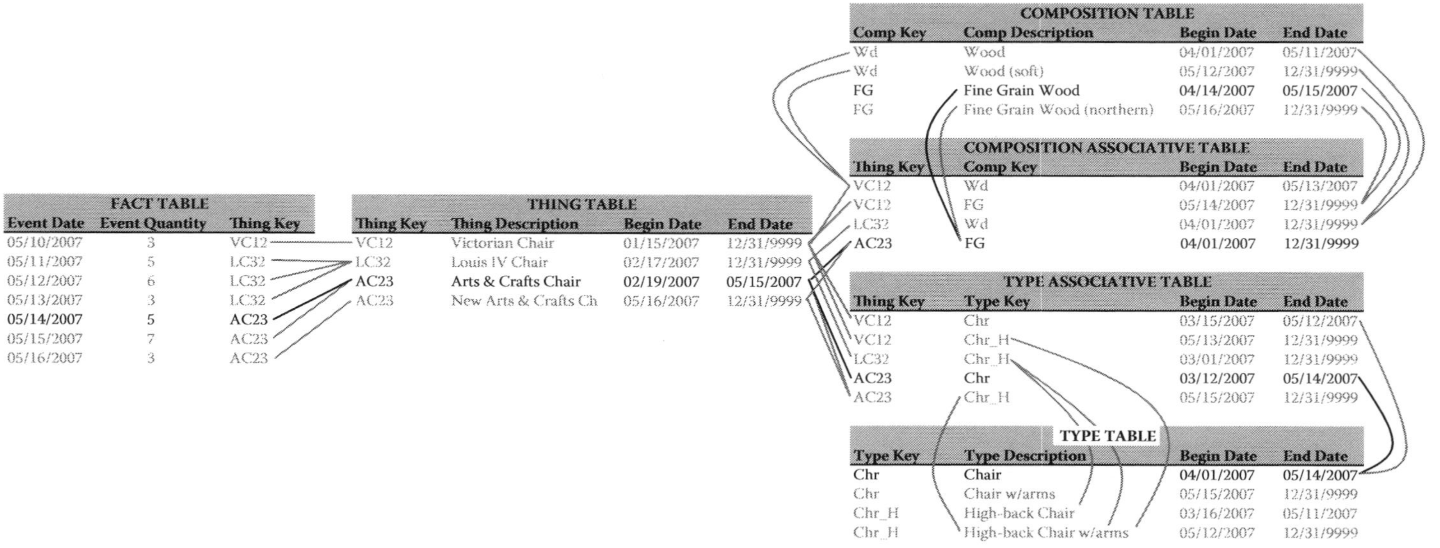

Figure 5.35 Transaction Five.

- The Thing Table joins to only one row in the Composition Associative Table (Thing Key = AC23, Comp Key = FG, Begin Date = 4/1/2007, and End Date = 12/31/9999).
- The Composition Associative Table joins to only one row in the Composition Table (Comp Key = FG, Begin Date = 4/14/2007, and End Date = 5/15/2007).
- The Thing Table joins to only one row in the Type Associative Table (Thing Key = AC23, Type Key = Chr, Begin Date = 3/12/2007, and End Date = 5/14/2007).
- The Type Associative Table joins to only one row in the Type Table (Type Key = Chr, Begin Date = 4/1/2007, and End Date = 5/14/2007).

Note that all of these dates surround inclusively the Event Date 5/14/2007. That Event Date provides the time-variant orientation for all of these joins to a single day.

Figure 5.36 demonstrates the time-variant effect of joining with the WHERE clause "Where Event Date between Begin Date and End Date" in the sixth Event row.

- The Fact Table joins to only one row in the Thing Table (Thing Key = AC23, Begin Date = 2/19/2007, and End Date = 5/15/2007).
- The Thing Table joins to only one row in the Composition Associative Table (Thing Key = AC23, Comp Key = FG, Begin Date = 4/1/2007, and End Date = 12/31/9999).
- The Composition Associative Table joins to only one row in the Composition Table (Comp Key = FG, Begin Date = 4/14/2007, and End Date = 5/15/2007).
- The Thing Table joins to only one row in the Type Associative Table (Thing Key = AC23, Type Key = Chr_H, Begin Date = 5/15/2007, and End Date = 12/31/9999).
- The Type Associative Table joins to only one row in the Type Table (Type Key = Chr_H, Begin Date = 5/12/2007, and End Date = 12/31/9999).

Note that all of these dates surround inclusively the Event Date 5/15/2007. That Event Date provides the time-variant orientation for all of these joins to a single day.

Figure 5.37 demonstrates the time-variant effect of joining with the WHERE clause "Where Event Date between Begin Date and End Date" in the seventh Event row.

- The Fact Table joins to only one row in the Thing Table (Thing Key = AC23, Begin Date = 5/16/2007, and End Date = 12/31/9999).
- The Thing Table joins to only one row in the Composition Associative Table (Thing Key = AC23, Comp Key = FG, Begin Date = 4/1/2007, and End Date = 12/31/9999).

FACT TABLE

Event Date	Event Quantity	Thing Key
05/10/2007	3	VC12
05/11/2007	5	LC32
05/12/2007	6	LC32
05/13/2007	3	LC32
05/14/2007	5	AC23
05/15/2007	7	AC23
05/16/2007	3	AC23

THING TABLE

Thing Key	Thing Description	Begin Date	End Date
VC12	Victorian Chair	01/15/2007	12/31/9999
LC32	Louis IV Chair	02/17/2007	12/31/9999
AC23	Arts & Crafts Chair	02/19/2007	05/15/2007
AC23	New Arts & Crafts Ch	05/16/2007	12/31/9999

COMPOSITION TABLE

Comp Key	Comp Description	Begin Date	End Date
Wd	Wood	04/01/2007	05/11/2007
Wd	Wood (soft)	05/12/2007	12/31/9999
FG	Fine Grain Wood	04/14/2007	05/15/2007
FG	Fine Grain Wood (northern)	05/16/2007	12/31/9999

COMPOSITION ASSOCIATIVE TABLE

Thing Key	Comp Key	Begin Date	End Date
VC12	Wd	04/01/2007	05/13/2007
VC12	FG	05/14/2007	12/31/9999
LC32	Wd	04/01/2007	12/31/9999
AC23	FG	04/01/2007	12/31/9999

TYPE ASSOCIATIVE TABLE

Thing Key	Type Key	Begin Date	End Date
VC12	Chr	03/15/2007	05/12/2007
VC12	Chr_H	05/13/2007	12/31/9999
LC32	Chr_H	03/01/2007	12/31/9999
AC23	Chr	03/12/2007	05/14/2007
AC23	Chr_H	05/15/2007	12/31/9999

TYPE TABLE

Type Key	Type Description	Begin Date	End Date
Chr	Chair	04/01/2007	05/14/2007
Chr	Chair w/arms	05/15/2007	12/31/9999
Chr_H	High-back Chair	03/16/2007	05/11/2007
Chr_H	High-back Chair w/arms	05/12/2007	12/31/9999

Figure 5.36 Transaction Six.

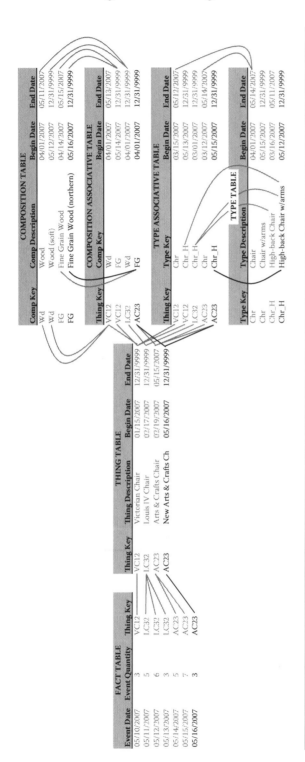

Figure 5.37 **Transaction Seven.**

■ The Composition Associative Table joins to only one row in the Composition Table (Comp Key = FG, Begin Date = 5/16/2007, and End Date = 12/31/9999).
■ The Thing Table joins to only one row in the Type Associative Table (Thing Key = AC23, Type Key = Chr_H, Begin Date = 5/15/2007, and End Date = 12/31/9999).
■ The Type Associative Table joins to only one row in the Type Table (Type Key = Chr_H, Begin Date = 5/12/2007, and End Date = 12/31/9999).

Note that all of these dates surround inclusively the Event Date 5/16/2007. That Event Date provides the time-variant orientation for all of these joins to a single day. The cumulative effect of these seven Fact table rows, each joined with Dimension, Dimension Attribute, and Associative tables based on the Event Date is a result set wherein all Fact rows are expressed in their historical context—a Type 2 time-variant result set. Multiple normalized Fact tables can also use this Type 2 time-variant method. The Fact tables in Figure 5.27 can join to Type 2 Dimension, Dimension Attribute, and Associative tables by orienting all joins around a single Fact Event Date field. A single SQL statement can only orient on one Date. The question that is answered by the SQL will probably indicate which Event Date to use as a point of orientation. For example:

■ When was the Payment made? The Payment Date provides the single point of orientation.
■ When did Underwriting approve the insurance policy? The Underwrite Date provides the single point of orientation.

When considered that way, the use of a single point of orientation seems to be mere common sense. The confusion occurs when confronted with multiple normalized Fact tables, each with their own Event Dates. The answer to the question is the question to the answer—The question being asked identifies the Event Date that will drive the Join with all the Dimension tables.

The same SQL that generated a Type 2 time-variant result set can also achieve a Type 1 time-variant result set by using the RDBMS Current Date function in place of the Fact Table's Event Date. The following SQL illustrates this method:

```
SELECT
FACT TABLE.EVENT DATE
, FACT TABLE.EVENT QUANTITY
, FACT TABLE.THING KEY
, THING TABLE.THING DESCRIPTION
, COMPOSITION TABLE.COMP KEY
, COMPOSITION TABLE.COMP DESCRIPTION
, TYPE TABLE.TYPE KEY
, TYPE TABLE.TYPE DESCRIPTION
FROM
```

```
FACT TABLE A
INNER JOIN THING TABLE B
ON A.THING KEY = B.THING KEY
AND CURRENT DATE BETWEEN B.BEGIN DATE AND B.END DATE
INNER JOIN COMPOSITION ASSOCIATIVE TABLE C
ON B.THING KEY = C.THING KEY
AND CURRENT DATE BETWEEN C.BEGIN DATE AND C.END DATE
INNER JOIN COMPOSITION TABLE D
ON C.COMP KEY = D.COMP KEY
AND CURRENT DATE BETWEEN D.BEGIN DATE AND D.END DATE
INNER JOIN TYPE ASSOCIATIVE TABLE E
ON B.THING KEY = E.THING KEY
AND CURRENT DATE BETWEEN E.BEGIN DATE AND E.END DATE
INNER JOIN TYPE TABLE F
ON E.TYPE KEY = F.TYPE KEY
```

This SQL will return a result set that includes only those rows that are in effect as of the moment the query is submitted. That is the purpose of a Type 1 time-variant query—to cast all of history in the current context. Remember, the Begin Date and End Date fields identify when a row is relevant to the data warehouse, not the operational application from which the data was extracted. So, a row in the data warehouse for a given Key may reference an entity that no longer exists in the enterprise. In that scenario, that operational nonexistence is the data in the data warehouse that is relevant to the data warehouse.

A Type 3 time-variant result set is best achieved by creating an alternate set of Dimension, Dimension Attribute, and Associative tables. An alternate set of tables is a safer option than embedding the alternate data values in a table with the real data values, demarcated by a flag or indicator field.

A time-variant Third Normal Form data warehouse must have one, and only one, row for every entity at a moment in time. If any Dimension, Dimension Attribute, or Associative table has multiple rows for a Key and Time, then the data warehouse could multiply its result sets for the affected Fact rows by the number of multiple rows. A data warehouse, therefore, must guard the time-variant integrity of its Dimension, Dimension Attribute, and Associative tables. The time-variant integrity is crucial to the success of a time-variant data warehouse.

Surrogate Key with Dates—Type 2 and Type 3 time-variant join strategies work the same regardless of the Key architecture: Source Native Key or Surrogate Key. In both architectures, a point in time date from a Fact table identifies the moment an event occurred. That single point in time is used in the SQL WHERE clause to select the Dimension rows relevant to the moment in time in the Fact table.

In both Key architectures, the foreign key in a Fact table joins to the primary key of a Dimension table. That first join between a Fact table and a Dimension table establishes the lowest hierarchical granularity possible for the joins associated with that Fact table. Thereafter, all other joins can only join hierarchically upward from the joined Dimension table.

Data Warehouse Dates Redux—As discussed previously in Data Warehouse Dates, a Dimension table can include multiple Date fields with distinct meanings. The use of multiple Date fields in a data warehouse is different from the multiple fields in an operational database. Typically, in an operational database, one Date field identifies when the data in a row became effective and another field identifies when the data in a row ceased being effective. These dates are basically operational metadata. A data warehouse will typically include additional metadata about each row. The additional Date metadata may include:

- The date or timestamp when the data in a row was extracted from a source system.
- The date or timestamp when the data in a row was transformed and ready to load.
- The date or timestamp when the data in a row was loaded into the data warehouse.
- The date or timestamp on which the data warehouse considers the data in a row to be relevant to the enterprise, i.e., Begin Date.
- The date or timestamp on which the data warehouse considers the data in a row to no longer be relevant to the enterprise. i.e., End Date.

Notice that none of these Date fields are the Effective and Not Effective operational metadata Date fields. In the context of a data warehouse, the Effective and Not Effective operational metadata Date fields are attributes of a row of data; they are not metadata of the data warehouse. The Begin Date and End Date fields in a data warehouse are not the operational Effective and Not Effective Date fields in operational data. Rather, the Begin Date and End Date fields are the dates within which a row of data is/was relevant to the enterprise and, therefore, the data warehouse.

Third Normal Form Data Model Summary

A Third Normal Form Data Model answers the questions of who, what, when, where, how, and possibly why by creating a normalized set of tables that join together as a cohesive logical unit to express a business event. These separate individual tables also create the possibility to capture the various grains of data within a single business event. Business entities are also captured in a set of normalized tables, which join together as a cohesive logical unit to express the hierarchy surrounding a business entity involved in a business event. Each set of entity hierarchy tables can be shared throughout the data warehouse to multiple sets of business event tables.

These tools (normalized tables that express business events and entities) allow a Third Normal Form Data Model to incorporate the Data Warehouse Philosophy.

- Subject Orientation: A set of tables that function as a logical cohesive unit to express a business event defines the subject for each section of a data warehouse.
- Data Integration: Conformed business entity tables express entity information in the same form, function, and grain across the data warehouse.
- Nonvolatility: New rows can be added to business event and business entity tables without destroying existing rows.
- Time Variant: Begin Date and End Date attributes allow business entity tables to join to historical entity rows in the past.
- One Version of the Truth: A table that captures a business event is the only table to capture that business event. A set of tables that capture a hierarchy is the only set of tables to capture that hierarchy.
- Long-Term Investment: Flexibility is a key feature of a Third Normal Form data model. This same flexibility also contributes to a long lifespan for a data warehouse.

Recursive Data Model

A Recursive Data Model is a Join method. Basically, a Recursive Data Model takes a set of Dimension tables and sets them on end. A basic Recursive Data Model is shown in Figure 5.38. On the left is an entity table and on the right is a recursion table. The two relation lines between these tables show that a single row in the entity can be a parent entity in multiple hierarchies (e.g., geographic, management, and team membership). Also, a single row in the entity can be a child entity in multiple hierarchies.[22]

The example in Figure 5.39 shows a simple management hierarchy, which includes a typical one-to-many relation.

In this example, Fred is the CEO and Sue's boss. Sue is a Director and boss of both Bill and Angela. Bill and Angela are staff members and boss of no one. The flexibility of a recursive table begins to pay off when additional hierarchies and

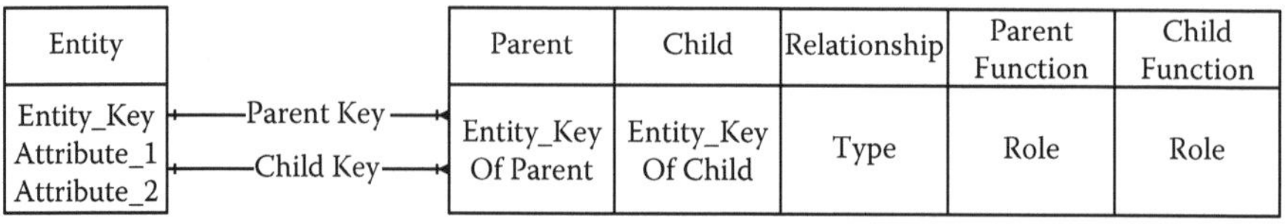

Entity		Parent	Child	Relationship	Parent Function	Child Function
Entity_Key Attribute_1 Attribute_2	├──Parent Key──→ ├──Child Key──→	Entity_Key Of Parent	Entity_Key Of Child	Type	Role	Role

Figure 5.38   Recursive Data Model.

Personnel			Personnel Recursion					
Employee_ID	Employee_Name		Parent_Key	Child_Key	Relationship	Parent_Function	Child_Function
1324	Fred		null	1324	Mgmt Hierarchy	null	CEO
2435	Sue		1324	2435	Mgmt Hierarchy	CEO	Director
3546	Bill		2435	3546	Mgmt Hierarchy	Director	Staff
4657	Angela		2435	4657	Mgmt Hierarchy	Director	Staff
			3546	null	Mgmt Hierarchy	Staff	null
			4657	null	Mgmt Hierarchy	Staff	null

Figure 5.39 Personnel Recursion with one dimension.

relationships are added to the data warehouse. No new physical data structures are added. Instead, only rows are added to the existing recursive table. The recursive table in Figure 5.40 shows that Fred, the CEO, has begun to mentor Bill and Angela. Interestingly, the recursive table allows multiple hierarchies to exist simultaneously, distinguished from each other by the Relationship field.

If a data warehouse can guarantee that each entity instance has a unique key throughout the entire data warehouse (or, at least a section or subject area), then a recursive table can also join entities from multiple tables. If a data warehouse cannot guarantee that each entity instance has a unique key throughout the entire data warehouse, then uniqueness can still be achieved by using a compound key: Entity and Entity Instance.

The addition of Insurance Provider demonstrates the ability of a recursive table to capture relations within entity tables and across entity tables (Figure 5.41).

In this example, the Personnel_Recursion table holds three dimension tables: Mgmt Hierarchy, Major Med Insur, and Dental Insur. The Personnel_Recursion. Relationship field functions as the name of each of these dimensions. The SQL for the Mgmt Hierarchy dimension looks like the following:

```
Select
Personnel_Recursion.Relationship
,Personnel_Parent.Employee_Id As Parent_Id
,Personnel_Parent.Employee_Name As Parent_Name
,Personnel_Recursion.Parent_Function
,Personnel_Child.Employee_Id As Child_Id
,Personnel_Child.Employee_Name As Child_Name
,Personnel_Recursion.Child_Function
From
Personnel_Recursion
Left Outer Join Personnel As Personnel_Parent
On Personnel_Recursion.Parent_Key = Personnel_Parent.
   Employee_Id
Left Outer Join Personnel As Personnel_Child
On Personnel_Recursion.Child_Key = Personnel_Child.
   Employee_Id
Where Personnel_Recursion.Relationship = 'Mgmt
   Hierarchy'
```

The result set, which is the Mgmt Hierarchy dimension, is in Figure 5.42. The SQL for the Major Med Insur dimension looks like the following:

```
Select
Personnel_Recursion.Relationship
,Insurance_Provider.Provider_Id As Provider_Id
,Insurance_Provider.Provider_Name As Provider_Name
,Personnel_Recursion.Parent_Function
,Personnel_Subscriber.Employee_Id As Subscriber_Id
```

| Personnel | | Personnel Recursion | | | | | |
Employee_ID	Employee_Name	Parent_Key	Child_Key	Relationship	Parent_Function	Child_Function
1324	Fred	null	1324	Mgmt Hierarchy	null	CEO
2435	Sue	1324	2435	Mgmt Hierarchy	CEO	Director
3546	Bill	2435	3546	Mgmt Hierarchy	Director	Staff
4657	Angela	2435	4657	Mgmt Hierarchy	Director	Staff
		3546	null	Mgmt Hierarchy	Staff	null
		4657	null	Mgmt Hierarchy	Staff	null
		1324	3546	Mentorship	Mentor	Apprentice
		1324	4657	Mentorship	Mentor	Apprentice

Figure 5.40 Personnel Recursion with two dimensions.

Personnel

Employee_ID	Employee_Name
1324	Fred
2435	Sue
3546	Bill
4657	Angela

Personnel Recursion

Parent_Key	Child_Key	Relationship	Parent_Function	Child_Function
null	1324	Mgmt Hierarchy	null	CEO
1324	2435	Mgmt Hierarchy	CEO	Director
2435	3546	Mgmt Hierarchy	Director	Staff
2435	4657	Mgmt Hierarchy	Director	Staff
3546	null	Mgmt Hierarchy	Staff	null
4657	null	Mgmt Hierarchy	Staff	null
1324	3546	Mentorship	Mentor	Apprentice
1324	4657	Mentorship	Mentor	Apprentice
13579	1324	Major Med Insur	Provider	Subscriber
13579	2435	Major Med Insur	Provider	Subscriber
24680	3546	Major Med Insur	Provider	Subscriber
24680	4657	Major Med Insur	Provider	Subscriber
132435	1324	Dental Insur	Provider	Subscriber
132435	3546	Dental Insur	Provider	Subscriber
132435	4657	Dental Insur	Provider	Subscriber
132435	5768	Dental Insur	Provider	Subscriber

Insurance Provider

Provider_ID	Provider_Name
13579	World Medical
24680	State Medical
132435	World Dental

Figure 5.41 Personnel Recursion with two dimension tables.

RELATIONSHIP	PARENT_ID	PARENT_NAME	PARENT_FUNCTION	CHILD_ID	CHILD_NAME	CHILD_FUNCTION
MGMT HIERARCHY	null	null	null	5768	MARY	CHAIR
MGMT HIERARCHY	1324	FRED	CEO	2435	SUE	DIRECTOR
MGMT HIERARCHY	2435	SUE	DIRECTOR	4657	ANGELA	STAFF
MGMT HIERARCHY	2435	SUE	DIRECTOR	3546	BILL	STAFF
MGMT HIERARCHY	5768	MARY	CHAIR	1324	FRED	CEO
MGMT HIERARCHY	3546	BILL	STAFF	null	null	null
MGMT HIERARCHY	4657	ANGELA	STAFF	null	null	null

Figure 5.42 Management hierarchy dimension.

```
, Personnel_Subscriber.Employee_Name As Subscriber_Name
, Personnel_Recursion.Child_Function
From
Personnel_Recursion
Left Outer Join Insurance_Provider As
    Insurance_Provider
On Personnel_Recursion.Parent_Key = Insurance_Provider.
    Provider_Id
Left Outer Join Personnel As Personnel_Subscriber
On Personnel_Recursion.Child_Key = Personnel_
    Subscriber.Employee_Id
Where Personnel_Recursion.Relationship = 'Major Med
    Insur'
```

The result set, which is the Major Med Insur dimension, is in Figure 5.43. The SQL for the Dental Insur dimension looks like the following:

```
Select
Personnel_Recursion.Relationship
, Insurance_Provider.Provider_Id As Provider_Id
, Insurance_Provider.Provider_Name As Provider_Name
, Personnel_Recursion.Parent_Function
, Personnel_Subscriber.Employee_Id As Subscriber_Id
, Personnel_Subscriber.Employee_Name As Subscriber_Name
, Personnel_Recursion.Child_Function
From
Personnel_Recursion
Left Outer Join Insurance_Provider As
    Insurance_Provider
On Personnel_Recursion.Parent_Key = Insurance_Provider.
    Provider_Id
Left Outer Join Personnel As Personnel_Subscriber
On Personnel_Recursion.Child_Key = Personnel_
    Subscriber.Employee_Id
Where Personnel_Recursion.Relationship = 'Dental Insur'
```

The result set, which is the Dental Insur dimension, is in Figure 5.44.

Figure 5.45 shows that, by adding Begin and End Dates, a recursive table can achieve a Type 2 time-variant relation. The SQL Where clause would look like the following:

```
Where Fact.Date between Recursion.Begin_Date and Recursion.
End_Date.
```

A Type 1 time-variant join can be achieved by using Current Date, where Current Date is between the Begin Date and End Date of each row in a Recursive table. The SQL Where clause would look like the following:

```
Where Current Date between Begin Date and End Date
```

RELATIONSHIP	PROVIDER_ID	PROVIDER_NAME	PARENT_FUNCTION	SUBSCRIBER_ID	SUBSCRIBER_NAME	CHILD_FUNCTION
MAJOR MED INSUR	13579	WORLD MEDICAL	PROVIDER	2435	SUE	SUBSCRIBER
MAJOR MED INSUR	24680	STATE MEDICAL	PROVIDER	4657	ANGELA	SUBSCRIBER
MAJOR MED INSUR	24680	STATE MEDICAL	PROVIDER	3546	BILL	SUBSCRIBER
MAJOR MED INSUR	13579	WORLD MEDICAL	PROVIDER	1324	FRED	SUBSCRIBER

Figure 5.43   Major Med Insur dimension.

RELATIONSHIP	PROVIDER_ID	PROVIDER_NAME	PARENT_FUNCTION	SUBSCRIBER_ID	SUBSCRIBER_NAME	CHILD_FUNCTION
DENTAL INSUR	132435	WORLD DENTAL	PROVIDER	5768	MARY	SUBSCRIBER
DENTAL INSUR	132435	WORLD DENTAL	PROVIDER	4657	ANGELA	SUBSCRIBER
DENTAL INSUR	132435	WORLD DENTAL	PROVIDER	3546	BILL	SUBSCRIBER
DENTAL INSUR	132435	WORLD DENTAL	PROVIDER	1324	FRED	SUBSCRIBER

Figure 5.44   Dental Insur dimension.

Personnel

Employee_ID	Employee_Name
1324	Fred
2435	Sue
3546	Bill
4657	Angela
5768	Mary

Insurance Provider

Provider_ID	Provider_Name
13579	World Medical
24680	State Medical
132435	World Dental

Personnel Recursion

Parent_Key	Child_Key	Relationship	Parent_Function	Child_Function	Begin Date	End Date
null	5768	Mgmt Hierarchy	null	Chair	05/11/2005	12/31/9999
null	1324	Mgmt Hierarchy	null	CEO	01/20/1998	05/10/2005
5768	1324	Mgmt Hierarchy	Chair	CEO	05/11/2005	12/31/9999
1324	2435	Mgmt Hierarchy	CEO	Director	09/27/2001	12/31/9999
2435	3546	Mgmt Hierarchy	Director	Staff	03/15/2006	12/31/9999
2435	4657	Mgmt Hierarchy	Director	Staff	05/18/2006	12/31/9999
3546	null	Mgmt Hierarchy	Staff	null	03/15/2006	12/31/9999
4657	null	Mgmt Hierarchy	Staff	null	05/18/2006	12/31/9999
1324	3546	Mentorship	Mentor	Apprentice	01/15/2007	04/15/2007
1324	4657	Mentorship	Mentor	Apprentice	01/15/2007	04/15/2007
13579	1324	Major Med Insur	Provider	Subscriber	01/01/2007	12/31/9999
13579	2435	Major Med Insur	Provider	Subscriber	01/01/2007	12/31/9999
24680	3546	Major Med Insur	Provider	Subscriber	01/01/2007	12/31/9999
24680	4657	Major Med Insur	Provider	Subscriber	01/01/2007	12/31/9999
132435	1324	Dental Insur	Provider	Subscriber	01/01/2007	12/31/9999
132435	3546	Dental Insur	Provider	Subscriber	01/01/2007	12/31/9999
132435	4657	Dental Insur	Provider	Subscriber	01/01/2007	12/31/9999
132435	5768	Dental Insur	Provider	Subscriber	01/01/2007	12/31/9999

Figure 5.45   Personnel Recursion with Dates.

A Type 3 time-variant join is best achieved by creating a separate Recursive join table, which reflects the Type 3 restatement of the past. Recursive tables are difficult enough on their own. The myriad joins possible with a Recursive table can be difficult to maneuver. The multiple Dimensions and Dimension Associations possible with a Recursive table can add to the confusion. Adding an alternate set of Dimensions for the same time frame is usually too much opportunity for erroneous joins. Rather, data warehouse customers are best served by representing an alternate set of Type 3 Dimension rows in an alternate Type 3 Recursive table.

Recursive Data Model Summary

A Recursive Data Model is actually a join table, a flexible and powerful join table. It creates the ability to add, remove, and modify hierarchies and relations with no changes to physical table structures. Typically, data warehouse customers need a view to correctly navigate the joins in a recursive table. Once correctly navigated, a recursive table presents two additional advantages.

- A recursive table is a very narrow table, which maximizes the number of rows that can be retrieved for every input/output (I/O).
- A recursive table localizes numerous joins in one table space and index space, which also reduces the number of I/Os necessary to retrieve the join data.

These two advantages typically yield impressive performance on most RDBMS platforms.

Physical Data Model Summary

The three Physical Data Models used in data warehousing are the Dimensional Data Model, Third Normal Form Data Model, and Recursive Data Model. Variations of these data models present a myriad of potential benefits and limitations. Each of these methods has proven itself in the data warehousing community.

So, for your data warehouse, which one is right? All of them. Which one is wrong? None of them. The decision to use a form of data model or a variation of that form must be based on the individual circumstance of each data warehouse, which can include:

- Existing infrastructure
- Data warehouse budget
- Available hardware
- Available software
- RDBMS platform
- Data warehouse developer skills

■ Data warehouse customer needs
■ Enterprise policy

At the end of the day, if a data warehouse is able to answer the customers' questions and add value to the enterprise, you chose the right data model.

Data Architecture

A Data Model (Dimensional, Third Normal Form or Recursive) is only half of a Database Design. Data Architecture is the other half. A data warehouse can consist of multiple databases, RDBMS platforms, and data models. Data Architecture completes the Database Design by defining the permutations of:

■ RDBMS Platform: What kind of machine?
■ RDBMS: What kind of relational software?
■ Data Model: What kind of data structure and organization?

This comprises the entire data warehouse. For most enterprises, the available options are quite numerous. No option is innately right or wrong. Every data warehouse designer must choose among the available options based on the goals, resources, and long-range plans of the enterprise.

The following sections outline the major and most common Data Architectures. These Architectures provide a framework within which data models exist. Data Architecture can span multiple RDBMS platforms, RDBMS applications, and data models. A data warehouse designer considers all the available options and environments to choose the Data Architecture that is best for the enterprise. From one enterprise to another, the available options and environments will be different. So, a Data Architecture that is optimal for one enterprise may not be optimal for another. The only best method is to be aware of all the options, do the homework, and pick the best set of options for the situation.

Enterprise Data Warehouse

An Enterprise Data Warehouse (EDW) is a single centralized database or set of databases on one platform. Typically, an EDW is the core of a data warehouse. The data in an EDW is owned, operated, and maintained by the data warehouse team. Other teams and applications may use the data in an EDW. They, however, do not manage or maintain the EDW. Rather, they are customers of the EDW.

Figure 5.46 shows an EDW containing six subject areas. EDW Data Architecture locates all the subject areas of a data warehouse inside the EDW. By locating all the subject areas in one RDBMS, a data warehouse facilitates cross-subject queries by its customers. Therefore, the subject orientation of a data warehouse does

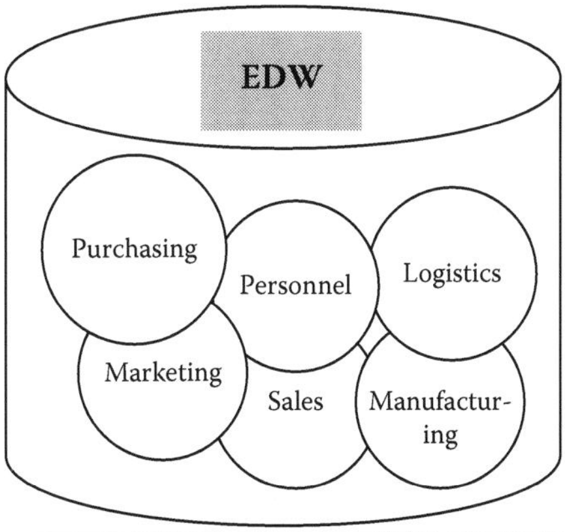

Figure 5.46   Enterprise Data Warehouse.

not prevent customers from querying across a data warehouse, rather, the subject orientation of a data warehouse facilitates data integration across a data warehouse. Data warehouse customers, therefore, can simultaneously query tables from multiple subject areas because they are integrated and co-located on one RDBMS.

An EDW can use any of the data models (Dimensional, Third Normal Form, and Recursive). The decision to centralize the data warehouse into a single RDBMS does not predetermine the data model. That and all other options (e.g., Business Intelligence Reporting, RDBMS Platform, RDBMS) are still available. EDW Data Architecture means that a decision has been made to centralize the data of a data warehouse into one RDBMS on one RDBSM platform.

A centralized EDW concentrates all the data volume and throughput into one RDBMS and RDBMS platform. The data volumes and throughput, therefore, are a major consideration in the design of an EDW. Data model interaction with a RDBMS and RDBMS platform are part of that consideration. Knowing that the hardware will be pushed to its maximum capacity and throughput, a data warehouse designer must do the homework necessary to optimize the databases, tables, and views on a specific RDBMS on a platform.

When all the data in a data warehouse is first integrated into an EDW, the data warehouse team is able to apply the rigor and discipline of Data Quality measurements and communication of metadata to that data. Otherwise, data orbits the EDW without actually integrating into the EDW. In the best-case scenario, data is extracted directly from a source system or operational data store (ODS) (which gets its data directly from a source system) and integrated into an EDW. Handled that way, the rigor and discipline of the ETL applications can be applied to the data, which will increase the value of that data. Once in an EDW, the data can be queried, reported, and disseminated throughout the enterprise from the context of all the data in the data warehouse.

Data Mart

A Data Mart is a separate database or set of databases, each with a specific focus. That focus can be either a subject area, which is shown in Figure 5.47, or that focus can be a decision support need (e.g., auditing, loss prevention, or profitability).[23] A Data Mart is created when an EDW cannot provide data in the manner required by data customers, and the business need for data in that form justifies the expense and overhead of a Data Mart. A common justification for a Data Mart is the need to allow input data from the business area. Frequently, such input data allows a "what if" analysis: What if the tax rate changed? What if productivity throughput changed? Obviously, input data is not enterprise data (i.e., the first Data Warehouse Principle). Another common justification for a Data Mart is data segregation. A business area needs to include sensitive data (e.g., proprietary, financial, medical, etc.), which cannot be available to anyone outside the business area. A business area needs to interact with an external business or government agency without allowing them access to all the other data. While RDBMS security functions can secure a database, table, or row of data, a Data Mart, which is physically or logically separate, provides a strong demarcation between the data in an EDW and the data in a Data Mart.

A Data Mart is physically or logically separate from the EDW from which it receives data. A Data Mart is a subset of an EDW and receives at least some of its data from an EDW. The load cycle of a Data Mart, therefore, is no faster than the load cycle of the EDW that feeds it. A Data Mart may receive data from other sources, including the customers who use it or organizations external to the enterprise. Sometimes that is a significant reason for a Data Mart. A Data Mart can simultaneously provide decision support functions required by data warehouse customers and shield the EDW from questionable data sources.

A Data Mart must be managed and maintained by someone, such as the data warehouse team who may provide the management and maintenance. The business area that uses a Data Mart may provide the management and maintenance of a Data Mart. This decision has more to do with intraenterprise politics than Data Architecture or Database Design. Customers who are savvy enough to use a Data Mart are also able to understand the implications of data as a business tool, regulated entity, and potential for power. For reasons such as these, a business area may want to exert authority over a Data Mart, or a data warehouse team may give a business area authority over a Data Mart. Regardless, the environmental and political context of an enterprise is very real, and must be included in the consideration of a Data Mart. The Data Mart customer may not be able to tolerate interaction with the data warehouse team for multiple reasons (e.g., HIPAA (Health Insurance

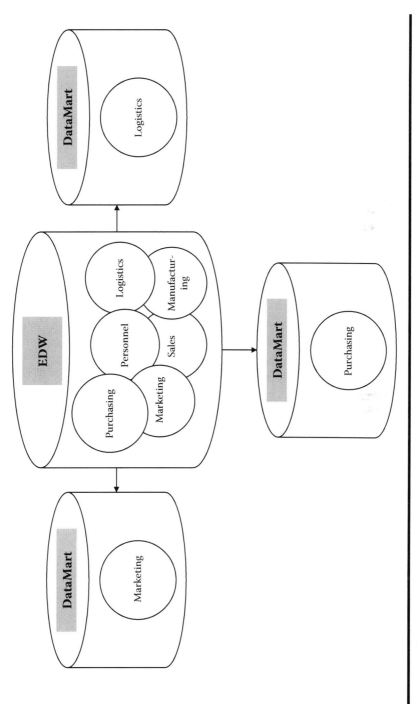

Figure 5.47   Data Mart.

Portability and Accountability Act) requirements, business cycles, logistics, etc.). In such circumstances a data warehouse team can divest itself of the ownership of a Data Mart. By providing the data that will go into a Data Mart, the data warehouse team can satisfy the requirements of such a Data Mart customer. These actions and reasons may seem on the surface to be contentious; however, they are cooperative in nature. A Data Mart is a tool by which a data warehouse team can give a customer what he wants when he wants too much, and they have the justification to get it.

A Data Mart can be achieved by two basic methods. The first method, mentioned above, is to create a physical set of databases and tables, which are located on a platform separate and removed from the data warehouse platform. This method provides the maximum possible isolation of the Data Mart. The data must be physically transported from the data warehouse platform to the Data Mart platform. The transportation of data to the Data Mart platform provides the opportunity to modify the data enroute to the Data Mart as required by the Data Mart customer. The resource consumption incurred by customers using the ODS have no impact on data warehouse customers. These advantages have a price. This method is also the most expensive, including the cost of a separate platform, data transport applications, and the maintenance of the separate platform and transport applications.

The second method is to define a set of views that draw their data from the data warehouse: a View Data Mart. A Data Mart based on views must, of course, be located on the data warehouse platform. While this method does not incur the overhead and cost of a separate platform, a View Data Mart does not have the independence of a separate Data Mart. A View Data Mart shares resources with the data warehouses. A View Data Mart still has the opportunity to introduce data not already in the data warehouse and the opportunity to isolate data via RDBMS security permissions. A table of sensitive or proprietary data can be located in the database, which otherwise holds views that point to the data warehouse. A View Data Mart can also reformat data from the data warehouse using SQL, displaying data in a format specifically needed by one business unit, but not the entire enterprise. These are the two basic methods of defining a Data Mart:

- A platform separate from the data warehouse
- Co-located with the data warehouse on the data warehouse platform

Operational Data Store

An Operational Data Store (ODS) reflects the data of a single subject area as it exists in the operational environment. This piece of data warehousing history is lost, but, looking at an ODS, someone must have said, "Well, that huge EDW is really impressive with all its data integration. I've got three subsidiary business units underneath my parent business unit. Can you tell me what's happening in just my business unit (which is really four business units, one parent and three subsidiary), without all that history? You know, what's going on right now?" The value of an ODS is that it leverages the strategic technologies of a data warehouse to answer tactical questions. ODS customers can see the data from their business unit without interrupting or interfering with their operational business applications, or incurring the performance degradation caused by five years of history and Type 2 dimensions.

Subject Orientation

An ODS focuses on a single subject area, which is typically a cohesive segment of the enterprise.[24] The example in Figure 5.48 shows an ODS that is focused on the Marketing department. This allows the department to have a decision support system, which reflects their department in its present state. Unlike a Data Mart, which can select data from an EDW to juxtapose data elements from different subject areas, an ODS receives its data directly from the business unit. An ODS, therefore, does not juxtapose data from multiple business areas. Rather, it is only a reflection of a single business area.

Data Integration

An ODS incorporates the data integration methods of the Data Warehouse Philosophy. The form, Function, and Grain of data in an ODS are consistent throughout that ODS.[25] Ideally, the Form, Function, and Grain of data in an ODS will also be consistent with the data warehouse, which helps avoid confusion among ODS and data warehouse customers.

Sequence

When an ODS is present, data acquisition and integration applications load the ODS from the operational environment. Then, a second layer of data acquisition and integration applications extract data from the ODS and load that data into the data warehouse.[26] An ODS receives its data from operational applications before the data warehouse receives its data from the ODS.

System of Record

The sequence of data from the operational environment to an ODS to a data warehouse necessarily and explicitly means the ODS is the System of Record of its subject for the data warehouse.[27] The data acquisition and integration applications gather data from the ODS for that subject area rather than the enterprise.

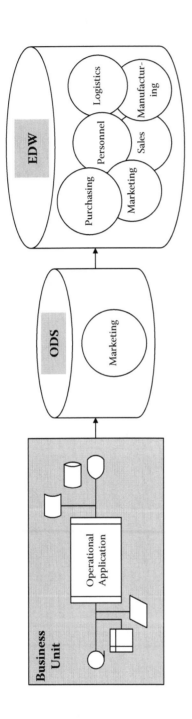

Figure 5.48   Operational Data Store.

Volatile

A data warehouse is nonvolatile. That means that once data is written into a data warehouse, it remains in the data warehouse regardless of what happens in the enterprise. An ODS is volatile. When a data element is updated, inserted, or deleted in the operational environment, that same update, insert, or delete also occurs in the ODS.[28]

Short History

A data warehouse typically retains years of data. Large histories of data are necessary to observe trends and patterns in data. An ODS, however, retains only a short duration of history.[29] An ODS does not need five years of history to reflect a business unit in its current state. Rather, the data volume necessary to store five years of history would interfere with the rapid response expected of an ODS. An ODS, therefore, holds only enough history to be considered current and up to date.

Detailed Data

An ODS stores operational data at its lowest grain. This allows the ODS to present a detailed reflection of the business unit.[30] An ODS does not aggregate or summarize data. The quick response time expected of an ODS removes the need to improve performance by preaggregating or presummarizing its data. The level of detail is limited by the granularity and detail available in the operational environment. So, an ODS will ideally reflect the grain and detail of the data already present in the operational environment.

Cycles

The applications that gather operational data and load it into an ODS occur on a scheduled frequency. That frequency can be determined by the needs of the business and the capacity of the applications.[31] If the applications can refresh an ODS every hour, and the business needs hourly updates, then the applications will refresh the ODS every hour.

The data warehouse will extract its data from the ODS. The data warehouse, therefore, cannot extract its data from the ODS more frequently than the data in the ODS is refreshed. If a data warehouse did extract its data from the ODS more frequently than the data in the ODS is refreshed, the data warehouse would extract identical sets of data, which would yield no updates to the data warehouse. The ODS refresh cycle, therefore, must be equal to or more frequent than the frequency of the data warehouse cycle.

Summaries and Aggregates

Data warehouse customers always have a common complaint—performance. Data warehouses always have a common problem—performance. Database tuning, SQL tuning, indexing, and optimizer improvements increase the performance of a data warehouse. Two methods, though, are applied in almost every data warehouse – Summaries and Aggregates.[32]

A Summary is a table that stores the results of a SQL arithmetic SUM statement that has been applied to a Fact table. The arithmetic portion of a Fact table is summed, while simultaneously one or more hierarchical levels of detail are removed from the data in a Fact table. For example:

- Intraday Fact data is summed at the Day level. The resulting data is stored in a Daily Summary table. For that data, the lowest grain is the Day.
- Store Fact data is summed at the Region level. The resulting data is stored in a Region Summary table. For that data, the lowest grain is the Region.

The intention of a Summary table is to perform the summation of arithmetic Fact data only once, rather than many times. By incurring the resource consumption necessary to summarize a Fact table, data warehouse customers will receive the previously summarized data they want quickly.

An Aggregate is a table that stores the results of SQL JOIN statements, which have been applied to a set of Dimension tables. The hierarchies and attributes above an entity are prejoined and stored in a table. For example:

- The Product entity, its levels of hierarchy and management area prejoined into a single table that stores the result set. The grain of this result set is the Product.
- The Facility entity, its levels of geographic and management hierarchy are prejoined into a single table that store the result set. The grain of this result set is the Facility.

The intention of an Aggregate table is to perform the joins of large sets of Dimension data only once. By incurring the resource consumption necessary to join a series of Dimension tables, data warehouse customers will receive data that uses those levels of hierarchy quickly.

An Aggregate is not a pure Dimension table as it would appear in a Dimensional Data Model. An Aggregate is a physical table that holds the result set of join statements, which are commonly used by data warehouse customers and are high system resource consumers. The point of an Aggregate is to incur the high system resource consumption once during off-peak hours to avoid multiple consumptions of system resources during peak hours. That being the case, an Aggregate table can denormalize along multiple hierarchies. The intersection of those multiple hierarchies is the grain of an Aggregate table. The hierarchical intersection and lowest level of granular detail must be the same because they are the grain of an Aggregate table.

Closing Remarks

Database Design achieves two major goals:

- Organize data structures within a database.
- Organize databases within a data warehouse.

The three forms of data model (Dimensional, Third Normal Form, and Recursive), and the permutations and variations within each, provide a set of strategies by which a Database Design can organize data structures within each database. The three forms of Data Architecture (EDW, Data Mart, and ODS) provide a set of strategies by which a Database Design can organize databases within a data warehouse.

RDBMS technology and data warehousing skills have advanced such that all permutations of data model and data architecture are viable options. Which set of options is the right set for a specific data warehouse? The answers (yes, a data warehouse can have multiple right answers) can only be found within the context of a specific enterprise and environment.

- What hardware is available?
- What software is available?
- What is the available budget to purchase hardware and software?
- What skills exist inhouse?
- What is the available budget to purchase additional skills?
- What is the long-term architecture plan of the enterprise?
- Who are the customers?
- How will they use the data warehouse?

These questions only scratch the surface, but they will guide a data warehouse designer to the right solutions. After that, a data warehouse designer has the task of choosing the best solution from among the right solutions. The only decision that has already been made is: A data warehouse resides on a RDBMS.

References

1. Claudia Imhoff, Nicholas Galemmo, and Jonathan G. Geiger, *Mastering Data Warehouse Design: Relational and Dimensional Techniques* (Indianapolis, IN: John Wiley & Sons, 2003).

2. Ibid.

3. Cindy Thousand (ed.), Logical Data Modeling Concepts, Information Resource Management Unit of WisDOT (http://enterprise.state.wi.us, 2002).

4. This is a good example of mixing physical and logical entities. Both entities (Real Estate and Function) are associated with no constraint from the fact that Real Estate is physical and Function is logical.

5. Actually, Date/Time should be modeled in a Calendar subject area. Inclusion of a Calendar subject area would distract, rather than enhance, this discussion. A Calendar subject area will be included during the discussion of Time Variance in a Physical Data Model.

6. A data warehouse would eventually run out of room, or hardware budget, if it forever retained all its data. For that reason, data retention periods must be used to free up space for new data to come into the data warehouse. This topic, data retention periods, while relevant to the maintenance of any database, is not relevant to a discussion of Physical Data Modeling.

7. Len Silverston, *The Data Model Resource Book, Volume 1*, Rev. ed., vol. 1 (New York: John Wiley & Sons, 2001).

8. David C. Hay, *Data Model Patterns: A Metadata Map*, Morgan Kaufmann Series in Data Management Systems (Amsterdam, Boston: Elsevier–Morgan Kaufmann, 2006).

9. Silverston, *The Data Model Resource Book.*

10. Ralph Kimball, *The Data Warehouse Lifecycle Toolkit: Expert Methods for Designing, Developing, and Deploying Data Warehouses* (New York: John Wiley & Sons, 1998).

11. Ralph Kimball and Joe Caserta, *The Data Warehouse Etl Toolkit: Practical Techniques for Extracting, Cleaning, Conforming, and Delivering Data* (Indianapolis, IN: John Wiley & Sons, 2004).

12. Type 1, Type 2, and Type 3 time-variant relations were discussed in the Time Variant section of Chapter 2 (Data Warehouse Philosophy).

13. The Surrogate Key and Surrogate Key Version fields can be defined as alphanumeric data types. The sequential numbers in these fields have no real arithmetic properties. You cannot add Key 123 to Key 234 to invent a new product with Key 357. So, an X in a Surrogate Key Version field that typically holds numbers is acceptable.

14. Kimball, *The Data Warehouse Lifecycle Toolkit.*

15. Ibid.

16. Laura Reeves, *Dimensional Modeling Beyond the Basics: Intermediate and Advanced Techniques*, TDWI World Conference (The Data Warehousing Institute, Renton, WA, 2002).

17. Ibid.

18. Ibid.

19. Kimball, *The Data Warehouse Lifecycle Toolkit.*

20. They had forms of normalization beyond the Third Normal Form. For general usage across the board, however, Third Normal Form provided the best balance of normalization and usage.

21. Ralph Kimball, A dimensional modeling manifesto — Drawing the line between dimensional modeling and ER modeling techniques, DBMS Online, August 1997, Vol. 10, Number 9.

22. Hay, *Data Model Patterns*.
23. William H. Inmon, Claudia Imhoff, and Ryan Sousa, *Corporate Information Factory* (New York: John Wiley & Sons, 1998).
24. William H. Inmon, *Building the Operational Data Store*, 2nd ed. (New York: John Wiley & Sons, 1999).
25. Ibid.
26. William H. Inmon and Richard D. Hackathorn, *Using the Data Warehouse* (New York: John Wiley & Sons, 1994).
27. Ibid.
28. Inmon, Imhoff, and Sousa, *Corporate Information Factory*.
29. Ibid.
30. Ibid.
31. Inmon, *Building the Operational Data Store*.
32. I include the word "almost" because there's probably one data warehouse that doesn't use these methods.

Chapter 6

Data Acquisition and Integration

Introduction

Data Acquisition and Integration is a name given to the set of applications that populate a data warehouse (Figure 6.1). This process consists of three main functions.

- Extract: Otherwise known as Data Acquisition, this function reaches into a source system to retrieve data. The data yielded by this function is known as Source Data.
- Transform: The first half of Data Integration, this function inspects, cleanses, and conforms Source Data to the needs of a data warehouse. The data yielded by this function is known as Load Data.
- Load: The second half of Data Integration, this function updates a data warehouse using the data provided in the Load Data.

These three functions (Extract, Transform, and Load) are more commonly known as ETL. An ETL application is the most comprehensive line between two points. These two points are the enterprise and all its source systems on one end and a data warehouse on the other.

The first concern of an ETL analyst, therefore, is these two points. The first point is the Source System. The enterprise and all its source systems are collectively referred to as the Source System, which may actually consist of multiple information

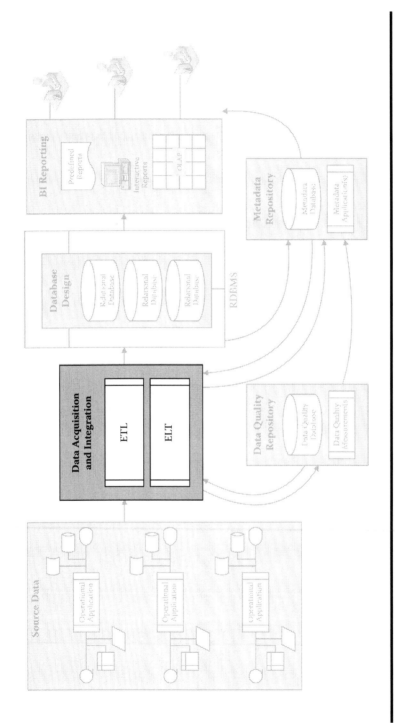

Figure 6.1 Data Acquisition and Integration.

systems, platforms, and geographies. For the purpose of discussion, however, they are referred to collectively as the Source System. The second point is the Target System. For an ETL application, the Target System is always a data warehouse or a section of a data warehouse architecture (e.g., Operational Data Store [ODS] or Data Mart). Prior to contemplating any ETL application design or architecture, an ETL analyst must first focus on and define the two points.

Source System Analysis

Chapter 3 focused solely on Source System Analysis. The principles of this analysis include:

- System of Record: The single authoritative statement of an entity or event
- Entity Data: The physical and logical members and agents of the enterprise
- Arithmetic Data: Measurements of enterprise activity
- Numeric Data That Isn't Arithmetic: Data with mismatched form and function
- Alphanumeric Data: Text and descriptive data
- Granularity: Hierarchical level of detail
- Latency: Delay in the arrival and availability of data
- Transaction Data: Conjunction of entity and arithmetic data to measure an event
- Snapshot Data: Conjunction of entity and arithmetic data to measure the net effect of multiple events over a period of time

The methods of Source System Analysis discussed in Chapter 3 include:

- Data Profile: A static view of the enterprise through its data
- Data Flow Diagram: A dynamic view of the enterprise through its data in motion
- Data State Diagram: A dynamic view of the enterprise through its data in motion and business relevance and meaning
- System of Record: A discernment of the authoritative data within an enterprise

If during the previous analysis activities, the Source System Analysis was omitted or abbreviated, an ETL analyst should return to the Source System Analysis. The potential of an ETL application failing to fulfill its requirements is greatly increased, if not completely assured, when the Source System Analysis is incomplete. The Source System Analysis provides an ETL analyst the information necessary to gather data from the source system. Even if the data warehouse has been designed without the advantage of the information provided by the Source System

Analysis, an ETL analyst should return to, and finish to completion, the Source System Analysis.

Target System Analysis

The Target System is a data warehouse, or a component of a data warehouse architecture. The data architecture, data model, and data warehouse design of that data warehouse are prerequisites for the design and creation of an ETL application. Usually, the design of a data warehouse stops at the data model. The data warehouse designer will usually choose a Relational Database Management System (RDBMS), Business Intelligence Reporting architecture, and data model. Data warehouse design should also indicate how the data warehouse will reflect the entities of the source system (e.g., purchase orders, machines, people, etc.) as those entities cycle through their states (e.g., reviewed, approved, commissioned, hired, etc.). For example:

- When the source system creates an instance of a data entity, how will the data warehouse reflect that instance?
- When the source system modifies the state of a data entity, how will the data warehouse reflect that modified state?
- When the source system removes an instance of a data entity, how will the data warehouse reflect the removal of that instance?
- When a business event occurs, how will the data warehouse reflect that event?
- When a business event cycles through its states (initiation, transaction, closure), how will the data warehouse reflect those states?

An ETL analyst asks such questions because the answers provide requirements that will be used to design and develop the ETL applications, which will load data into a data warehouse. The process of gathering these answers is the Target System Analysis.

The purpose of Target System Analysis is to identify and document expectations of the data in a data warehouse. These expectations come from multiple constituents. The data warehouse designer has expectations of the data in a data warehouse. Some of the data warehouse designer's expectations will be explicitly stated in the data architecture, data model, and data warehouse design deliverables. Target System Analysis will reveal and clarify the data warehouse designer's implicit expectations of a data warehouse. Data warehouse customers also have explicit and implicit expectations of the data in a data warehouse. The Target System Analysis will also reveal and clarify the expectations of data warehouse customers. Finally, when the expectations of the data warehouse designer contradict the expectations of the data warehouse customers, the Target System Analysis provides an opportunity to recognize and resolve such discrepancies. The goal of Target System Analysis is to create a set of expectations (i.e., requirements) so explicit that these expectations can be compared directly to the data in the data warehouse. The customers will compare the data in the data warehouse to their expectations. Therefore, an ETL analyst would be wise to perform that comparison during development and testing.

Data warehouse customers have explicit and implicit expectations of the data in a data warehouse. Looking at a data element named SALES, data warehouse customers explicitly expect to see sales data in a SALES table. Explicit expectations are easy to gather. Implicit expectations, however, can be more difficult. An ETL analyst, therefore, must pursue implicit expectations (i.e., assumptions) about the data in the SALES table. For instance, implicit expectations can be found with the following questions:

- Do you expect to see all sales data (i.e., complete)?
- When sales data is incomplete, would you like to know what data is missing (metadata)?
- Do you expect to never see the sales data duplicated (data quality)?
- Would you like to know when the next batch of sales data becomes available (metadata)?

For questions such as these, data warehouse customers typically answer, "Well, yes." Requirements such as these are not addressed in the creation of a data model because they do not contribute to an understanding of entities, attributes, and relationships. Requirements questions such as these are discussed in the following sections:

- Direct Requirements
- Indirect Requirements

Direct Requirements

Direct Requirements can best be understood as the explicit expectations of data warehouse customers. The meaning of each data element and how to achieve that meaning are the focus of Direct Requirements. An ETL analyst must investigate completely the meaning of each and every data element in a data warehouse as perceived by data warehouse customers.

Sometimes multiple populations of data warehouse customers have different and irreconcilable expectations for a data element. For example, a derived data element (Gross Profit) can have multiple meanings. The process of gathering ETL Direct Requirements typically discovers a few instances of multiple meanings. This is no reason to panic. Two meanings for Gross Profit indicate that there are multiple Gross Profit data elements. The ETL analyst should pass such anomalies back to the data warehouse designer for resolution. Once the anomaly is resolved, the ETL analyst can continue gathering the business meaning (i.e., customer expectation) of all data elements.

Direct Requirements are captured during Target System Analysis. That is when the meaning and behavior of a data warehouse and, therefore, all its data elements, are gathered. Figure 6.2 illustrates the progression of customer expectations to Direct Requirements.

An ETL analyst cannot assume without question that the Target System Analysis defines all Direct Requirements. If a Target System Analysis is expected to serve the purpose of documenting all Direct Requirements, then the Target System Analysis document should be audited to determine whether or not it meets that expectation. More realistically, an ETL analyst can use the Target System Analysis as a foundation for an ETL Direct Requirements document, which can provide definitions and customer expectations that are missing from the Target System Analysis document. Regardless of the requirements documents, an ETL analyst must understand data warehouse customer expectations of the data they will see in a data warehouse. That is the goal and focus of Direct Requirements.

Indirect Requirements

Indirect Requirements can best be understood as the information customers need for them to use a data warehouse to do their job. Indirect Requirements address the implicit expectations of data warehouse customers. Unless told otherwise, data warehouse customers assume the data in a data warehouse matches their expectations. An ETL application, therefore, has a responsibility to stipulate when a data warehouse does not match their expectations.

Indirect Requirements come directly from the Data Quality Service Level Agreement (SLA) and Metadata SLA (Figure 6.3). The Data Quality SLA and

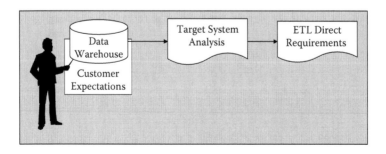

Figure 6.2 Direct Requirements.

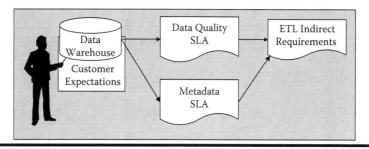

Figure 6.3   Indirect Requirements.

Metadata SLA gather requirements from data warehouse customers specifically for the purpose of helping them use a data warehouse.

Frequently, implicit expectations are not known until after a data warehouse has had the opportunity to violate these assumptions. As data warehouse customers come to understand their own implicit expectations, the Data Quality SLA and Metadata SLA documents can be updated to include these implicit expectations. This progression is normal and should not be viewed as a problem. A data warehouse team, in conjunction with data warehouse customers, will continue to identify and add new Data Quality and Metadata requirements throughout the life of a data warehouse.

Throughout the life of a data warehouse, the focus and goal of Indirect Requirements is the information customers need to use a data warehouse to do their job. The people, jobs, and skill levels may change. As these changes occur, the Data Quality and Metadata Programs must maintain their focus on deriving the maximum value possible from a data warehouse.

Direct and Indirect Requirements

The Direct and Indirect Requirements together (Figure 6.4) capture all expectations of data warehouse customers. At the conclusion of the requirements-gathering effort, all customer expectations, explicit and implicit, should be in one of these two documents.

During the subsequent design and development phases in the creation of an ETL application, no new customer expectations can be added to the design or development deliverables. Instead, any new customer expectations must be added to either the Direct or Indirect Requirements and then brought forward.

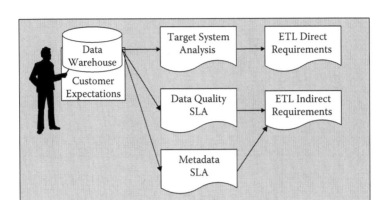

Figure 6.4   Direct and Indirect Requirements.

Language

The language of a Target System Analysis must be painstakingly precise. As with all requirements documents, a Target System Analysis is an agreement between an ETL analyst and data warehouse customers. By accepting a Target System Analysis deliverable, both the ETL analyst and data warehouse customers agree on its contents and meaning.

If the data warehouse does not match the expectations of the data warehouse customers, they will refer to the Target System Analysis and declare, "The data in the data warehouse does not match the data as described in the Target System Analysis." In such a circumstance, if the verbiage in the Target System Analysis allows any room for interpretation, the data warehouse customers will interpret it in their own way and by their own understanding, which will probably not match the data warehouse. For example:

- The ETL will respond appropriately.
- The row will change its state.
- When the data is ready.

These phrases are so vague that they can only be interpreted. A Target System Analysis that uses such language will communicate more confusion then information. A Target System Analysis written with explicit and precise language will communicate clearly, allowing no room for interpretation. Such language should:

- Name the exact database, table, and field.
- Name the exact data values and their locations, which constitute a prerequisite for any action.

- Name the exact sequence of processes, including predecessors and successors.
- Name the exact data values, which constitute each state and their meanings.

After all the work necessary to gather a complete set of requirements, the language with which these requirements are communicated can limit or enhance their success.

Data Profile

All ETL applications share the risk of loading wrong data into a data warehouse. A data profile of the Target System allows an ETL analyst to define or describe the data that will be loaded into a data warehouse before actually loading the data. The Data Profile includes three sections similar to the data profile from the Source System Analysis. Each section is intended to provide a cross-section description of data warehouse data elements in terms of the intended nature of the data (Inventory of Data Elements) and how the data warehouse data elements will relate to each other (Data Model).

- Inventory of Data Elements
  - Name
  - Format
  - Domain of values
  - Range of values
  - Frequency of distinct values
- Inventory of Data Entities
  - Combined data elements that define logical data
  - Core data element
  - Descriptive data elements
  - Associative data elements
- Data Model of the Target System
  - Logical
  - Physical
  - ETL keys
  - Foreign key relationships
  - Data Entity relationships

The purpose of a Data Profile is to define or describe the data elements in a data warehouse. The inventory of data elements is based on the intentions of the data warehouse designer and the expectations of the data warehouse customers. The logical and physical data models are provided by the data warehouse designer. The definition of the ETL keys enables an ETL application to uniquely identify every

Table 6.1   Data States

Data Element	Source System Data State	Data Warehouse Data State
Product	Proposed	Excluded: n/a
Manufacturing Design	Finalized	Included as Finalized
Invoice	Paid in Full	Included as Complete

business instance within a data entity, which is different from a primary key that identifies every row.

An ETL analyst must be able to explain the data that was loaded into a data warehouse. The Data Profile captures cross-section descriptions of the data in the data warehouse. Knowledge of the Target System allows an ETL analyst to demonstrate how well the data in a data warehouse conforms to expectations.

Data State

Data State Analysis is used to capture the various business meanings of data elements as they flow through a data warehouse. A data warehouse may not include all the data states present in the operational source system. Therefore, the presence of data states in a source system does not imply the presence of these data states in the data warehouse. Also, data states in the source system may be different from the data states in the data warehouse. The Data State Analysis identifies these data states that are intended to be captured in the data warehouse (Table 6.1). For example:

An ETL analyst must be able to explain the data that was loaded into a data warehouse. The Data Profile captures cross-section descriptions of the data in the data warehouse, excluding time and data state. Knowledge of the Target System allows an ETL analyst to demonstrate how well the data in a data warehouse conforms to expectations. Data State Analysis further enables an ETL analyst to identify expectations of a data warehouse by identifying the path within a data warehouse through which a data entity travels as it changes business meanings and relevance.

Data Mapping

Data Mapping is the process by which an ETL analyst identifies the source data, specific to location, state, and timing, which will be used to satisfy the data requirements of a data warehouse. Transformations necessary to create the data elements, as they will be stored in a data warehouse, are also included in a Data Mapping. Data Mapping documents can be in the form of a spreadsheet, a diagram, or text document. The form is not important. The important aspects of a Data Mapping document are:

- The participants in the Data Quality SLA must easily understand the Data Mapping document. The Data Mapping document will be an input into the Data Quality SLA and the Metadata SLA. If the participants in the Data Quality SLA cannot understand the Data Mapping document, they will be less effective addressing data quality problems.
- The Data Mapping document must clearly and precisely identify the source data element that will be used, such that there is no ambiguity about the location, state, or timing of the extract of a data element.
- The Data Mapping document must clearly and precisely identify the target data element that will be populated, such that there is no ambiguity about the location and state of the data element as stored in the data warehouse.
- The Data Mapping document must clearly and precisely define the transformations necessary to create the data element as it will be stored in the data warehouse.

Figure 6.5 illustrates, at a conceptual level, these four elements.

Simple data mappings may require no transformation at all, such as the mapping in Table 6.2.

Derived data mappings may require simple transformations, such as the mapping in Table 6.3.

Derived data mappings may cause recursive data mappings, such as the mapping in Table 6.4.

The entire lineage from specific source data elements to specific target data elements is captured in a Data Mapping. That lineage includes all transformations, modifications, and recursive mappings. Any new source or target data elements introduced to an ETL application must begin in the Data Mapping.

The Data Mapping must satisfy all Direct Requirements. Any Direct Requirement not satisfied in a Data Mapping will not be satisfied in a data warehouse either. Tracing Direct Requirements to the Data Mapping, therefore, can help verify that no Direct Requirements were missed.

The Data Mapping is the basis for the Physical Design. The purpose of the Physical Design is to achieve the lineage shown in the Data Mapping, which satisfies all Direct Requirements. Physical Design, therefore, must wait for completion of the Data Mapping.

Business Rules

Finally, the Target System Analysis is the opportunity to document the business rules that will govern data in the data warehouse. The Data Profile, Data State Diagram, and Data Mapping provide the best opportunity to identify the business rules of the data warehouse. These business rules come in three basic varieties.

DATA MAPPING FROM SOURCE TO TARGET

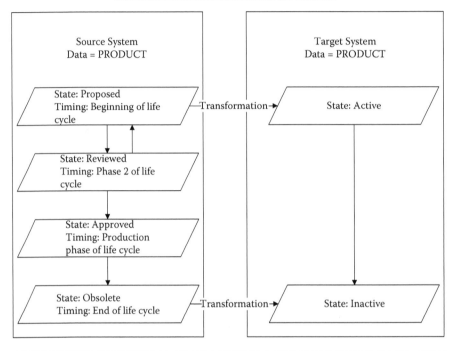

Figure 6.5   Data Mapping.

Table 6.2   Simple Data Mapping

Source Data Element	Transformation	Target Data Element
Length in kilometers	n/a	Length in kilometers

Table 6.3   Derived Data Mapping

Source Data Element	Transformation	Target Data Element
Length in kilometers	Multiply by 1,000	Length in meters

■ Intrarow Business Rules: Column A + Column B = Column C. The business rule exists entirely within each individual row. All the data and information necessary to validate the business rule is present in a single row. An Intrarow business rule can only be validated one row at a time because that business rule applies to only one row at a time.

Table 6.4   Recursive Data Mappng

Source Data Element	Transformation	Target Data Element
Length in kilometers	n/a	Length in kilometers
Price per meter	n/a	Price per meter

Source Data Element	Transformation	Target Data Element
Price per meter	Multiply by 1,000	Price per kilometer

Source Data Element	Transformation	Target Data Element
Length in kilometers	Multiply	Total Price
Price per kilometer		

- Intratable Business Rules: Row 1.Column A + Row 2.Column A = Row 3.Column B. This business rule spans across rows within a data warehouse table, but still remains within the table. All the data and information necessary to validate the business rule is present in a single data warehouse table. An Intratable business rule can only be validated one table at a time because that business rule applies to only one table at a time.
- Cross-Table Business Rules: Table 1.Column A = Table 2.Column B. The business rule spans across sets of data warehouse tables. The data and information, therefore, may not be available in the data warehouse. The data may be late arriving. Cross-Table business rules, therefore, require more effort to define.

Business rules will be used to create the Data Quality validations of data as it flows through the ETL application on its way to the data warehouse. Therefore, any data elements in the data warehouse that should maintain a consistent behavior, and can affect the perceived quality of the data warehouse, should be included in the list of Business Rules.

Architecture

Early ETL applications were physically designed on the assumption that three platforms were involved:

- Source system platform
- ETL platform
- Data Warehouse platform

These three platforms equated to three physically separate and individually whole computers (Figure 6.6).

Since then, ETL analysts realized they could leverage the computing power of a target RDBMS (i.e., a data warehouse). ETL analysts moved the Transform application over to the data warehouse RDBMS (Figure 6.7). This physical design is called ELT because the Load application had been moved in front of the Transform application.

Within a Load application, the final Update function will always be the last function because the final purpose and destination is a data warehouse. All physical designs, therefore, culminate at the update of a data warehouse.

So, all physical designs begin with an Extract application and end with an Update function. First, all ETL/ELT physical designs must extract data from a source system, otherwise, there is no data to transform, load, or update. Second, all ETL/ELT physical designs must update a data warehouse, otherwise, they do not fulfill their final purpose. Everything that happens between the Extract and Update is up to the discretion of the ETL analyst (Figure 6.8). Any operation can happen on any platform most capable of that operation, and the operations performed on various platforms are typically Transform operations.

A physical design that crosses multiple Transform platforms must observe two caveats:

- Load: Any function that pushes data from a sending platform to a receiving platform has the responsibility to verify that all transported data was received exactly as intended.

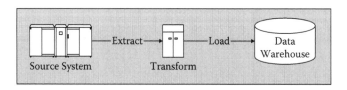

Figure 6.6 Extract, Transform, and Load (ETL) platform.

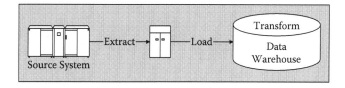

Figure 6.7   Data Warehouse Relational Database Management System (RDBMS).

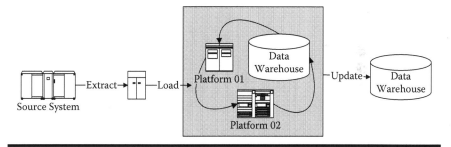

Figure 6.8   Multiple Extract, Transform, and Load (ETL) platforms.

■ Extract: Any function that pulls data from a source platform has the responsibility to verify that all transported data was received exactly as intended.

Extract, Transform, and Load (ETL)

In an ETL application (Figure 6.9), data is extracted (i.e., acquired) from an operational system. The extracted data is captured on a platform that is controlled by the ETL application. This process of capturing data on a controlled platform is called Staging, and the platform is called a Staging Platform or Staging Environment. At this point, the staged data is in its raw form, which is identical to its form and state when it was in an operational application. In this raw, pretransform state, the staged data is called Source Data.

A Transform application performs all data modifications to the Source Data necessary to conform it to the rules, layout, and format of a data warehouse. The transformed data is also captured on a platform that is controlled by the ETL application. The posttransform data is also captured on a Staging Platform or Staging Environment. In this posttransform state, however, the staged data is called Load Data.

A Load application bridges the gap between the ETL and Staging Platforms and the data warehouse platform. A Load application reads the Load Data and

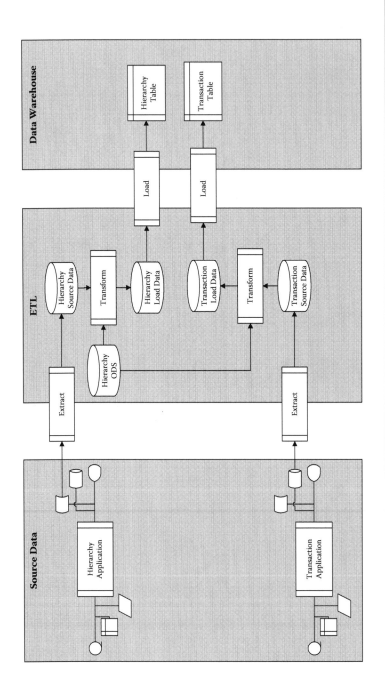

Figure 6.9   Extract, Transform, and Load (ETL).

performs the necessary inserts, updates, and deletes to a data warehouse. When the Load application has finished, the ETL application has completed.

Extract, Load, and Transform (ELT)

An ELT application (Figure 6.10) performs all the functions and purposes of an ETL application. The difference between an ETL application and an ELT application is the platform on which the application performs it functions.

An ELT application uses the ELT platform as a momentary hub enroute to the data warehouse RDBMS platform. The ELT platform extracts operational data, and loads it directly to staging tables on the data warehouse RDBMS platform. All the transform functions are performed on the data warehouse RDBMS platform. Finally, the data warehouse is loaded from within the data warehouse RDBMS platform.

ELT has two advantages.

■ A data warehouse RDBMS platform is a powerful platform. All the resources (CPU seconds, throughput, etc.) of a data warehouse RDBMS platform are available to an ELT application.
■ A copy of look-up data need not be kept and maintained on the ELT platform because the data warehouse RDBMS has access to all the data in the data warehouse.

ELT has one disadvantage.

■ A portion of the data warehouse's resources (CPU seconds, throughput, etc.) are consumed by someone other than a data warehouse customer. Given sufficient data volumes and transformation complexity, this could adversely affect data warehouse customers

For discussion purposes, ETL and ELT applications will be referred to collectively as ETL. The principles and methods discussed in the following sections apply to ETL and ELT equally.

ETL Design Principles

The following ETL Design Principles are a set of lessons learned. ETL applications are subject to unexpected circumstances and, therefore, should expect the unexpected to occur. An ETL analyst must work hard to assure an ETL application is bulletproof, knowing each ETL application will behave as intended, even if the source system does not.

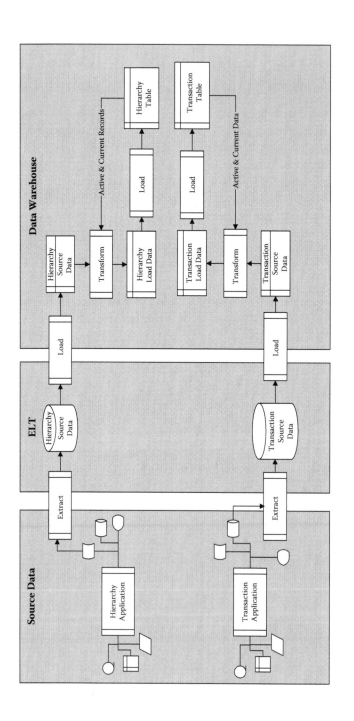

Figure 6.10 Extract, Load, and Transform (ELT).

ETL Process Principles

ETL Process Principles 1 through 6 address specifically the executable part of an ETL application, i.e., the code that moves, copies, and transforms data. The executable part of an ETL application is similar to a manufacturing plant. Raw materials come in one door and finished products go out another. Inside the manufacturing plant, an assembly line is the path by which raw materials are converted to finished products by means of many independent and interdependent manufacturing functions (stamping, dyeing, casting, trimming, etc.).

The same concepts that apply to manufacturing also apply to ETL. Data anomalies can enter an ETL application as raw data or transformed data. Some anomalies only manifest themselves deep into the manufacturing process. Therefore, the ETL manufacturing processes that convert and transform raw data (i.e., materials) into a data warehouse (i.e., finished product) must manage and control the data within each manufacturing function. The strength and robustness of that control are a function of a Data Quality SLA, Metadata SLA, and discretion of the ETL analyst designing the application.

ETL Process Principles provide six design principles by which an ETL analyst can manage and control data as it passes through an ETL application. An ETL application can avoid data anomalies by incorporating ETL Process Principles throughout the entire manufacturing process. The following topics describe each of the ETL Process Principles on a conceptual level.

Principle 01: One Thing at a Time

Multitasking, the ability to perform two or more tasks simultaneously, is perceived as a positive characteristic both in people and computer applications. Multitasking conserves time and resources and is contrary to all things ETL. Applications that multitask are built with the assumption that all will go as planned, that all input values will be reasonable and valid. An ETL application, however, assumes that nothing will go as planned, and that some input values will be unreasonable and invalid.

Efficiency through multitasking is a basic principle of application design. In operational applications, the benefits of efficiency have been always been obvious, and the risks have been few. For these reasons, efficiency through multitasking is a standard design principle for all application design, except ETL application design. The benefits and risks of multitasking in ETL application design are difficult to notice because they are so different. The following example highlights the difference.

Many applications are built on a relational database (RDBMS) platform. Relational applications manipulate data using SQL. The following is an example of a SQL statement that can be found in any operational application.

```
SELECT
    EMPLOYEE.EMPLOYEE_ID
,SUBSTR(EMPLOYEE.LNAME & ',' EMPLOYEE.FNAME & ' ' &
EMPLOYEE.MNAME) AS NAME
, (PAYROLL.BASE_SALARY*TAX_MATRIX.TAX_RATE) AS
TOTAL_TAX_AMT
,((PAYROLL.BASE_SALARY*TAX_MATRIX.TAX_RATE) /PAY_
CALENDAR.NUM_WEEKS) AS WEEKLY_TAX_AMT
FROM EMPLOYEE
INNER JOIN PAYROLL
    ON EMPLOYEE.EMPLOYEE_ID = PAYROLL.EMPLOYEE_ID
INNER JOIN TAX_MATRIX
    ON EMPLOYEE.TAX_REGION_ID = TAX_MATRIX.TAX_REGION_ID
    AND EMPLOYEE.DECUCTION_ID = TAX_MATRIX.DEDUCTION_ID
    AND EMPLOYEE.EXEMPTION_ID = TAX_MATRIX.EXEMPTION_ID
INNER PAY_CALENDAR
    ON PAYROLL.PAY_DATE = CALENDAR.DATE
WHERE EMPLOYEE.STATUS IN ('FT', 'PT')
    AND EMPLOYEE.DRUG_TEST = 'PASS'
```

This SQL calculates, for all Full-Time and Part-Time employees, the total and weekly tax amounts. In a closed-loop payroll application, this sort of SQL statement would be valid. This SQL, in an ETL application, would not be wise. This SQL is performing numerous actions simultaneously. Each of those actions implicitly incurs one or more assumptions. Some of those simultaneous actions and assumptions are listed in Table 6.5.

In an ETL application, simultaneous actions are not a problem. Assumptions that accompany simultaneous actions are a problem. If any assumption is violated, then the set of simultaneous actions fails to deliver a complete and accurate set of data. The cause of such a failure, a violated assumption, is usually extremely difficult to discern. The occurrence of such a failure may go unnoticed because no part of this SQL would expose a violated assumption. A better approach would be to perform each action individually and then combine the separate result sets into one set of data.

This example of multitasking within a SQL statement can also occur in any other language and platform. For example:

■ An ETL application written within an ETL tool can transform event transaction records, write them to a file, and load them to a table, all in one piece of code. When questionable event transaction records are in the data warehouse:
  – Was the source data bad?
  – Did the fact transformation malfunction?
  – Was the problem in the creation of the load file?
  – Did the load modify the data?
  – Which assumption was violated?

Table 6.5 Simultaneous Assumptions

SQL Statement	Action	Assumption
INNER JOIN PAYROLL ON EMPLOYEE.EMPLOYEE_ID = PAYROLL.EMPLOYEE_ID	Join the Employee and Payroll tables on Employee_ID	1. All applicable employees are in the Employee table 2. All employees receiving a salary are in the Payroll table 3. Referential Integrity between the Employee and Payroll tables is complete
INNER JOIN TAX_MATRIX ON EMPLOYEE.TAX_REGION_ID = TAX_MATRIX.TAX_REGION_ID AND EMPLOYEE.DEDUCTION_ID = TAX_MATRIX.DEDUCTION_ID AND EMPLOYEE.EXEMPTION_ID = TAX_MATRIX.EXEMPTION_ID	Join the Employee and Tax_Matrix tables on Tax_Region_ID, Deduction_ID and Exemption_ID	1. All applicable employees have valid values in the Tax_Region_ID, Deduction_ID, and Exemption_ID fields of the Employee table 2. Referential Integrity between the Employee and Tax_Matrix tables is complete
INNER PAY_CALENDAR ON PAYROLL.PAY_DATE = CALENDAR.DATE	Join the Payroll and Calendar tables on Date	1. The Payroll table has the correct Pay_Date 2. Referential Integrity between the Payroll and Calendar tables is complete
((PAYROLL.BASE_SALARY *TAX_MATRIX.TAX_RATE) /PAY_CALENDAR.NUM_WEEKS) AS WEEKLY_TAX_AMT	Calculate Weekly_Tax_Amt	1. Tax_Rate will be available from the Tax_Matrix table 2. Num_Weeks will be available from the Pay_Calendar table 3. Num_Weeks from the Pay_Calendar table will not equal zero

Table 6.5 Simultaneous Assumptions (continued)

SQL Statement	Action	Assumption
WHERE EMPLOYEE.STATUS IN ('FT', 'PT')	Include only Full-Time and Part-Time employees	1. All Full-Time employees have Status = 'FT' 2. All Part-Time employees have Status = 'PT' 3. The Status value for all Full- and Part-Time employees is spelled correctly
WHERE EMPLOYEE.DRUG_TEST = 'PASS'	Include only employees who have passed the drug test	1. All employees have a valid value in the Drug_Test field of the Employee table 2. All employees who have passed the Drug Test have the value 'PASS' spelled correctly
WHERE PAYROLL.PAY_CLASS IN ('A', 'B', 'D')	Include only employees with applicable payroll classes	1. All employees have a valid value in the Pay_Class field of the Employee table 2. All employees who have an applicable pay class, have the Pay Class value spelled correctly

▪ An ETL application written in COBOL can extract a list of manufacturing processes, transform manufacturing specifications, and write them to a load file. When questionable specification records are in the data warehouse:
- Was the source data bad?
- Did the transformation malfunction?
- Was the problem in the creation of the load file?
- Did the load modify the data?
- Which assumption was violated?

Principle 01: One Thing at a Time is basically a granular modular approach. Benefits of using a granular modular approach include:

▪ Create the opportunity for Data Quality and Metadata functions to integrate within an ETL application.
▪ Create the opportunity to isolate violated assumptions.
▪ Remove any question about the sequence and precedence of ETL functions, regardless of the language or platform.

A granular modular design that does one thing at a time is inefficient. Capacity analysts and resource planners will most likely challenge such an inefficient design, as well they should. An ETL analyst must find that delicate balance between the benefits of modular granularity and the risks of violated assumptions.

At the lowest total cost of granular modularity (Figure 6.11), not all functions will be isolated in a modular fashion. The functions with any real risk of violated assumptions, however, will be isolated.

Principle 02: Know When to Begin

Operational systems rely on operational job schedulers to know when the conditions have been satisfied for a job to begin. Typically, those conditions are expressed in terms of jobs and completion codes. A satisfactory completion code from a precedent job will trigger the beginning of a subsequent job, as shown in Figure 6.12.

ETL applications, however, rely on conditions within precedent data (i.e., Begin Conditions). When precedent Begin Conditions have been satisfied, subsequent applications relying on those conditions can safely begin. In the example above (Figure 6.12), Job 02 would examine data created by Job 01, not just the return code generated by Job 01, and Job 05 would examine data created by Job 01, Job 02, Job 03, and Job 04.

An Extract application will examine an operational source system prior to extracting data (Figure 6.13). Examination of source data and associated data within an operational source system can provide clues as to whether or not the

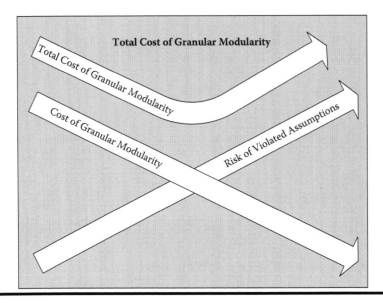

Figure 6.11 **Cost of Granularity.**

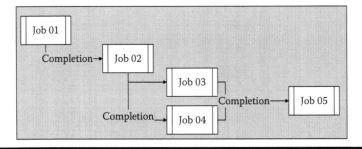

Figure 6.12 **Know When to Begin.**

source data is truly ready for extraction. Data elements associated with source data may include flags, inventories, or exceptions present in operational source data.

A Transform application will examine data provided by preceding Extract applications, as shown in Figure 6.14. A Load application will examine data provided by preceding Transform applications to determine whether or not Begin Conditions have been satisfied. In these circumstances, Data Quality and Metadata information prove to be extremely helpful, and subsequent applications may require preceding applications (within an ETL application) to provide Data Quality or Metadata information.

Principle 02: Know When to Begin is basically a backward-looking design principle. Rather than place all trust in return codes and job schedulers, an ETL

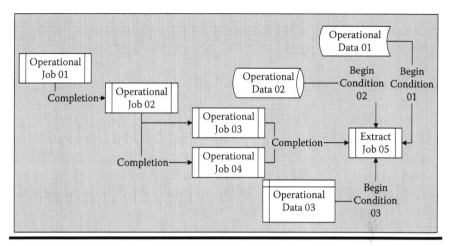

Figure 6.13   Operational Source System.

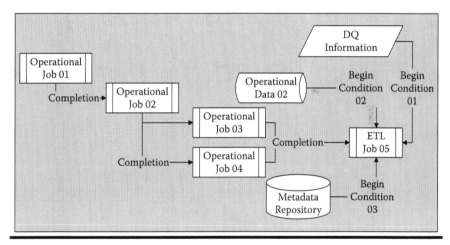

Figure 6.14   Preceding Extract Applications.

application can look backward to examine the data associated with precedent conditions to determine whether or not Begin Conditions have been satisfied. Begin Conditions mitigate the risk and cost of errors in input data. The choice to include Begin Conditions is a balance between the probability, risk, and cost of input errors and the expenses incurred by implementing Begin Conditions.

Principle 03: Know When to End

Principle 03: Know When to End is a forward-looking design that requires an ETL application to examine data it has created. An individual ETL application is best equipped to know what it intended to create. After completing the core functions of an ETL application, that same application can review its own output, as shown in Figure 6.15. A post-application review of output data gives an ETL application the opportunity to warranty data prior to passing it on to subsequent applications or data warehouse customers.

An Extract function examines data prior to releasing it to a Transform application. The Transform application also reviews load-ready data prior to warranting that data as ready for a Load application. A Load application can query a data warehouse to determine whether or not data was successfully loaded. If the data created, or loaded, by an ETL application fails to pass this final review, an ETL application has many options, depending on the severity of the failure. Those options include data remediation, rebuild the output data completely, and interrupt the job stream.

Principle 03: Know When to End is a forward-looking design principle. An ETL application can verify, by examining its own output data, whether or not that ETL application has completed satisfactorily. Then, the results of that final review can be captured as Data Quality or Metadata information, and shared with subsequent ETL applications. End Conditions mitigate the risk and cost of errors in output data. The choice to include End Conditions is a balance between the probability, risk, and cost of output errors and the expenses incurred by implementing End Conditions.

Principle 04: Large to Medium to Small

Principle 04: Large to Medium to Small is a design principle that typically spans across an entire ETL application. Large to Medium to Small is one of three overall

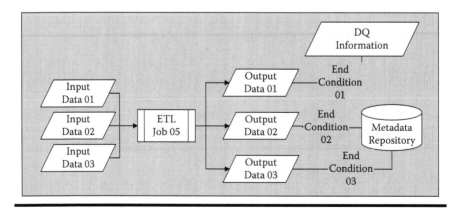

Figure 6.15　Know when to end.

design methods. Coincidentally, Large to Medium to Small happens to work the best.[1] The three overall design methods are:

- Small to Medium to Large
- Just In Time
- Large to Medium to Small

Small to Medium to Large functions like a river. Typically, rivers begin from a small spring or melting glacier. Then, as other rivers join, the initial river grows by the volume of additional rivers. Likewise, Small to Medium to Large begins with a "driver" data element. As data is added to that data element, the data that flows through an ETL application grows to its final form, as shown in Figure 6.16.

An inherent weakness of this design is the absence of the excluded data. Applications bring data into the data stream, but only the data that is perceived to be needed by that data stream. If data not included in the data stream becomes relevant and necessary later in the data stream, then that ETL application will not have the data it needs. Small to Medium to Large also hides excluded data by disallowing its entry into an ETL application. The ETL application is not allowed to capture or measure the disallowed data and, therefore, can neither report nor control data exclusions.

Just in Time is a design method wherein data enters and leaves an ETL stream of data, without significantly altering the nature of that data. An ETL application includes data that is needed when it is needed and dismisses data that is not needed when that data is no longer needed, which is shown in Figure 6.17.

An inherent weakness of this design is the lack of a big picture. Throughout an ETL application, that application only looks at the data necessary to perform the next function. Data that was dismissed early in an ETL application is no longer available to juxtapose against data that arrives later in that same application.

Finally, Large to Medium to Small design assembles all applicable data elements and entities. Data that is no longer required is dismissed. The final data set is a load-ready file that will be loaded to a data warehouse (Figure 6.18).

Inherent strengths of this design are the reverse of the weaknesses of the previous designs. Excluded data is initially present and, as excluded data is dismissed

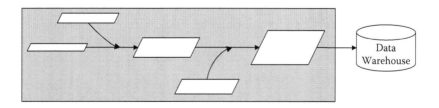

Figure 6.16   Small to medium to large.

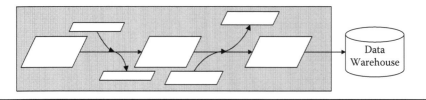

Figure 6.17   Just in time.

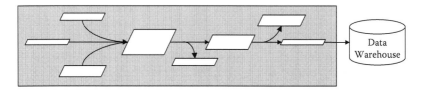

Figure 6.18   Large to medium to small.

from the data stream, it is dismissed within the context of all applicable data. At the initial stage, all applicable data is juxtaposed simultaneously. The decision to exclude data, therefore, is made in the broadest context possible, which allows the greatest possible control of data exclusions.

Principle 05: Stage Data Integrity

Principle 05: Stage Data Integrity is a design principle that maintains the integrity of a set of stage data. Once created, a set of stage data can only be consumed as a single contiguous set by subsequent applications. When multiple logical sets of data share common characteristics (including format, layout, data types, meaning, and usage), storing them together in a single set of stage data seems reasonable; however, storing them together creates unnecessary risk for an ETL application.

For example, the following list describes a single set of stage data (Manufacturing Raw Materials) containing raw materials from Companies A, B, and C (Figure 6.19). This list can also be perceived as three logical sets of data—raw materials from Companies A, B, and C.

- Manufacturing Raw Materials
  - Sourced from Company A
  - Sourced from Company B
  - Sourced from Company C

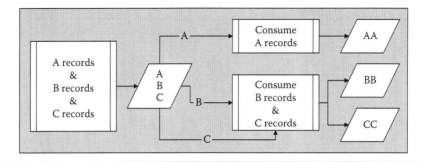

Figure 6.19 Stage Data Integrity: one dataset.

Any function that retrieves a subset of data from an existing dataset is, in essence, an extract function. An application needing data describing raw materials from Company A must extract that data from the entire set of Manufacturing Raw Materials. This is an extract function and is vulnerable to the problems faced by all extract functions.

- Did the extract retrieve all records?
- Did the extract retrieve only the required rows?
- Did the extract retrieve rows already retrieved by a previous extract (i.e., duplicate)?

Rather than introduce an extract function where it does not belong by storing multiple logical sets of data in a single physical dataset, ETL applications store data as it will be used by subsequent applications. By storing data physically, as it will be used, an ETL application establishes and maintains the integrity of individual sets of stage data.

A single application writes A, B, and C records to multiple data sets (Figure 6.20). Datasets A, B, and C are each consumed, without modification, by immediately subsequent applications. Dataset ABC is consumed by a later application. All four datasets (A, B, C, and ABC) can be used by subsequent applications without the intervention of an extract function.

Principle 05: Stage Data Integrity is a design principle by which precedent applications create stage data as it will be consumed by subsequent applications. This design avoids unnecessary risk and increases the overall integrity of an ETL application.

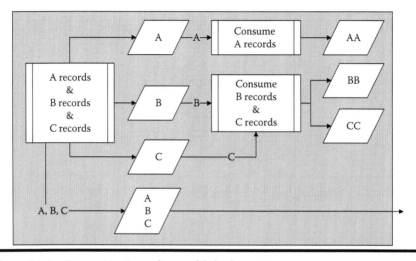

Figure 6.20 Stage Data Integrity: multiple datasets.

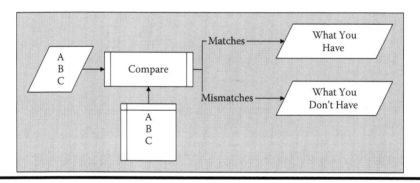

Figure 6.21 Know what you have.

Principle 06: Know What You Have

Principle 06: Know What You Have is a design principle that prompts an ETL application to take inventory of inbound data, rather than assume inbound data contains all that is expected. An ETL application can compare the contents of inbound data with expected data (Figure 6.21).

Information describing contents of inbound data is available through two sources. The first source is Metadata. The precedent application that created the data can also capture an inventory of that data as Metadata. Requirements to perform an inventory of data, while creating that data, can be included in the Metadata SLA. That's how a subsequent application can require precedent applications provide Metadata to accompany created data.

The second source of information describing contents of inbound data is the data itself. If no Metadata describing inbound data is available, then the only remaining option is to profile the inbound data. To profile inbound data, an application may need to read every record of the inbound data. Statistical methods, including sampling, may not provide the required information. If an application requires the inclusion of all 40,000 raw materials, a sample of 500 records will not provide a reasonable inventory of the inbound data. If possible, the profile of inbound data occurs simultaneously as the inbound data is processed. Then, if the inbound data is satisfactory, the inbound data (which has been processed) can be released to the next application or function.

The reverse of Know What You Have is Know What You *Don't* Have. The second output of the comparison of inbound data and expected data is a list of mismatches, i.e., missing data. Knowledge of missing data provides an ETL application the opportunity to apply a threshold. If the impact of missing data exceeds an applied threshold, that application has the opportunity to choose its response. Responses can include a reduced Data Quality rating, a default value as substitute data, or termination of a job stream.

An application incorporates Principle 06: Know What You Have to shield itself from the possibility of missing data and other anomalies. Both methods, data profile and Metadata, incur additional cost in the forms of application development, maintenance, and resource consumption. The decision to include either method, therefore, is a balance between the risk of data anomalies and the cost of mitigating that risk. Three key factors in that balance are:

- History: Has the inbound data demonstrated a probability of data anomalies?
- Threshold: What is the threshold? What is the probability that threshold will be exceeded?
- Response: What is the required response when the threshold is exceeded?

Process Principles Conclusion

ETL Process Principles describe the logical processes that contribute to a bullet-proof ETL application.

- Principle 01: One Thing at a Time describes how to isolate individual functions along with their actions and assumptions.
- Principle 02: Know When to Begin describes how to use prerequisite conditions in data to determine whether or not an application or function should begin.

- Principle 03: Know When to End describes how to use requisite conditions in data to determine whether or not an application or function has completed its purpose.
- Principle 04: Large to Medium to Small describes how to manage a set of data throughout all its transformations.
- Principle 05: Stage Data Integrity describes how to establish and maintain whole and self-contained data throughout an ETL application.
- Principle 06: Know What You Have describes how to inventory inbound data to determine what is present and missing.

ETL Process Principles, of course, neither supplant nor replace best practices of operational applications. ETL Process Principles, in addition to best practices of operational applications are intended to contribute to a bulletproof ETL application. These principles can insulate an ETL application from unexpected variations that can occur in source data. Rather than expect every day to be like yesterday, ETL Process Principles can provide sufficient granular control to notice when variations occur, including variations that would adversely affect either the ETL application or the data warehouse.

ETL Staging Principles

The analogy between a manufacturing process and ETL breaks down in one place: stage data.

- In a manufacturing process, when a bolt is used to fasten two pieces of metal together, that bolt is now embedded in the finished product. Afterward, that manufacturing process can only describe the bolt that is now in the finished product by saying, "It was a type XYZ123 bolt."
- In an ETL application, however, when a set of stage data is used to fasten two pieces of data together, that stage data is still stage data. Afterward, that ETL application can describe stage data that is now in the finished product by saying, "I used exactly this row of data and none other."

For this reason, the useful lifespan of stage data in an ETL application goes much longer than the application that consumes the stage data. Data Quality and Metadata applications can measure stage data. Support analysts can inspect stage data.

The properties of stage data that extend its lifespan are its integrity and continuity. The integrity and continuity of stage data also increase the control and integrity of an ETL application. ETL Staging Principles provide design principles by which an ETL analyst can manage and control the creation and use of stage structures, which also increases the control and integrity of an ETL application and the useful lifespan of the stage data. The following topics describe each of the ETL Staging Principles on a conceptual level.

Principle 07: Name the Data

Identification is a key element of control. Granular identification is in direct proportion to precise control. Data (as well as a person, car, airplane, boat, etc.) is identified by its name. A name, however, ceases to identify one dataset when two datasets share the same name. To achieve granular identification, datasets of the same type must have a method of unique identification.

Principle 07: Name the Data is a design principle that prompts an ETL application to choose the level of granularity at which data will be named and, therefore, controlled. For example:

- Look at the nearest bottle of headache or sinus pain relief. There is a lot number on the bottle. That lot number corresponds to a batch of product that was created at one time. The most granular identification a manufacturer has of that product is the lot number. The most granular identification, and control, available for that product, therefore, is the lot number.
- Look at the nearest car (manufactured for the United States). If you look closely enough, there is a Vehicle Identification Number (VIN). That car's VIN uniquely identifies that car from all other cars. The license tag can, and probably will, change; however, the VIN will never change. The most granular identification, and control, available for that product, therefore, is the individual car.

In each of these instances, a decision was made to identify one product (bottle of medicine) at the lot number (i.e., batch lot), and another product (automobile) at the individual product level. Likewise, an ETL analyst chooses the level of granularity by which data will be named.

A data name should not identify the instance of a dataset. If the operating system allows long names, a date, timestamp, or other uniquely identifying text can be embedded in a file name. Mainframe operating systems allow names with multiple nodes (a node is a text string eight characters long between two periods), and Generation Data Groups (GDGs) with their uniquely identifying generation number. These and other methods will allow a data name to uniquely identify an instance of a data name.

Specific data names can include a wide variety of specific identifying features. Typically, specific data names are embedded in data records rather than file names. Identifying data names can include elements such as:

- Unique identifier of the function that created the data.

- Unique version of the function that created the data.
- Unique identifier of the function for which the data is intended.
- Unique version of the function for which the data is intended.
- Unique batch number of the data.
- Unique row number of each row.
- Metadata key as a foreign key to a Metadata Repository.
- Data Quality key as a foreign key to a Data Quality Repository.

Data names have specific meaning, purpose, and use. All data names should satisfy a real requirement. Otherwise, any data names that do not satisfy a requirement should not be included.

The advantage of specific data names is clarity. Specific data names applied correctly can remove any doubt about the nature of a set, row, column, or cell of data. The disadvantage of specific data names is cost. As identifying features, of increasing granularity, are embedded into a dataset, the level of control and integrity increase in direct proportion.

Principle 08: Own the Data

An ETL application is one occasion when sharing (the instruction all parents give their children) becomes a bad design. Operational applications frequently share datasets. Rather than continuously synchronize multiple datasets, operational applications share common datasets. When an operational application updates a shared dataset, those updates are available to other operational applications without incurring synchronization overhead.

A feature of data warehousing that distinguishes data warehouses from other data constructs is time variance. Time variance is the feature by which a data warehouse reports changes in data through time. For example, a time-variant data warehouse can capture the following:

- **May 13**: Candy XYZ123 began using Dye Color #34.
  - Sales averaged 500,000 units weekly.
  - Returns average 10,000 units weekly.
- **July 24**: Candy XYZ123 switched to Dye Color #67.
  - Sales averaged 4,500,000 units weekly.
  - Returns average 2,000 units weekly.
- **November 30**: Candy XYZ123 switched to Dye Color #35.
  - Sales averaged 750,000 units weekly.
  - Returns average 12,000 units weekly.

Based on this time variant information, the manufacturer of Candy XYZ123 would probably prefer to use Dye Color #67. For an ETL application to provide time variant data to a data warehouse, that ETL application must be able to control time by freezing a dataset at a moment in time. An ETL application uses a frozen dataset to capture, at a moment in time, the data in that dataset. Subsequent updates to the source dataset will be captured in the next ETL cycle or batch. For the time variant purposes of a data warehouse, however, an ETL application will create its own instance or copy of a source dataset. By restricting access to that dataset copy, the ETL application using that dataset copy can be assured that no operational updates have been introduced.

ETL applications use exclusive dataset copies to isolate operational source data, interim transformed data, and load-ready data. So, ETL applications can refuse to share with operational source systems and other ETL applications. By freezing time in a dataset, which is then compared to data frozen at a different time, an ETL application can transform time-variant data.

Principle 09: Build the Data

Datasets are used throughout an ETL application. The creation of those datasets, therefore, significantly affects the success of an ETL application. The creation of a dataset is similar to the creation of a house.

- Pour the concrete foundation
- Assemble the frame on top of the foundation
- Attach the roof and walls to the frame
- Apply paint, fixtures, and furnishings to the interior.

Notice the sequence goes from the outside to the inside. The area of the house is defined by the foundation. The perimeter of the house is defined by the frame. The perimeter is sealed by the walls and roof. Then, finally, the details are attached to an existing framework.

The creation of a dataset uses the same sequence, from the outside foundation and frame to the inside data.

- Create the foundation of a dataset.
  - Sequential file, logical record length, and storage method.
  - XML file.
  - Relational table.
- Define the frame on top of the foundation.
  - COBOL copybook.
  - XML layout.
  - Relational data definition.
- Define the structure within the layout.
  - Define the meaning of each field or column.

- Define the accepted domain, range, and relational integrity for each field or column.
- Determine the expected cardinality of the dataset.
■ Attach data to the interior of the dataset.
- Insert data using the COBOL copybook, XML layout, or relational data definition.
- Verify the data conforms to the structure within the layout.

This probably seems to be over-thinking the creation of a dataset. All applications create datasets. So, why this attention to detail in an ETL application? The answer is simple—control. By isolating the logical steps in the creation of a dataset, Principle 09: Build the Data allows an ETL application to control the creation of a dataset.

Rather than allow a dataset to inherit its properties from existing constraints or classes, define a new dataset and its properties. Rather than allow a dataset to inherit its demographics from the data within, define and control these demographics before any data is added to that dataset. Rather than propagate the properties of an existing dataset by copying that dataset, define a dataset and its properties (even if those properties are identical).

An ETL application can best control the data within an ETL application by controlling the creation of datasets, which are best controlled from the outside (foundation and frame). Rather than allow a SQL Select or COBOL Read statement to define a dataset from the inside, a dataset is best defined and controlled from the outside, by defining the structure, properties, layout, and expectations, and then applying the data.

Principle 10: Type the Data

Data type mismatches, numeric data overflows, and null violations can stop an ETL application. Principle 10: Type the Data is a design principle intended to protect an ETL application from data that can cause an abnormal end. The principle is very simple—verify that the data type of inbound (or transformed) data is compatible with the data type of the destination before moving inbound (or transformed) data to its destination (Figure 6.22).

This principle is simple. The *application* of this principle, however, is not so simple. During the initial design of an ETL application, the data types of source and destination datasets are known. When those data types are incompatible, a decision must be made. What will the ETL application do with records containing incompatible data types? Instances of incompatible data types include the following:

■ A source field allows alpha characters. Assurances from the source system indicate the source field always contains only numeric values. The destination

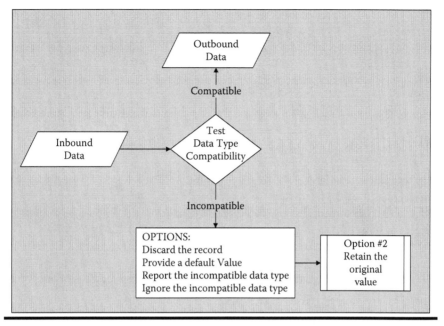

Figure 6.22 Type Data.

field is numeric. What will the ETL application do with inbound records containing alpha characters?

■ A transformation multiplies two values. The product should always be less than 5,000. The destination field is defined as Small Integer. What will the ETL application do with transformed records that exceed the numeric range of a Small Integer field?

Some of the options are:

■ Option #1: Discard the record
■ Option #2: Provide a default value
■ Option #3: Report the incompatible data type
■ Option #4: Ignore the incompatible data type (and allow the application to end abnormally)

Each of these decisions has implications for the behavior of the entire data warehouse, Data Quality SLA, and Metadata SLA. So, these decisions must be made with the consensus of data stewards and data warehouse designers. While it may seem more expedient to make these decisions alone, in the long run these decisions are best made with a consensus of data warehouse constituents.

Option #2 includes an additional element. Before overwriting an incompatible data value with a default value, capture the original data value. The original data value can be captured as part of a Data Quality record, Metadata record or within the outbound data in a field that is compatible with the inbound data type. The storage location for discarded data is not important; the ability to retrieve discarded data is important. This is not a Recycle Wheel nor should it be considered a Recycle Wheel. Rather, the retention of discarded incompatible data is insurance against the prospect that a discarded data element might actually be vitally important data without which the sky will come crashing down.

After an ETL application has been implemented, operational source systems may introduce variations in source data that did not exist during the initial design. Operational source systems may change data types, domains, ranges, etc. Such changes can cause an ETL application to end abnormally. Changes in source system data, however, do not constitute a violation or failure of Principle 10: Type the Data, rather, they constitute a change in source data. A change in source data capable of adversely affecting an ETL application should cause a revision of the data warehouse and ETL application to accommodate the change in source data.

Principle 11: Land the Data

Operational application best practices suggest that interim data should only be retained in a cataloged dataset when a subsequent person or application will need that interim data. Otherwise, if no person or application will need the interim data, then interim data should be passed from one function to another function via temporary datasets. When the last person or application has finished using a cataloged interim dataset, that dataset should be decataloged and removed, releasing storage space and resources. Figure 6.23 illustrates the practice of not retaining interim data.

For ETL applications, however, the best practice is to land (i.e., retain in a cataloged dataset) interim data.[2] After the last person and application have finished using an interim dataset, that dataset is still available. Figure 6.24 illustrates the practice of retaining interim data.

The purposes for retaining interim data include the following:

■ Problem Investigation: Abnormal problems in an ETL application rarely occur within the function that reported the problem-causing data. Allowing interim data to evaporate in a temporary dataset removes the possibility of using interim data to triage an abnormal problem.
■ Principle 09: Build the Data: In combination with Principle 09: Build the Data, defining the dataset in which interim data will be stored strengthens the structure of that data.

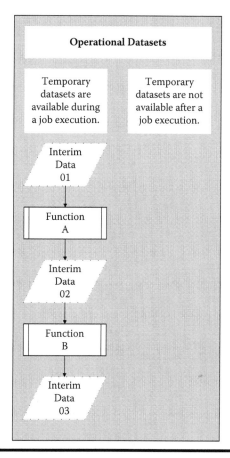

Figure 6.23   Operational datasets.

- Data Quality and Metadata: Data Quality and Metadata applications can profile interim data. The profiles and measurements applied to interim data are defined in the Data Quality SLA and Metadata SLA.
- Restart and Rerun: If an abnormal problem requires an ETL job stream be restarted or rerun from a step that has already completed, a retained dataset can be used again. Otherwise, a nonretained dataset must be created again, which would increase the scope and risks of a restart or rerun.

An interim dataset should never be updated. An update to an interim dataset changes the data and, therefore, means that interim data is not really retained. Rather, updates should be captured in another interim dataset.

Principle 11: Land the Data consumes a respectable amount of disk and catalog space. For that reason, an ETL platform should have significant disk storage

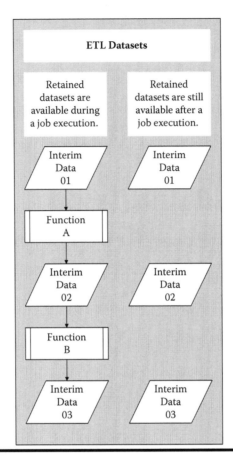

Figure 6.24   Extract, Transform, and Load (ETL) datasets.

available for interim data. Also, an ETL application needs a clearly defined method of archiving and removing interim data. Otherwise, too much of a good thing can get in the way. Landing interim data contributes to a bulletproof, yet flexible, ETL application. Landed interim data must be managed and controlled, like all other resources, otherwise it will get in the way.

Staging Principles Conclusion

ETL Staging Principles describe the physical manipulation of interim data in an ETL stage environment.

- Principle 07: Name the Data describes how to identify data and its features, origin and destination with an appropriate level of granularity and control.
- Principle 08: Own the Data describes how to secure data to prevent interference by other applications, including ETL and operational applications.
- Principle 09: Build the Data describes how to create a dataset from its foundation.
- Principle 10: Type the Data describes how to protect ETL functions from incompatible data types.
- Principle 11: Land the Data describes the need to retain interim data beyond its immediate use.

An ETL staging environment is the factory in which data is captured and transformed into what will become a data warehouse. Visibility and control, features of an effective and efficient manufacturing assembly line, are also features of the ETL Staging Principles. By incorporating ETL Staging Principles in the Extract, Transform, and Load applications an ETL application can know what is on the assembly line now, where and how it came from, where and how it is going, and what to do about it.

ETL Functions

ETL is not a nebulous cloud wherein miracles occur. Rather, ETL applications tend to share a similar set of functions (Figure 6.25). At first glance, these ETL functions look different from functions that typically occur in operational applications because they are different. ETL functions are designed to discern what has happened in the enterprise, and bring that information to the data warehouse. An ETL analyst needs a set of functions, like a carpenter needs a set of tools. Once an ETL analyst masters a specific function, he or she will be able to use that function as needed. The ETL functions listed below are standard in every ETL environment. These functions comprise the majority of functions in ETL applications. An ETL analyst must understand, and be able to apply, the following ETL functions in order to have a successful ETL application.

Extract Data from a Contiguous Dataset

This is the simplest Extract function (Figure 6.26). A contiguous dataset may be a flat file, relational table, or XML file. The dataset is stationary and self-contained. An Extract function is able to retrieve all the data from the dataset without any modifications, conditions, or extraneous functions. Once the data is in the ETL environment, a Transform function can filter or modify the data.

The difficulty of such a simple Extract function is to keep it simple. As though they can exert a vacuum of complexity, simple Extract functions attract additional

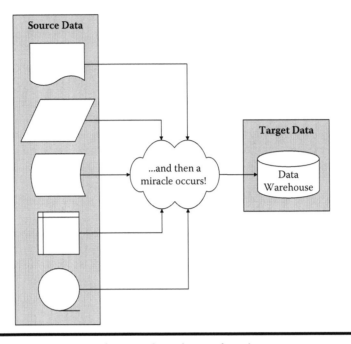

Figure 6.25 Extract, Transform, and Load (ETL) functions.

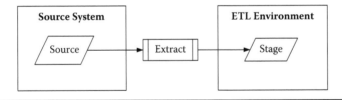

Figure 6.26 Contiguous data.

functions and complexity to them. Resist this temptation at all costs. A simple Extract function is a beautiful and elegant design, and should be allowed to remain that way.

Extract Data from a Data Flow

Asynchronous messaging and real-time transactions have introduced a class of data, which is both infinite and bounded. Extracting such data is really a matter of catching it as it goes by. This is, of course, real-time ETL (Figure 6.27).

When a data warehouse customer expresses the requirement that an ETL application retrieve data in real-time, the first question that should come from the ETL analyst is: "Why?" Why would a data warehouse customer, armed with the years of data, including trends, seasonality, and the most recent data available through batch ETL, change a business decision, strategy, or tactic based on the information that arrived in the past two seconds?

Real-time ETL usually feeds real-time data to an ODS. This fits the mission of an ODS.

- Capture and store only data values that are current and effective.
- Reflect the current state of the operational environment.

All that said, an ETL application must be able to know:

- Each message has been caught
- Once
- Only once

If the source system, which is creating the data flow, includes a control mechanism, the ETL application should try to leverage that control mechanism. If the source system does not have a control mechanism for a data flow, an ETL application should create a control mechanism of its own. Control mechanisms are at the heart of every ETL application. In real-time ETL, control mechanisms must be able to control the flow of data and, therefore, control the granularity of the flow of data. If a data flow sends records in bundles of ten, then the control mechanism must log and record bundles of ten. If a data flow sends records in bundles of a thousand, then the control mechanism must log and record bundles of a thousand. The control mechanism must be able to directly associate each record within a bundle, with that bundle.

Real-time ETL often works best by employing the technology or tool that created the data flow to read the data flow. Using an XML tool to get XML files and convert them from Tool A format to Tool B format is a violation of Principle 01: One Thing at a Time. Instead, get the XML files using the same technology that

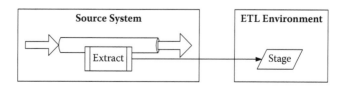

Figure 6.27   Data flow.

put the XML files. Once the XML files have been extracted from the real-time data flow, then the ETL application can transform them.

Row-Level Transformation

Row-level transformations are the simplest transformations (Figure 6.28). A row (or record) of data is in the memory of the ETL application. Based on conditions within that data, an ETL application will perform (or not perform) an update on the row.

A row-level update function is typically applied to every row in a staged dataset. The data row presents all the input data values needed by the row-level function to perform the required updates. The difficulty of such a simple Transform function is to keep it simple. As though they can exert a vacuum of complexity, simple Transform functions attract additional functions and complexity to them. Resist this temptation at all costs. A simple Transform function is another beautiful and elegant design, and should be allowed to remain that way.

Dataset-Level Transformation

Some transformations are performed within the context of a whole set of data (Figure 6.29). In these situations the entire dataset is read into memory. The Transform function must address the whole dataset at a time to derive the information necessary to update each individual row (or record).

Transform functions that summarize Fact data and aggregate Dimension data operate at the dataset level. They use the entire dataset to derive data values, which arithmetically represent a set of Fact data or they use an entire dataset to derive a subset of Dimension values that represent a set of Dimension data. A Dataset-Level Transform function should be isolated to that dataset and not attempt to include other datasets or portions of other datasets in the iteration of the Transform function.

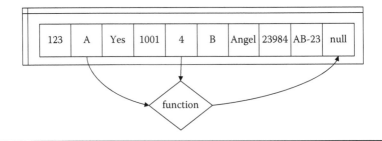

Figure 6.28 Row-level transformation.

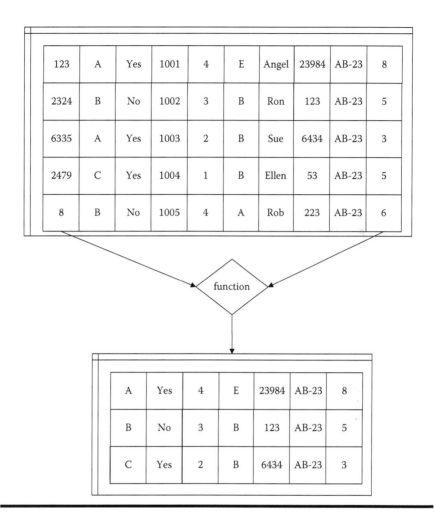

Figure 6.29   Dataset transformation.

Surrogate Key Generation: Intradataset

A Transform function can generate a sequential numeric value that uniquely identifies each row/record of a dataset (Figure 6.30). The numeric unique identifier supplants the need for a unique key, hence, the name Surrogate Key. A Transform function can generate a Surrogate Key that will be unique within the boundary of that dataset.

Usually, a Surrogate Key is needed because the data lacks a key that uniquely identifies each row, and sometimes in that iteration of ETL, the ETL application will need to uniquely identify each row. The presence of a Surrogate Key allows the

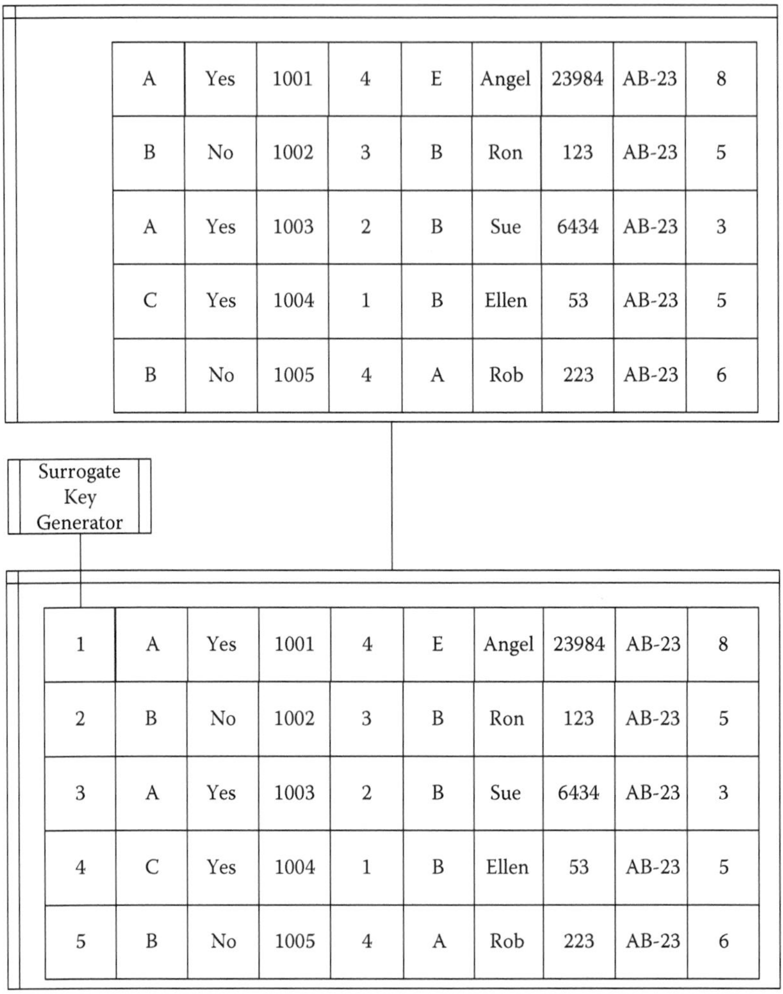

A	Yes	1001	4	E	Angel	23984	AB-23	8
B	No	1002	3	B	Ron	123	AB-23	5
A	Yes	1003	2	B	Sue	6434	AB-23	3
C	Yes	1004	1	B	Ellen	53	AB-23	5
B	No	1005	4	A	Rob	223	AB-23	6

Surrogate
Key
Generator

1	A	Yes	1001	4	E	Angel	23984	AB-23	8
2	B	No	1002	3	B	Ron	123	AB-23	5
3	A	Yes	1003	2	B	Sue	6434	AB-23	3
4	C	Yes	1004	1	B	Ellen	53	AB-23	5
5	B	No	1005	4	A	Rob	223	AB-23	6

Figure 6.30   Surrogate Key: Intradataset.

ETL application and the data warehouse to identify and isolate each row of that dataset.

Data Warehouse-Level Transformation

Sometimes, a transformation must be performed within the context of the data warehouse. The Transform function does not have all the input data necessary to derive the data required of that Transform function. The data warehouse has the data that will allow the ETL application to perform its required updates. In such a circumstance, a Transform function must perform its task by using both the input data and data from the data warehouse.

Surrogate Key Generation: Intra-Data Warehouse

A Transform function can assign a unique identifier to each row/record in a dataset. When the resulting row, with a surrogate key, will eventually be loaded into a data warehouse (including the key), the identifier key must be unique throughout the data warehouse (Figure 6.31). The best way to achieve this uniqueness is to retrieve the maximum unique identifier in the data warehouse. Then, begin assigning a unique identifier to new rows/records starting from the maximum unique identifier in the data warehouse, incremented by one.

Look-Up

An ETL application may need to find the unique identifier in the data warehouse for a specific row/record (Figure 6.32). The input data provides enough information to allow a Transform function to find the uniquely identifying key within the data warehouse. A Transform function uses the input data values to query the data warehouse. The returning result set includes the unique identifier for the row/record of input data.

If the input row/record has values that will identify the correct unique identifier, why did the ETL application need the unique identifier? Apparently, the data native to the row/record identifies each record uniquely enough. The data values that uniquely identified each row/record may not persist with the row/record as it is modified by a later Transform step. Or a data warehouse may include data from three different subsidiaries. Dimension data within the three subsidiaries may require customized look-up logic. The performance of the look-up function and the subsequent assignment of the unique key that uniquely identifies all rows/records for that Dimension across all subsidiaries facilitates the Data Integration of a data warehouse.

Changed Data Capture

A common requirement of ETL applications is to identify and capture Dimension updates that have been performed by the source system. An ETL application will typically perform this function by juxtaposing Dimension data from the data warehouse against corresponding Dimension data from the source system (Figure 6.33). The result set is:

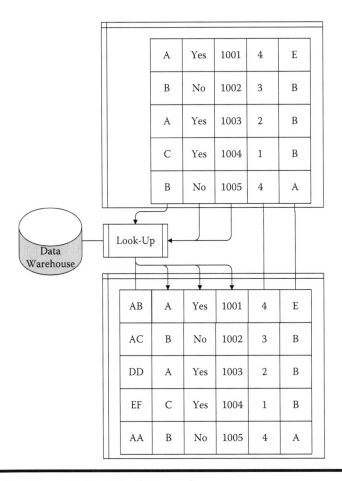

Figure 6.31 Surrogate Key: Intradata warehouse.

■ The rows in the data warehouse and the operational application that share the same key values, but different attribute values. This scenario indicates rows that have been updated.

■ The rows in the data warehouse, but not in the operational application. This scenario indicates rows that existed yesterday, but not today.

■ The rows in the operational application, but not in the data warehouse. This scenario indicates rows that did not exist yesterday, but do exist today.

■ The rows that are identical in both the operational environment and data warehouse. This scenario indicates rows in which no data has changed.

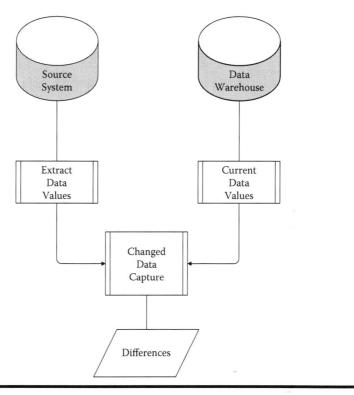

Figure 6.32   Look-Up.

ETL Key

The key values by which each and every instance of a Dimension entity can be identified are called the ETL Key. An entity from the source system is juxtaposed against an entity from the data warehouse by finding corresponding entities that share the same ETL Key. The ETL Key is usually similar to the Logical Key of an entity or the Physical Key of the Dimension table. The Logical Key or Physical Key may satisfactorily identify each and every instance of a Dimension entity.

If, however, the Logical Key and Physical Key of a Dimension entity is not granular enough to identify each and every instance of a Dimension entity, the ETL Key will derive a level of granularity sufficient to identify each and every instance of a Dimension entity. Common examples of Logical Keys and Physical Keys that do not necessarily identify each and every instance of a Dimension entity include:

■ Social Security Number: People can change their Social Security Number.
■ Name: People can change their name.

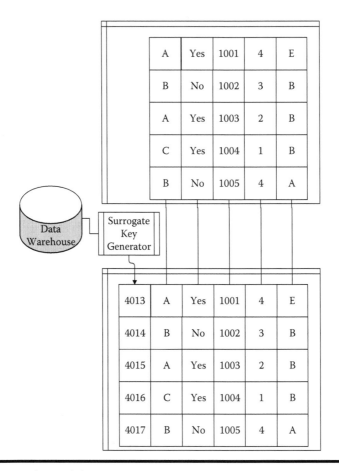

Figure 6.33 Changed data capture.

- Universal Product Code (UPC): UPC numbers are recycled.

These Keys may suffice as Logical or Physical Keys. Depending on the volatility of these Keys and the data warehouse's exposure to risk by using them, an ETL analyst may choose to investigate possible other Keys that can be used as ETL Keys. For example:

- In lieu of Social Security Number or Name: The person's birthday, place of birth, mother's maiden name, and mother's birthday. These data values are not wont to change and may have a high probability of identifying an individual person.

- In lieu of UPC: The product's manufacturer, distributor, internal product code, retail pack code, and country of origin. The data values may have a high probability of identifying an individual product.

The selection of an ETL Key, therefore, requires a bit more thought than just leveraging the Logical Key or the Physical Key. Instead, the ETL Key is the set of data values by which the ETL application can identify each and every instance of a Dimension entity. The ETL Key may be the Logical Key, it may be the Physical Key, it may be a more granular and precise key than either the Logical or Physical Key.

Universe to Universe and Candidate to Universe

Changed Data Capture (CDC) basically occurs in two forms: Universe to Universe and Candidate to Universe. Universe to Universe CDC is the best practice. In Universe to Universe CDC, the entire universe of data values from moment #1 is compared to the entire universe of values from moment #2. The differences between Universe of Data Values #1 and the Universe of Data Values #2 is the net effect of the changes in the source system that occurred between moment #1 and moment #2. Because the Universe to Universe CDC uses all the data values available from the source system, no source system updates can inadvertently escape the notice of the ETL application. That is why Universe to Universe CDC is the preferred CDC design.

When the volume of data is too large to allow Universe to Universe CDC to occur or when the data is available and required on a real-time basis, the Candidate to Universe CDC method will allow an ETL application to compare individual source system rows (i.e., Candidate rows) to the universe of data values in the data warehouse. An ETL application will bring individual Candidate rows to itself for one of two reasons:

- A real-time ETL application delivers individual rows or groups of individual data rows to itself.
- The universe of data values is too large to allow normal ETL processing to occur within the allowed time frame.

A single record, or set of records, is delivered to the ETL application. The ETL application compares the Candidate row to the enterprise. If they are different, the data value in the Candidate row is delivered to the data warehouse. Candidate rows can be selected for delivery to the ETL application for multiple reasons:

An operational transaction Log indicates update activity occurred on a specific row.

The Effective or Not Effective dates in an operational dataset indicate something happened to a specific row.

Business Rules and business relations within the operational data indicate that a change occurred in the source system that will modify a data value derived from a table without actually updating the source system table (i.e., a back-door update).

The gap in Candidate to Universe CDC is its inability to detect when a source system row is terminated. When a row disappears, that row cannot become a Candidate row. Without a Candidate row, the Candidate to Universe CDC will not consider the deleted source system row because it does not receive a Candidate row.

Load Data from a Stable and Contiguous Dataset

A Load function loads data from a stable and contiguous dataset (Figure 6.34). This is the simplest and most common method of loading data. The Load function interacts physically with the data warehouse. So, a Load application must be as simple and bulletproof as possible. The best method for a simple and bulletproof Load application is to load a data warehouse from a stable and contiguous dataset.

Load Data from a Data Flow

Real-time Load applications use data that was created by an ETL application (Figure 6.35). This gives an ETL analyst the opportunity to embed the necessary control mechanisms into the data. A real-time Load application should checkpoint on a basis frequently enough to be meaningful, but not so frequently as to interfere with the ETL application.

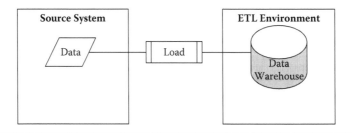

Figure 6.34   Stable and contiguous data.

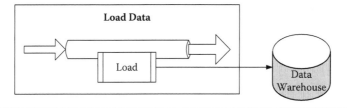

Figure 6.35   Data flow.

Control mechanisms are the key to a successful real-time Load application. An ETL application must be able to recognize when and where a hiccup occurred in the real-time data. The ETL application will probably not be able to recover lost or corrupted data. But, at a minimum, an ETL application should be able to notify the data warehouse team when a discrepancy occurs in the load data.

An ETL application must be able to know:

- Each row has been loaded
- Once
- Only once

A Transform application creates the real-time load data. The Transform application that generates the Load records also generates control data (Metadata) for the Load data. The control data will be used to control the Load application as it loads the data to a data warehouse. Control mechanisms are at the heart of every ETL application. Load control mechanisms also work best in bundles; individual records are far too numerous to log and control individually. Thus, Load control mechanisms work best in bundles, albeit very small and rapid bundles. Each bundle is logged and monitored. Each record within a bundle is directly associated with that bundle. In that way, a Load application can log and monitor the movement of data as it moves from a data flow to a data warehouse.

Transaction Summary

A Transaction Summary arithmetically sums numeric measurements in granular-detailed Event data. This Event data can be any quantifiable measurement of enterprise activity.

- Productivity throughput
- Sales (retail or wholesale)
- Customer activity

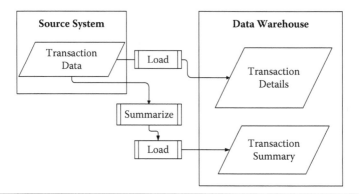

Figure 6.36 Transaction Summary.

The goal of a Transaction Summary is to increase the query response time of a data warehouse. Query response time is improved when a Transaction Summary reduces the volume of data the data warehouse RDBMS must manipulate to return the result set. Query response time is also improved when a Transaction Summary reduces the arithmetic processes the data warehouse RDBMS must perform to return the result set.

These goals are best met when a Transaction Summary precalculates an arithmetic summation, which is queried frequently by the data warehouse customers, and then stores the result set as a physical table (Figure 6.36). When data warehouse customers submit a query for that arithmetic summation, they can query a Transaction Summary table and receive the result set faster with reduced CPU cycles and input/output (I/O) consumption.

A Transaction Summary applies an arithmetic summation by summing together the numeric data from rows that share a common attribute. For example, Transaction data can be summarized in Time (Day-Level Summary), Geography (City-Level Summary), and Hierarchy (Department-Level Summary). Transaction summaries, therefore, remove a level of granular detail.

- Time: Remove the hours, minutes, and seconds in Transaction data, leaving only Day-Level data.
- Geography: Remove the Zip Code, street address, and apartment number in Transaction data, leaving only City-Level data.
- Hierarchy: Remove the individual employee name and number in Transaction data, leaving only Department-Level data.

By removing granular detail, a Transaction Summary also reduces the number of rows manipulated in a result set. In that reduced result set, the required arithmetic summation has already been achieved. The result is the data warehouse RDBMS manipulates fewer rows and avoids performing the arithmetic summation process (again and again and again) while returning the answer to the data warehouse customer faster, and with reduced CPU cycles and I/Os.

The return on investment (ROI) of a Transaction Summary increases with the popularity and frequency of the arithmetic summation in the Transaction Summary. System CPU and I/O resources are consumed once to create the data. Then, System storage resources are consumed throughout the day to store the data. The ROI is then based on how often data warehouse customers will query that data. If a single data warehouse customer queries that data once a day, it was not worth the system resources consumed to create and store it. But, if many data warehouse customers query that data every five minutes, the ROI is extremely high.

Dimension Aggregation

A Dimension Aggregate holds the result set of a query that joins multiple Dimension tables. The goal of a Dimension Aggregate is to increase the query response time of a data warehouse. Query response time is improved when a Dimension Aggregate reduces the volume of data the data warehouse RDBMS must manipulate to return the result set. Query response time is also improved when a Transaction Summary reduces the relational join processes the data warehouse RDBMS must perform to return the result set.

These goals are best met when a Dimension Aggregate prejoins multiple Dimension tables, which are queried frequently by the data warehouse customers, and then stores the result set as a physical table. When data warehouse customers submit a query for that set of joined Dimension tables, they can query a Dimension Aggregate table and receive the result set faster with reduced CPU cycles and I/O consumption.

The example in Figure 6.37 shows Dimension data from the Product, Geography, Hierarchy, and Distribution subject areas. These tables are joined once. The result set is stored in a physical table. Then, when a data warehouse customer queries the data warehouse for the Sales data for a Product that was sold in a Geographic location by someone in the Hierarchy dimension and shipped by the Distribution Department, the data warehouse RDBMS is able to avoid joining all the Dimension tables because that join has already been done.

The ROI of a Dimension Aggregate increases with the popularity and frequency of the Dimension tables joined in the Dimension Aggregate. System CPU and I/O resources are consumed once to join the data. Then, System storage resources are consumed throughout the day to store the data. The ROI is then based on how often data warehouse customers will submit a query that uses data from this join path. If a single data warehouse customer queries that data once in a day, it was not worth the system resources consumed to create and store it. But, if many data warehouse customers query that data every five minutes, the ROI is extremely high.

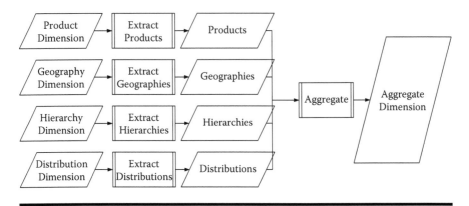

Figure 6.37   Dimension aggregation.

Common Problems

An ETL application, once installed, is static while the changing world is dynamic. Listed below are a few problems that occur when either the data or business rules change.

Source Data Anomalies

Garbage In Garbage Out (GIGO) refers to the reality that outbound data is no better than the inbound data by which the outbound data was created. An ETL application suffers this same reality. Unfortunately, unless an ETL application can detect and resolve inbound data anomalies, these anomalies become data warehouse anomalies.

Incomplete Source Data

A common data anomaly is incomplete data. Incompleteness occurs in three forms:

> Records in a set of data are missing.
> Fields in a record are not populated.
> A set of data is missing completely.

An ETL application can detect the third form of incomplete data rather easily. The second form can be detected if the unpopulated fields are key fields or directly associated with other populated fields.

The first form of incomplete data is the most common and most difficult to detect. Typically, missing records occur in transaction event data. Detection of a transaction event, that is independent of other transaction events, that did occur, but was not recorded, is a common circumstance and difficult to detect.

Redundant Source Data

Operational applications frequently resolve their own missing records problem by restating a set of data, yielding a set of data with missing records that are now present, and present records that are now repeated. These repeated and redundant sets of data can result in repeated and redundant data in a data warehouse, unless an ETL application can detect and resolve the repeated and redundant condition.

Misstated Source Data

Another common anomaly occurs when source data contains errors. Source data may identify the wrong physical plant, object, or person. Detection of source data errors varies in feasibility and treatment. Some source data errors can be detected while the source data is still within an ETL application. Unfortunately, some source data errors can only be detected within the context of other data in a data warehouse. Unless detected and treated by an ETL application, source data errors become data warehouse errors.

Business Rule Changes

Operational applications can (and do) change the logic by which data is manipulated and understood. Such changes may require no alteration of the physical manifestation of source data. Changes in logic or business rules are typically subtle and difficult to detect.

Obsolete Data

A common manifestation of changing business rules is the discontinued use of a dataset. The physical dataset may remain extant for purposes associated with historical data. Current operations, however, do not include the discontinued dataset. Meanwhile, an ETL application may not know to refer to the new dataset rather than the discontinued dataset. The result is incorrect data within a data warehouse.

Redefined Data

An operational application may continue using a dataset with a different format or layout. Hopefully, a new format or layout will cause abnormal problems in an ETL application, which will be noticed. A redefined dataset, however, may cause no operational problems, but may cause data errors. Unless detected, these data errors will become part of a data warehouse.

Unrecorded Data

All organizations, large and small, have a handful of codes and values that are known and understood by all relevant organization members. Because these codes and values are known and understood, no one records them in a stable operational dataset. These are the unrecorded data of an organization.

An ETL application may record these codes and values for its own purposes. Without a record of the existence and meaning of these codes and values, an ETL application cannot know when these codes and values change, and they do change. Changes in an organization's unrecorded codes and values may result in data warehouse errors.

Closing Remarks

An ETL application (Figure 6.38) begins and ends with data warehouse customers. They are the reason for a data warehouse. A data warehouse designer captures customer expectations in the design of a data warehouse. A Target System analysis captures the behavior of data in a data warehouse design. The behavior of data is a result of actions performed by an ETL application. These behaviors are expressed as Direct Requirements. The Data Mapping is a road map showing how an ETL application will achieve data behaviors. Typically, a Data Mapping starts at a source system and ends at a data warehouse.

The Data Quality SLA and Metadata SLA capture the information necessary for customers to use the data in a data warehouse.

- Is the data complete?
- Are there any anomalies?
- When is the data available?
- What is the profile of today's data?

All of these questions are captured as Indirect Requirements. The Direct Requirements (data behavior) and Indirect Requirements (information about data behavior) meet together in a single physical design. That physical design declares the physical hardware, platforms, datasets, and jobs that are the ETL application,

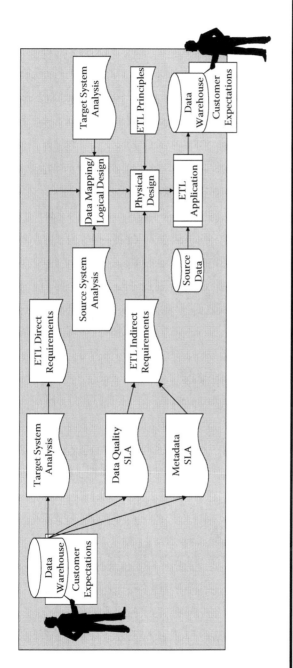

Figure 6.38 ETL beginning to end.

which delivers data to a data warehouse. The data in that data warehouse meets the expectations of data warehouse customers, which is the original intent.

References

1. Mark Beyer, personal communication, 2002.
2. Ibid.

Chapter 7

Business Intelligence Reporting

Introduction

Business Intelligence Reporting, otherwise known as BI Reporting, or just BI, is the face of a data warehouse (Figure 7.1). BI Reporting is what the data warehouse customers see. All the hardware, software, data architectures, data models, Source System Analysis, Target System Analysis, and ETL applications culminate in data displayed on a computer monitor or printed on a piece of paper. All that work, the effort and investment, will be counted a blazing failure if the BI Reporting fails to deliver or all of that work, the effort and investment, will be counted a tremendous success if the BI Reporting delivers the data and value expected of a data warehouse, which will lead to subsequent iterations of data warehouse development.

BI Reporting Success Factors

The success factors of BI Reporting include performance, the user interface, presentation of the data architecture, alignment with the data model, ability to answer questions, mobility, flexibility, and availability. These success factors and their business relevance are discussed below.

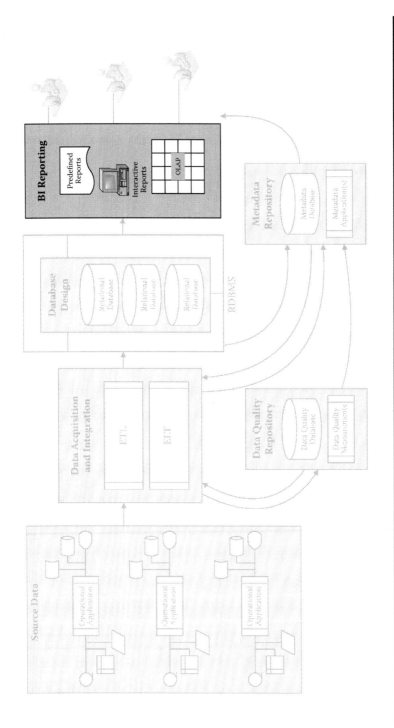

Figure 7.1 Business Intelligence (BI) Reporting.

Performance

A successful BI Reporting application will return answer sets in a consistent time frame. Initially, data warehouse customers will accept only subsecond response time as reasonable. In the early days of a data warehouse, subsecond response time may actually occur. That is unfortunate because as new and additional customers begin to use a data warehouse, each will consume central processing unit (CPU) cycles and input/output (I/Os), degrading the response time for all data warehouse customers. The CPU cycles and I/Os of a data warehouse are a finite resource. As one customer consumes CPU cycles and I/Os, those CPU cycles and I/Os are taken from another customer. A successful BI Reporting application manages the finite resource of CPU cycles and I/Os by managing the customers' use of them. Data warehouse customers will eventually accept subminute response time in lieu of subsecond response time, as long as the response times are consistent. A BI report will become, in the minds of a customer, a two-minute report. A successful BI Reporting application will manage the consumption of resources so that a two-minute report is always a two-minute report.

An unsuccessful BI Reporting application fails to manage the consumption of data warehouse resources. When a customer is allowed to adversely affect all other data warehouse customers, then for those other customers a two-minute report will become a one-hour report. Data warehouse customers will not accept the inconsistent response times because it does not allow them to plan their work. If a customer has an assigned task that must be finished by the afternoon, which requires the result set of a two-minute report, the customer must plan enough time for the result set of that two-minute report. An unsuccessful BI Reporting application will allow that two-minute report to become a two-hour report (by letting Fred from Logistics submit forty-two high impact queries), which will send that data warehouse customer to his or her afternoon meeting without the result set required to complete the assigned task.

User Interface

A successful BI Reporting application is intuitive and easily understood. A successful user interface is organized along the thought processes and methods already present in the enterprise. A business question native to the enterprise (How profitable is my business unit? How many personnel hours are required to fulfill a customer order? Where are the capital assets of my business unit?) is native to the BI Reporting application. The Source System Analysis was performed so the data warehouse designer could accurately architect and model the data warehouse to reflect the enterprise. The ETL applications were designed and developed to reflect the enterprise within the data elements of the data warehouse. A successful BI Reporting application continues this philosophy—the data warehouse is a reflection of the enterprise into the User Interface. When a data warehouse customer is looking at the User Interface of a BI Reporting application, that customer is looking at his or her enterprise in data.

An unsuccessful BI Reporting application requires data warehouse customers to "learn the tool". Data warehouse customers are first and foremost business people. They understand and operate their business. An unsuccessful BI Reporting application will require data warehouse customers to translate their business questions into "tool" queries and then translate the "tool" result sets into business information.

Presentation of the Data Architecture

A successful BI Reporting application presents data from the Operational Data Store (ODS) as operational data, data from a Data Mart as information assembled for a specific purpose and business unit, and data from a Data Warehouse using the guidelines in the Data Warehousing Philosophy. Each of these three sets of data (ODS, Data Mart, and Data Warehouse) is distinguished from each other, so the customer understands the meaning and intention of the data he or she is viewing.

An unsuccessful BI Reporting application presents these three sets of data (ODS, Data Mart, and Data Warehouse) with a homogenous User Interface, so that customers are not sure of which set of data they are viewing. Or, a BI Reporting application may mix data from the three sets of data (ODS, Data Mart, and Data Warehouse). If the three sets of data physically exist on the same platform, a BI Reporting tool may join data elements from one data set with data elements from another data set. The User Interface in which this occurs most frequently is an ad hoc Open Database Connectivity (ODBC) interface. A data warehouse customer will search for a data element with a foreign key that matches the data element he or she wants to use. Unaware of the distinction between ODS, Data Mart, and Data Warehouse data as presented in the ODBC interface, a data warehouse customer can inadvertently join an ODS Dimension table (which has no history) to a Data Warehouse Fact table (which does have history) and then wonder where all that history went.

Alignment with the Data Model

A successful BI Reporting application synchronizes with the relations and relational integrity of a data model. The relations and cardinalities embedded in a data model are intentional. They reflect the relations and cardinalities of the enterprise. By synchronizing with the data model, a BI Reporting application continues this reflection of the enterprise through the data reported to the data warehouse customer.

An unsuccessful BI Reporting application violates the relations and relational integrity of a data model. By introducing relations where none exist and cardinalities that are not true, a BI Reporting application distorts the reflection of the enterprise. At best, a data warehouse customer will recognize the distortion and refuse to accept the data. At worst, a data warehouse customer will not recognize the distortion and use the data to form tactical or strategic decisions.

Ability to Answer Questions

A successful BI Reporting application is able to use the data in a data warehouse to answer the questions posed to it. This requires the ability to identify the data elements that will contribute to an answer set, join them correctly, and present the result set in the business terms understood by the customer. Also, but no less important, the answer set is correct.

An unsuccessful BI Reporting application is not able to generate the correct answer set with the data elements available. The BI Reporting application may not be able to identify all the data elements that will contribute to an answer set or, having identified all the correct data elements, a BI Reporting application may not be able to leverage them correctly. The end result is either no answer or an incorrect answer.

Mobility

A successful BI Reporting application empowers data warehouse customers to take the answer set with them. Having generated the information necessary to answer a business question, a data warehouse customer can then save, print, copy/paste the information to any destination.

An unsuccessful BI Reporting application requires data warehouse customers to carry their computer monitor around and say, "Look at this monitor. That's the answer to our question." This is, of course, absurd. But, a BI analyst must define the mobility threshold below, which a BI Reporting application is considered unsuccessful. Does the enterprise require BI reports be printed, copy/pasted into spreadsheets, captured as permanent documents, published through an intranet, published real-time through an Internet Web site to enterprise agents around the globe? Each of these levels of mobility includes a cost and a return on investment (ROI). An enterprise requires, and is willing and able to invest in, mobility within it BI Reporting application, but how much mobility?

Flexibility

A successful BI Reporting application can answer questions that have never before been asked. The world is a dynamic and changing business environment. New players are coming into the marketplace all the time. Existing players are constantly redefining themselves within the marketplace. A BI Reporting application should help its customers to keep up with the dynamic and changing marketplace by allowing them to ask questions that are framed in the present state of the marketplace.

An unsuccessful BI Reporting application expects the world to remain static and frozen; expecting the world will always look as it does now. A BI Reporting application that only allows business questions framed in the enterprise as it existed on a date in the past will find it has no future with the enterprise.

Availability

A successful BI Reporting application is available during the active cycles of the enterprise. Implicitly, availability of the BI Reporting application also includes availability of the data that will be used by the BI Reporting application. Data availability requires coordination with Extract, Transform, and Load (ETL) applications that load the data. ETL Load applications can interfere with a BI Reporting application in two ways. First, an ETL Load application might lock a table required by the BI Reporting application. Second, an ETL Load application, if loading during a BI Reporting cycle, might update the data being reported. The results of a data update during a BI Reporting cycle cause confusion (Why did the data change?) and suspicion of the BI Reporting application (Is this thing working right?).

An unsuccessful BI Reporting application fails to match the active cycles of the enterprise. The customers are not sure if they are looking at the most recent data or if the most recent data is still on its way. Customers may also experience significant delays in report delivery if the BI Reporting application is down during the enterprise active cycle. By failing to accommodate the active cycles of the enterprise, a BI Reporting application communicates to the customers that they need to find another alternative, which they will.

A BI Reporting application is limited in its ability to excel at these success factors by the data architecture, data model, and data that precede it. The query performance of a BI Reporting application cannot exceed the query performance it inherits from the Relational Database Management System (RDBMS). The ability of a BI Reporting application to answer questions cannot exceed the ability of a data model to answer questions. The flexibility of a BI Reporting application cannot exceed the flexibility of a data model. The seeds of a BI Reporting applications success, therefore, are planted in the RDBMS and data model of its data warehouse.

If the performance, answers, and flexibility are feasible given the Database Design, the BI application has the job of harnessing and leveraging these features to their fullest extent possible. If, however, the performance, answers, or flexibility are not feasible given the Database Design, the BI application should not be expected to compensate for the lack of these features in the data warehouse.

BI Customer Success Factors

BI Reporting customers leverage a BI Reporting application as they perform their business functions within the enterprise. Each BI Reporting customer has individual assignments and functions within the enterprise. The cost of providing every member of the enterprise with their own individual BI Reporting application, on its own server, with its own data warehouse, and its own network infrastructure is, of course, prohibitively high. That is why these are all shared resources. So, rather than an individual BI Reporting application, a BI Reporting analyst presents each customer with an individualized BI Reporting application. The success factors of an individualized BI Reporting application include its ability to support the processes and satisfy the needs of individual BI Reporting customers.

Proactive Processes

The enterprise needs to know when a problem is approaching with the maximum possible lead-time. Once an approaching problem has been observed, the lead-time allows the enterprise to align its resources to prepare the best possible response to the approaching problem. Some members of the enterprise have a responsibility to monitor conditions within the enterprise that could harm the enterprise.

For proactive processes, a BI Reporting application should relieve customers of the need to remember to query enterprise data. The risk is that the customer will be too busy or just forget to run the query at the exact moment a problem emerges. A BI Reporting application's ability to mitigate this risk by performing the proactive processes is a success factor for the customers as they use the BI Reporting application.

Reactive Processes

The enterprise needs to assess its recent past in the context of long-term and seasonal trends. The information from these assessments helps the enterprise know whether short-term tactics and long-term strategies are currently working as intended or should they be modified in the near future. Business processes such as these are reactive because they allow the enterprise to react to recent events.

BI Reporting customers need the toolsets necessary to review and analyze recent events in the context of long-term and seasonal trends. Is a spike in activity the beginning of an upward trend or a seasonal pattern? A BI Reporting application's ability to give its customers the toolset necessary to answer the questions that support the reactive processes of the enterprise is a success factor for the customers as they use the BI Reporting application.

Predefined Processes

Some business processes are well defined, repeated, and stable. Predefined business processes could include such queries as:

■ How many units did we sell?
■ How much cash came in, and out, in the past week?
■ What is the net present value of investments held by each customer?

In predefined processes, everything is known, except the answer. The time frame, query, and audience are all known. A predefined process has very few, if any, variables that require the help or participation of a member of the enterprise.

A BI Reporting application should be able to remember and execute a predefined process. Programmatic responses to the result set of a predefined process can be included in a BI Reporting application, including report distribution and sending alerts. The ability of a BI Reporting application to support customers' predefined reporting processes is a success factor for the customers as they use the BI Reporting application.

Ad Hoc Processes

Not all questions have been identified and programmed into a BI Reporting application because not all questions are known. Regardless, the enterprise's need for the answer to a question must be satisfied. The enterprise may not be able to wait for a BI Reporting developer to gather the requirements, develop, test, and release the report back to the enterprise. When the enterprise cannot wait for the answer, a member of the enterprise must be able to ask the question in the timeframe of the enterprise. A BI Reporting application's ability to support ad hoc processes is a success factor for the customers as they use the BI Reporting application.

Data Needs

Data is the granular minutia values that document the existence of an enterprise entity or measure an enterprise event. For example:

■ The date, time, place, and product of each individual sales transaction
■ The number of warehouses in the southeast region
■ The name of a building

Members of the enterprise sometimes require the data of the enterprise. On these occasions, the question asks for the most granular minutia information available within the enterprise. A BI Reporting application's ability to present enterprise data is a success factor for the customers as they use the BI Reporting application.

Information Needs

Information is data interpreted within a context.[1] Information questions juxtapose two or more data points to answer a question that is expected to yield an answer that will help the enterprise. For example:

- Profitability: What was the recent margin between revenues and expenses?
- Trends: Did the business unit sell more or less product this quarter as compared to last quarter?
- Ratios: What is the ROI of the data warehouse?

These and similar questions are asked by members of the enterprise on a frequent basis. A BI Reporting application's ability to answer informational questions is a success factor for the customers as they use the BI Reporting application.

Analytic Needs

Sometimes, the question that must be answered is, "What question should I ask?" BI Reporting processes begin their lifecycle as a search for the question. Much like scouts searching for something, anything, they'll know it when they see it, business analysts search the enterprise and its environment for a question. This search is the analytic process, searching for a correlation between events, for an association between factors within and around the enterprise. Business analysts need a toolset that will enable them to search for the questions that will lead to the answers. A BI Reporting application's ability to empower and enable analytic processes is a success factor for the customers as they use the BI Reporting application.

BI Reporting Application

A BI Reporting application is a tool, or set of tools, that provide the user interface between a data warehouse and its customers (Figure 7.2). The architecture, features, and functions vary between the different BI Reporting tools. In general, BI Reporting tools provide a layer of abstraction that allows the data warehouse customers to interact with a data warehouse without learning the Structured Query Language (SQL) syntax, network address, or database connectivity required to query a data warehouse.

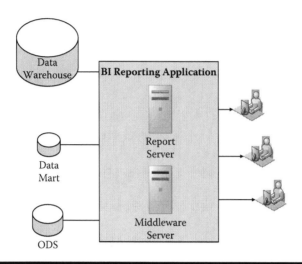

Figure 7.2   Business Intelligence (BI) Reporting Application.

Architecture

The architecture of BI Reporting tools includes one or more servers between the data warehouse and customers. These servers have a roadmap of the data warehouse. Through its user interface, customers tell a BI Reporting application the required information. The BI Reporting application submits the SQL to the data warehouse. When the result returns from the data warehouse, the BI Reporting application returns it to the customer.

BI Reporting tools market themselves on their ability to connect with RDBMS platforms. The companies that develop and own BI Reporting tools negotiate partnerships with the companies that develop and own RDBMS platforms. The partnership means that the owners of the RDBMS platform have shared their proprietary information, including application programming interfaces (APIs) and other interfaces, which allow a BI Reporting tool to connect with the most possible features and efficiency. When the owners of a RDBMS platform are not quite so forthcoming with the keys to their kingdom, they may share proprietary information that is not quite so close to the operating system, but is also not quite as packed with features and efficiency. The intent behind these partnerships is symbiotic. By including themselves in an architecture that is more efficient than others, they hope to attract newcomers to the marketplace to purchase their platform as well as customers who have already purchased the platform that is the other half of the partnership. The least efficient connectivity is through ODBC. A BI Reporting tool will use ODBC when no other connectivity is available. In their marketing literature, BI Reporting tools will usually state they have a direct ODBC connection.

BI Reporting Methods

BI Reporting tools interact with data warehouse customers using one of the following three methods. Each method has its own advantages and disadvantages. None of these methods addresses all the data warehouse customers' needs and skills. For that reason, most BI Reporting tools combine these methods. Some of the combinations have produced stellar results, some are still working on it. As a potential BI Reporting tool customer, a BI Reporting analyst must be well-versed on all the features and options, so that he or she can choose a BI Reporting tool with the best fit for the enterprise.

Predefined Reports

Predefined reports are basically SQL statements with a label. The BI Reporting tool has a library of predefined reports. A large selection of reports may compensate for the lack of interactive or menu-driven report creation. Data warehouse customers need to be able to find the exact permutation of Fact and Dimension data in a report. If that is not available, the BI Reporting team has the responsibility of creating that report. Either way, the report required by the data warehouse customer must be provided by the BI Reporting application.

The SQL in all the reports can be optimized for maximum query efficiency. The BI Reporting team can test and validate each report, verifying it does indeed return the data that it promises to return. Also, the BI Reporting team can own and catalog all the BI reports, thus avoiding redundant reports.

Interactive Reports

Interactive reports require the BI Reporting tool translate the list of data elements required by the customer into a SQL statement. Then, the BI Reporting tool submits that SQL to the data warehouse and returns the result set back to the data warehouse customer. A BI Reporting tool usually uses drop-down lists, menus, and user input boxes to indicate the list of data elements and WHERE clauses required by the data warehouse customer. To achieve the translation of data elements and WHERE clauses, a BI Reporting tool must have its own roadmap of the data warehouse. That roadmap of the data warehouse must be maintained and synchronized with the data warehouse; if the data warehouse changes, the BI Reporting roadmap changes.

Interactive reports provide flexibility and ad hoc reporting that does not exist with predefined reports. The interactive BI Reporting tool uses the list of data elements and WHERE clauses provided by the customer and its own roadmap to generate a SQL statement. That SQL statement is submitted to the data warehouse. The result set is returned to the data warehouse customer.

The price for that flexibility is the roadmap of the data warehouse, which includes the cost of a BI Reporting server, probably a middleware server, development and maintenance of the BI Reporting tool, and the roadmap. All in all, this flexibility is not inexpensive. This flexibility must also be managed. If the data warehouse customers are allowed free reign with a BI Reporting application, they will create redundant reports (e.g., 100+ copies of one report), incorrect reports, and inefficient reports.

Online Analytical Process (OLAP) Reports

Online Analytic Processing (OLAP) applications precalculate and store the answers (i.e., result sets) to permutations of Dimensions. The precalculated result sets are stored in a multidimensional structure, which is referred to as a Cube. The multidimensional cube is able to navigate directly to the cell that holds the result set associated with the permutation of Dimensions indicated by the customer. As a result, the answer set comes back to the customer with nearly instant response time.

The multiplication table in Table 7.1 illustrates the precalculated and stored result sets. The numbers on the left and top are the Dimensions. The numbers inside the table are the result sets. When a customer indicates the permutation 2 × 3, the OLAP application does not calculate 2 × 3. Rather, the OLAP application finds the cell that is the intersection of 2 and 3. That cell holds the answer. Without calculating or knowing the answer, the OLAP application simply returns the value held in the cell at the intersection of 2 and 3 to the customer.[2]

Table 7.1 Precalculated Result Sets

X	1	2	3	4	5	6	7	8	9	10	11	12
1	1	2	3	4	5	6	7	8	9	10	11	12
2	1	2	3	4	5	6	7	8	9	10	11	12
3	3	6	9	12	15	18	21	24	27	30	33	36
4	4	8	12	16	20	24	28	32	36	40	44	48
5	5	10	15	20	25	30	35	40	45	50	55	60
6	6	12	18	24	30	36	42	48	54	60	66	72
7	7	14	21	28	35	42	49	56	63	70	77	84
8	8	16	24	32	40	48	56	64	72	80	88	96
9	9	18	27	36	45	54	63	72	81	90	99	108
10	10	20	30	40	50	60	70	80	90	100	110	120
11	11	22	33	44	55	66	77	88	99	110	121	132
12	12	24	36	48	60	72	84	96	108	120	132	144

The tradeoff is a limited set of Dimensions. Because the result sets are precalculated and stored in the multidimensional cube, storage capacity is a limiting factor. To offset this, OLAP applications actually precalculate and store only a portion of the intersecting cells. Because 2 × 3 is the same as 3 × 2, the OLAP application need only store the result of one permutation, knowing that the stored result set will hold the answer to both permutations. Table 7.2 illustrates this method by which a result set can be stored only once.

The final, and best, feature of an OLAP application is the user interface. An OLAP application uses a GUI interface. The customer is able to point-and-click on a cell that is a reference to a permutation of Dimensions. The result set returns immediately because the result set has been precalculated and stored, allowing the customer to ask questions (via point-and-click) and receive answers in a near stream of consciousness.

OLAP is purely an analytic tool. The result set is rarely mobile. The analyst using an OLAP application must have a deep understanding of the business and the enterprise to achieve the stream of consciousness analysis. The result set and the path by which the analyst achieved the result set are usually not repeatable. An OLAP application is good at finding where to look to find the permutation of Dimensions that is likely to yield helpful results. A presentable report of information (information that was first detected by an OLAP application) is best created in a BI Reporting application intended to create reports that will be understood by a wider audience.

OLAP applications offer three permutations of storage capacity requirements and performance. These permutations allow the customer to make the decision,

Table 7.2 Nonredundant Result Sets

X	1	2	3	4	5	6	7	8	9	10	11	12
1	1											
2	1	2										
3	3	6	9									
4	4	8	12	16								
5	5	10	15	20	25							
6	6	12	18	24	30	36						
7	7	14	21	28	35	42	49					
8	8	16	24	32	40	48	56	64				
9	9	18	27	36	45	54	63	72	81			
10	10	20	30	40	50	60	70	80	90	100		
11	11	22	33	44	55	66	77	88	99	110	121	
12	12	24	36	48	60	72	84	96	108	120	132	144

the final tradeoff between storage capacity and performance. At the time an OLAP cube is built, the customer can choose one of three OLAP technologies.

MOLAP

Multidimensional OLAP (MOLAP) stores all the result sets of all the permutations of Dimension in an OLAP cube. MOLAP requires significant storage capacity. The creation of all the result sets in a MOLAP cube requires significant CPU cycles, I/Os, and memory capacity. MOLAP provides the fastest performance for the customer.

ROLAP

Relational OLAP (ROLAP) stores no result sets. Rather, ROLAP identifies the data within an associated data warehouse by which it can calculate at runtime all result sets. When a customer indicates an intersection of Dimensions, the ROLAP cube translates that information into a SQL statement, which is submitted to a data warehouse. The result set comes back as a data value that is reflected in the OLAP GUI (graphical user interface). A ROLAP cube requires the least storage capacity on the OLAP server; however, ROLAP transfers consumption of CPU cycles and I/Os over to the data warehouse. ROLAP provides the slowest performance and the maximum number of Dimensions for the customer.

HOLAP

Hybrid OLAP is a combination of MOLAP and ROLAP. By precalculating and storing most, but not all, of the result sets within an OLAP cube, a HOLAP cube achieves a compromise between capacity, performance, and permutations of Dimensions available to the customer.

Drilling

Within OLAP, Drilling is the concept whereby the customer is able to ask the same question (Number of units manufactured?) at successively lower hierarchical levels. Through a series of point-and-click queries, the customer Drills down to lower and lower levels of granularity. For example:

- A customer can begin by asking, "How many widgets did the enterprise manufacture today?"
- A customer can drill down by asking, "How many widgets did the Eastern Division manufacture today?"

- A customer can drill down farther by asking, "How many widgets did the Southeastern Region manufacture today?"
- A customer can continue drilling down by asking increasingly precise, and hierarchically lower, questions. Drilling stops when the customer gets to the bottom of the hierarchy, "How many widgets did Plant #236 manufacture today?"

The Drilling concept of OLAP is not original to OLAP. Analysts queried up and down hierarchies before the creation of OLAP cubes. What OLAP cubes added to Drilling as a concept is an understanding of the power of drilling up and down hierarchies. As a result, the concept of Drilling has matured in other BI Reporting technologies and methods.

Push versus Pull

Push

BI Reports are pushed to members of the enterprise on a scheduled basis. Other than the schedule, no event triggers a pushed report. Typically, pushed reports are integral to, and designed for, recurring business processes. A pushed report looks the same, answers the same questions, and presents the same data from day to day.

Pull

A member of the enterprise also can request BI Reports. An enterprise event occurs that requires information in a BI Report. In response, a member of the enterprise requests that BI Report. Pulled BI Reports are typically canned reports, but with input parameters. The input parameters allow the report to answer the question posed by the enterprise event.

Printed on Paper

Despite all the advances in technology, BI Reporting applications are still required to include the functionality that prints reports on paper. Although increasingly fewer people distribute reports by walking around with pieces of paper in their hands, a printed page from a report will always provide a concrete record of a report and the information on that report.

Report Archives

BI reports chronicle the activities and history of an enterprise. At a point in time, they record the questions that were asked, and the answers. BI reports can be archived electronically or optically in addition to publication to their intended audience. The result is a history of the enterprise. By capturing the information available at the time of a decision, archived reports create a context for historical decisions.

Web-Based BI Reporting

BI Reporting applications publish reports via corporate intranets and the Internet.[3] This method allows a BI Reporting application to span physical and geographic boundaries. The Push, Pull, and Interactive features of BI Reporting are viable options across a corporate intranet and the Internet. The connective capacities of BI Reporting tools and networks have removed the physical and geographic constraints that had previously tied BI Reporting to a physical location or local network.

Operational BI Reporting: From an ODS

BI Reporting applications leverage the operational data in an ODS. BI reports generated from the data in an ODS relieve the operational source system of the responsibility to publish reports. By letting the BI Reporting application do what it does best, the operational source system is allowed to do what it does best.

The business cycles of the operational system provide the cycles by which the ODS gathers, and the BI Reporting application reports, operational data. The ODS and BI Reporting application should not allow operational data to go stale by moving slower than the operational system. The ODS and BI Reporting application also should not repeat operational reports by gathering and reporting operational data faster than the operational source system generates it. Rather, the ODS and BI Reporting application should be synchronized with the operational source system. The periodicity of this synchronization can be as slow as daily, or as fast as real-time.

Operational BI Reporting: From an Operational System (Real-Time)

When an ODS is not available, but operational BI reports are still required, a BI Reporting application can retrieve its data directly from an operational source system. Used this way, a BI Reporting application becomes a reporting module of an operational system. This method leverages the reporting capabilities of the BI Reporting tool, while still removing reporting responsibilities from the operational system. The risk to this approach is that the BI Reporting application may interfere with the operational system. This is a risk that must be managed and mitigated. The business cycles of the operational system provide the cycles by which the BI Reporting application reports operational data. The BI Reporting application should not allow operational data to go stale by moving slower than the operational system.

The BI Reporting application also should not repeat operational reports by reporting operational data faster than the operational source system generates it. Rather, the BI Reporting application should be synchronized with the operational system. The periodicity of this synchronization can be as slow as daily or as fast as real-time.

Operational BI Reporting: EDI, Partnerships, and Data Sharing

BI Reporting applications can share data and information with partners of the enterprise. Electronic Data Interchange (EDI) is the sharing of documents, data, and information. An enterprise will share specific data and information for prearranged purposes. Typically, an enterprise will share orders, inventory levels, and near-term plans to allow its partners to supply product and materials at the time and place they are needed.

BI Reporting: Thus Far

In the early days of BI Reporting, the reporting tools, infrastructures, and applications we presently associate with BI Reporting were not yet created. BI Reporting was limited to the printing functions inherent in operational applications. Then, as BI Reporting tools developed and matured, they found three fast paths to ROI.

Customer Relationship Management (CRM)

Without customers, any business or enterprise will die—quickly. So, it is no surprise that BI Reporting tools found a niche by enhancing interaction with customers. Customer Relationship Management (CRM) systems allow the enterprise to recognize the customer, regardless of the agent actually talking to the customer. By providing customer-specific information to the agent, the agent is able to give the impression of a personal interaction with the customer. By referencing the name of the customer's business, line of work, or other details, the agent is able to communicate to the customer that the enterprise remembered these details about the customer.

CRM systems also remember the buying patterns and seasonality of the customer. If the customer seems to miss a typical buying period, a CRM can alert the enterprise that a potential transaction has not yet happened. CRM systems can also associate a transaction event to typical buying behavior; when the customer purchases nails, the CRM can suggest the customer also consider a product typically purchased with nails. CRM systems can also remember birthdays and anniversaries. By sending out cards congratulating a customer on a birthday or anniversary, an enterprise is able to simultaneously remind the customer that the enterprise exists and generate a small measure of good will. Clearly, BI Reporting has, and continues to, serve well in CRM.

Business Metrics Measure the Enterprise

BI Reporting applications also achieve immediate ROI by giving visibility to the state of the enterprise. Published reports disclose the activity levels, benchmark measurements, and key performance indicators of the enterprise. The visibility allows an enterprise to recognize its position in the marketplace and respond to that information. Rather than remain blind to it, BI Reporting applications illuminate the enterprise in the context of the marketplace.

Decisions and Decision Making Closer to the Action

An interesting effect of BI Reporting applications is the availability of information at all hierarchical levels of the enterprise. In the early days, only those managers within walking distance of the carbon impact printer, which printed the reports of the enterprise, would receive the reports generated by operational applications. When BI Reporting applications disseminated operational reports, these reports could be distributed to members of the enterprise closer to the action. Managers back in the office no longer had to tell the workers on the floor and in the field what was in the report; instead, those workers could see the report for themselves.

BI Reporting: Coming Soon

Recent and upcoming developments in BI Reporting have less to do with the technology of BI Reporting and more to do with the use of that technology. Although the technology continues to advance and improve, the analysts and developers using BI Reporting technology are still finding ways to achieve their potential in BI Reporting.

Reporting around the Event

For those BI Reporting applications that report a specific event or condition, BI Reporting analysts know someone will ask, "Why?" In an effort to streamline the "why" question and its answer, BI Reporting analysts have begun to include related and relevant information with the BI report of an event. They have begun to report around the event. The net effect is to simultaneously provide the enterprise event and its context. By providing the context of the event in the first report, the enterprise agent addressing the event can dispense with the request to generate a report of the context of the event.

BI Search

BI reports that have already been designed and coded can be cataloged and indexed.[4] When a member of the enterprise needs a specific piece of information, that person can scan the catalog and index of existing BI reports.[5] If a BI report already exists that presents the required information, that person has simultaneously avoided the creation of a new BI report and obtained the required information.

Sarbanes–Oxley and BI Reporting

The Sarbanes–Oxley (SOX) legislation that addresses recent corporate tragedies applies to the applications that create the data of the enterprise, and to the applications that report the data of the enterprise.[6] BI Reporting applications that are regulated by the SOX legislation now must conform to the following guidelines.

- Quality Assurance (QA): A BI report must be thoroughly tested to validate the data it presents.
- Change Management: The BI report that generates the information viewed by the enterprise must be the BI report that is intended to generate that data.
- Security: The information disclosed by a BI report must be visible to, and used by, only the intended target audience.
- Operations Management: The execution of a BI report and distribution of its result must occur via the infrastructures that are controlled by the enterprise information systems.

Data Mining

Data Mining is a search for patterns and associations within data that are not immediately obvious or may be hidden altogether. Data Mining is a very dynamic exercise. As a pattern emerges, it may lead to a question that will lead to another pattern that may open up a new line of inquiry and discovery.[7] The inquiry and discovery in Data Mining follows one of two paths:

- Exploratory Analysis: This is the search for a hypothesis, a business rule that can predict future events and conditions.
- Confirmatory Analysis: This is the test of a hypothesis. A business rule has been found that requires validation and verification.[8]

An enterprise performs data mining to achieve a competitive advantage.[9] The enterprise that can decipher the tea leaves of information within itself and its environment to be able to predict the near, and not so near, future possesses a competitive advantage over those in the marketplace who can only react to events and conditions after they have happened.

At first glance, Data Mining has the appearance of a second semester statistical time-series class project. The professor distributes to the class a data file containing thousands of rows of comma separated values (CSV) data. In each row, the first value is the dependent value; all the other values are the independent values. The assignment is find the independent variables and statistical algorithm that best predict the dependent variable; remembering to include the confidence measurements.

Data Mining is similar to that assignment. An enterprise wants to be able to predict an event or condition, i.e., what function and factors in $f(x, y, z) = A$? In the best case scenario, factors x, y, and z are within the power of the enterprise to manipulate. In that case, the enterprise can cause result A to occur by manipulating factors x, y, and z. In the next best-case scenario, factors x, y, and z are known by the enterprise. The enterprise can know result A is about to occur whenever factors x, y, and z have occurred.

In the second semester statistical time-series class, the assignment was testing the students' ability to perform and measure statistical time-series functions on an almost infinite set of permutations of independent and dependent variables. That may have actually been the point, considering how difficult it was.

Statistics Concepts

Data Mining uses many of the concepts and terminology found in Statistics. This does not mean that Data Mining is a statistical exercise. It does, however, mean that Data Mining is an exercise that includes elements of statistics. The foundational and most prevalent of these concepts and terms are explained in the following sections.

Random Error

Slight fluctuations occur constantly in the universe. These fluctuations manifest themselves in our daily lives. We experience these fluctuations all the time. Sometimes we're aware of them, sometimes not. For example:

■ In the morning, we take varying durations of time to eat breakfast, dress, and get out the door, for no apparent reason.
■ The morning commute using the same route consumes varying durations of time, for no apparent reason.
■ The number of people in the elevator going to work varies from one morning to the next, for no apparent reason.

These slight fluctuations that occur everywhere and all the time were illustrated by W. Edwards Deming.[10]

In Deming's example, he held a handful of coins and tried to drop them, one at a time, onto a single spot in the floor. Marking first the target spot on the floor and then all the spots where the coins actually fell, Deming observed:

- Most coins did not fall on the same spot.
- Most coins did not fall on the target spot.
- Most coins fell very close to the target spot.

Was Deming's aim poor with the coins? No, because his results and observations can be repeated. In fact, they can only be repeated. No one is able to stand over a spot in the floor and hit it exactly with a handful of coins. Why? The answer is Random Error.

While Random Error is random, it is not error. Rather, Random Error is the naturally occurring variance between a target value and an actual value. Random Error is ubiquitous and unavoidable. Any process, therefore, that proclaims it achieves perfect results is not measuring itself well enough to identify its own Random Error.

Data Mining experiences Random Error. In the case of Data Mining, Random Error is the naturally occurring variance between the data value derived by an algorithm and the actual data value. Since Random Error occurs everywhere all the time, including Data Mining algorithms, all Data Mining algorithms will rarely derive the correct answer. But, a good Data Mining algorithm will consistently derive an answer that is closest to the correct answer. Random Error, measured, recorded, and graphed, should render a graph that looks like a bell curve, preferably a tall, narrow, bell curve (Figure 7.3).

So, it may seem counter-intuitive, but a good Data Mining algorithm is not the algorithm that derives the right answer, but the best answer. Why not the right answer? The right answer also experiences the ubiquitous Random Error.

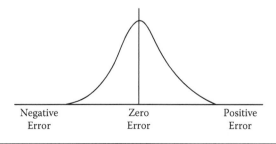

Figure 7.3   **Random Error.**

Statistical Significance

So, the goal of Data Mining, therefore, is not to find an algorithm that derives the right answer, but to find an algorithm that derives the best answer. The best answer is described as the answer that is Statistically Significant. An algorithm is Statistically Significant when it adds the least possible Error, in addition to the unavoidable Random Error.

For example, the top graph in Figure 7.4 illustrates the Error generated by an algorithm that derives expected values that are more prone to Error than Random Error. The difference between Random Error and Actual Error is a measure of an algorithm's Statistical Significance. The algorithm that adds the least Error in addition to Random Error (i.e., Actual Error − Random Error) is the most Statistically Significant algorithm.

Variables: Dependent and Independent

An algorithm uses multiple input data values to predict an output data value. The multiple input data values are the Independent Variables. They are independent because their data value does not rely on any other data value. The output data value is the Dependent variable. It is dependent because its data value depends on

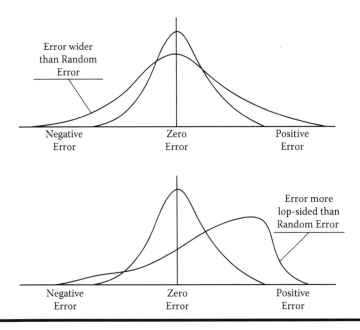

Figure 7.4   Nonrandom Error.

the data values in the Independent Variables. An algorithm can be expected to have multiple Independent Variables, but only one Dependent Variable.

Hypothesis

The Hypothesis of every algorithm is that the algorithm is able to accurately predict the Dependent Variable using the Independent Variables. The measured Error between the predicted Dependent Variable and the actual Dependent Variable, adjusted for Random Error, is the Error associated directly with the algorithm and the measure of its Statistical Significance. The algorithm with the greatest Error is the least Statistically Significant. But, the algorithm with the least Error is the most Statistically Significant. An algorithm, therefore, may never derive the right answer, but be the most Statistically Significant algorithm by which answers can be derived.

Data Mining Tools

Data Mining tools have mitigated the difficulty of performing and measuring statistical time-series functions. Generally available Data Mining tools handle all the statistical and time-series functions as well as the confidence measurements. These Data Mining tools are powerful software packages that enhance and accelerate the Data Mining process. They include the statistical algorithms and functions that are at the center of Data Mining.

Data Mining tools, like all competing software packages, can be compared to each other. The criteria on which to compare Data Mining tools are:[11]

- Platform: The computers and operating systems on which the Data Mining tools will operate.
- Algorithm: The library of statistical functions inside each Data Mining tool.
- Data Input options: File layouts accepted by the Data Mining tool.
- Model Output options: Methods by which the Data Mining tool presents its results.
- Usability: The least skill set necessary to use the Data Mining tool.
- Visualization: The graphic representation of a predictive model.
- Automation Methods: The power of the Data Mining tool to perform and measure the statistical functions and the final hypothesis without human intervention.

By comparing Data Mining tools along these criteria, a BI analyst can determine which Data Mining tool best fits his or her skills and needs. Regardless of which Data Mining tool is selected, a BI analyst must have a strong understanding of the statistical principles and methods used by the Data Mining tool and the business meaning of the methods and data. As always, no amount of tool can compensate for a lack of knowledge.

Data Mining Activities

Data Mining is a specific activity. A BI analyst does not accidentally mine data. In a data warehouse full of gigabytes or terabytes of data, a BI analyst cannot simply bump into a golden nugget. Rather, a BI analyst has to intentionally search for the correlations and associations in those gigabytes and terabytes of data. The first step is to recognize that no Data Mining tool is going to mine these gigabytes or terabytes of data. Data Mining tools, despite all of their statistical power, actually, because of all their statistical power, require the data be brought to them. Data Mining tools require data be brought to them in specific formats (hence, the similarity to the CSV file in that second semester statistical time-series class).

Data Preparation is similar to preparing a house for painting. The preparation work is usually two or three times the work of painting. Data Preparation is usually two or three times the work of Data Mining. But, if enough attention is given to the preparation, the final product will be much better.

Data Cleansing

The Data Mining tool is going to derive correlations between independent variables, dependent variables, and algorithms that may or may not explain their association. To do this, a Data Mining tool needs a clean set of data, without any "noise" data that might cause confusion or distraction.[12] This is not the data warehouse. This is not data that will be presented to data warehouse customers. Rather, this data will be used by the Data Mining tool and no one else. So, the constraints in the Data Warehousing Philosophy do not apply. That being said, some of the Data Cleansing methods are:

- **Missing Values**: Identify missing values in the data. Fill them in with a reasonable value. This mitigates the risk that an empty spot in the data that does not normally occur may lead the Data Mining tool to believe that empty spot always occurs.
- **Outliers**: Identify unreasonable data values. In the data warehouse, these outliers are retained. But, in the data presented to a Data Mining tool, these values are modified to a more reasonable value. This mitigates the risk that an outlier in the data that does not normally occur may lead the Data Mining tool to believe that outlier always occurs.
- **Sample Bias**: Preferably, feed a Data Mining tool with a universe (a whole and complete set) of data, not just a sample. A sample of data should *only* be used when the delivery of a universe of data is physically and logistically impossible (including asking that person fours doors down and two doors over, who can move mountains of data, to help gather the universe of data). If, and only if, the universe of data is impossible, use a sample of data for Data Mining. If a sample is used, check the bias of that sample. For example:

- A sample of customers throughout the world should not be used to investigate patterns in Georgia sales tax.
- A sample of customers in Georgia should not be used to investigate time-of-day purchasing behavior in Scandinavia.

These examples of sample bias are obvious. The sample bias in data used in Data Mining is usually far subtler. The point is to realize the act of sampling data applies a logic algorithm to the universe of data. The Data Mining tool is not aware of this logic algorithm. Even if a Data Mining tool were aware of the logic algorithm used to sample data, the Data Mining tool could not compensate for bias of that sample.

Remember, you do not want the Data Mining tool to derive unusual or biased behavior of the enterprise. Instead, you want the Data Mining tool to derive the normal behavior of the enterprise.

Data Inspection

A Data Mining tool perceives data as variables. A Data Mining tool understands two kinds of variables: Independent Variables and Dependent Variables. In the cause–effect concept of the world wherein every effect is preceded by one or more causes, Independent Variables are the cause and a Dependent Variable is the effect. In Data Inspection, a BI analyst reviews the meaning, content, and inconsistencies within each Variable. The methods applied in Source System Analysis can also be applied to Data Inspection:

- Data profile
- Histogram
- Business Rule validation

Compound Variables

Variables that are composed of two or more discreet data elements (e.g., shoe style and size, date and time, etc.) can be separated into their distinct data elements. The result would be two new Variables and the removal of the compound Variable.

Lag Variables

When an Independent Variable affects subsequent periods, but not the period in which it occurs, that Independent Variable must be displaced in time to the time period it affects. A Lag Variable can be expressed as an Independent Variable (one period prior). The BI analyst doesn't know the length of the trail of effect following a Lagging Variable. Therefore, a single Lagging Variable can become Independent

Variable (one period prior), Independent Variable (two periods prior), Independent Variable (three periods prior), Independent Variable (x periods prior). The creation of Lag Variables is an educated guess. Thus, it is best to guess many times and let the Data Mining tool find the best correlation.

Numeric Variables

Numeric Variables quantify the measurements applied to enterprise entities. These could be the number of units is a transaction, the size of a building, or the temperature of molten iron ore. In each case, the Numeric Variable quantifies a single aspect of an enterprise entity. To inspect a Numeric Variable, the mathematical mean, mode, and median of all the measurements of a Variable will identify the mathematical center of that Numeric Variable.[13] Does that mathematical center look correct? If the Numeric Variable represents the height of people and the mathematical center is 12 feet, that Numeric Variable is wrong.

A Distribution Histogram of a Numeric Variable is also helpful. The Distribution Histogram of a Numeric Variable should resemble a bell curve, centered on the mathematical center of the Numeric Variable. If it is not a bell curve, or if it is not centered on the mathematical center of the Numeric Variable, then the Numeric Variable requires further investigation. Either, the Numeric Variable means something other than was originally represented or is just plain wrong. By juxtaposing a Distribution Histogram over the mathematical center of a Numeric Variable, a BI analyst is able to derive some level of confidence in that Numeric Variable.

Categorical Variables

Categorical Variables qualify enterprise entities into groups by directly associating one of a set of mutually exclusive attributes to an entity. For example:

- Blue: From the set Red, White, and Blue
- Yes: From the set Yes and No
- Upper Midwest: From the set Northeast, Southeast, Upper Midwest, Lower Midwest, Northwest, and Southwest
- Female: From the set Male and Female

A BI analyst can measure the distribution of Categorical Variables. That distribution compared to the expectations of the Variable provides some level of confidence in it.

Hypothesis

Inherently, the set of Independent Variables is a hypothesis within themselves. That inherent hypothesis is that these Independent Variables have some sort of connection to the Dependent Variable. Beyond that ambiguous hypothesis, Exploratory Analysis is a search for an explanation as to how (not necessarily why) some subset of these Independent Variables relates to, or associates with, the Dependent Variable. The relation, or association, derived from Exploratory Analysis is an algorithm. For example:

- Growth in sales is inversely proportional to changes in price.
- Increases in manufacturing throughput are directly proportional to certification levels.

These algorithms are also hypotheses. Exploratory Analysis uses the input data to discover the algorithm (i.e., hypothesis).

Confirmatory Analysis begins with the hypothesis. In Confirmatory Analysis, the BI analyst tries to predict the Dependent Variable by using the Independent Variables and the hypothesized algorithm. The variance between the predicted value and the actual value is a measurement of the confidence in the hypothesized algorithm.

The goal is important. The goal of Data Mining is the achievement of a competitive advantage. Inside the data is a key by which the enterprise can identify approaching opportunities and threats. That key, finding it, validating it, and using it to the advantage of the enterprise is important, and the reason for Data Mining.

Data Mining Algorithms

Data Mining tools offer many different algorithms because Data Mining is not a one-size-fits-all methodology. A BI analyst must come to the Data Mining exercise with a knowledge of the data and a knowledge of the algorithms. Data Mining does not work by just throwing algorithms at data and then waiting to see what works. The best-fit algorithm will not work to some degree. Therefore, a BI analyst should begin the Data Mining exercise with an understanding of the independent variables, dependent variable, and the available algorithms. From that perspective, a BI analyst can begin to select an algorithm, or set of algorithms, that might be able to predict the dependent variable with sufficient confidence.

Five of the myriad Data Mining algorithms are discussed in the following sections. The purpose of these sections is not to disseminate all possible knowledge of these algorithms, but rather, the purpose is to provide a sense of what algorithms are, how they work, and how a BI analyst works the algorithms.

Neural Network

The Neural Network algorithm is based on the processes of cognitive learning in the neurological infrastructure of the human brain (Figure 7.5).[14] The Neural Network begins when a BI analyst defines a set of neurons (hence, Neural), otherwise known as nodes. These nodes are lined up in multiple rows, or layers. Within each node is a function. That function will use as input the data values that comes into the node. The output is the result of the function having been applied to the input data.

Nodes are connected by links. Links serve two purposes. First, they pass data values from:

■ An input to a node
■ A node to another node
■ A node to an output

Each input is linked to all nodes in the first layer. All nodes in the first layer are linked to all nodes in the second layer. All nodes in the subsequent layers are linked to all nodes in the next layer. Finally, all nodes in the last layer are connected to the output. The result looks like a Cartesian join from input to nodes, from nodes to nodes, and from nodes to output.

The second purpose of links is that they apply a weight to the data values that pass through them. This is how the Neural Network "learns." By iteratively applying varying weights to the data values as they pass through, the Neural Network is able to adjust its decision-making process.

This is very similar to priorities and their application to decision making by humans. For example:

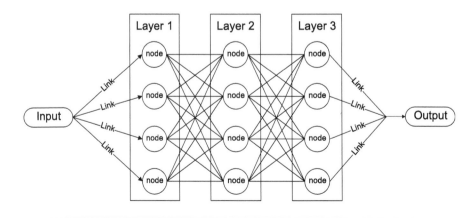

Figure 7.5   Neural Network.

- Node 1: I want to play flag football.
- Node 2: I just stepped on a nail. It is sticking up through my foot.
- Outcome: Zero weight is applied to the data value from Node 1. Node 2 receives 100 percent weight. The decision is: Go to the doctor.

In this scenario, had the value from Node 2 been: "I have a cramp in my leg," then Node 1 would have received some weight. Interestingly, the Neural Network would require iterations of training to learn the correct weight to apply.

There is no guarantee a Neural Network will be able to predict the dependent variable. After several iterations of learning (i.e., adjusting the weights applied by the links), a Neural Network may be no closer to predicting the dependent variable with any level of confidence. In these situations, a BI analyst can throw away that set of neurons and links and start over. This is perfectly acceptable, albeit annoying. A BI analyst can start over by creating a whole new set of neurons with new functions, lined up in new rows, and connected by new links.

Decision Tree

A Decision Tree is a stack of binary decision boxes (Figure 7.6). Within each box is a categorical question, which separates the input values based on their answers. For example:

- Are you greater than five feet tall?
  - Yes
  - No

- Are you left-handed?
  - Yes
  - No

- What is your annual salary?

  - < 50,000
  - > 50,000

Each decision box yields two outputs. These outputs either lead to another decision box or a termination point. When the answer to a decision box is statistically significant, the set of independent variables proceeds to the next decision box. When the answer to a decision box is statistically insignificant, the set of independent variables goes immediately to a termination point. Based on their answers, a set of independent variables will either pass all the way to the bottom of the Decision Tree or cause that set of independent variables to terminate the Decision Tree.

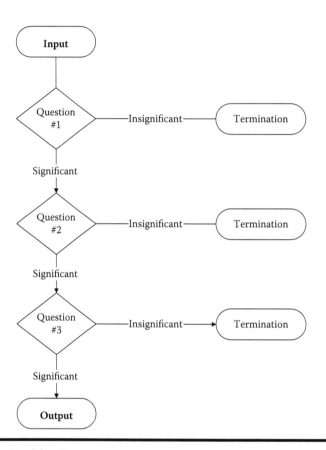

Figure 7.6   Decision Tree.

A Decision Tree also has no guarantee of predicting the dependent variable. If all rows of independent variables terminate the Decision Tree, then none of them will yield a prediction for the dependent variable. A BI analyst can redefine, recreate, and restructure the Decision Tree many times before finding a permutation that predicts the dependent variable with an acceptable level of confidence.

CHAID

CHAID (Chi-squared automatic interaction detector) is also a decision tree, a non-binary decision tree.[15] That means every decision box can simultaneously output multiple (i.e., more than two) branches (Figure 7.7). A CHAID tree applies one independent variable at a time. Each independent variable is treated categorically. Numeric independent variables are banded into categories so the CHAID statistical test can treat them categorically. The categories in each layer of CHAID have an

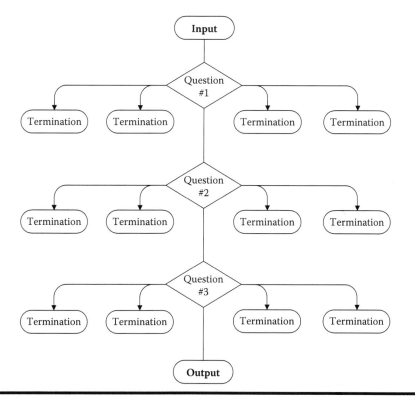

Figure 7.7   Chi-squared automatic interaction detector (CHAID).

equal probability of occurring. If they did not have an equal opportunity of occurring, the CHAID tree would be self-prophetic and useless because the outcome would be built into the tree. For example:

- Layer 1 Independent Variable is Profession. The categories are
    - Government employee
    - Educational employee
    - Student
    - Private Sector

- Layer 2 Independent Variable is Income level. The categories are
    - 0 to 10,000
    - 10,001 to 50,000
    - 50,001 to 250,000
    - > 250,001

■ Layer 3 Independent Variable is Housing. The categories are
  – Homeowner
  – Condominium owner
  – Renter

An input record is tested using the Chi-squared method to determine the Layer 1 category for which it is most significant. If the Chi-squared test directed the input record to a Layer 1 category, which is not exploded into Layer 2, then that record terminates the CHAID tree. One category in Layer 1, the statistically most significant and, therefore, least independent category, is exploded into the categories of the next independent variable in Layer 2. This process continues until the record either terminates or exhausts all independent variables.[16]

CHAID is a nonbinary decision tree. Input records are Chi-squared tested to determine down which branch in the tree they will travel. If the input record goes down an insignificant branch in the tree, that record is terminated. If the input record continues to go down a significant branch, that record will eventually reach a prediction of the dependent variable.

Nearest Neighbor

The Nearest Neighbor algorithm is an interesting application of the old saying "Birds of a feather flock together." The idea behind Nearest Neighbor (Figure 7.8) is that if I'm trying to predict the dependent variable for a single row, I'll go find another row that looks just like it, and use the dependent variable from that row.[17] The independent variables in the other row, by some unknown means, lead to the dependent variable in that row. By correlating the two rows based on their similarities, the same unknown means that yielded the dependent variable in the other row will also yield the same, or at least extremely similar, dependent variable in the row in question.

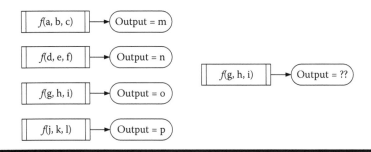

Figure 7.8   Nearest Neighbor.

This method is invalidated when the independent variables have no direct connection or association with the dependent variable. For example:

- Height, Weight, and Annual Salary → Left-Handed
- Left-Handed, Favorite Movie, and Mother's Maiden Name → Hair Color

But then, if the dependent and independent variables were so disconnected from each other, the whole Data Mining exercise was doomed to not find a connection, regardless of the algorithm.

If, however, a direct and strong connection does exist between the independent and dependent variables, Nearest Neighbor may be able to predict the dependent variable. Nearest Neighbor does not make any attempt to explain why the dependent variable is connected to the independent variables. Rather, Nearest Neighbor simply borrows the dependent variable from another record to predict the dependent variable for the record in question.

Rule Induction

The Rule Induction method is basically Data Mining by brute force. All the input records are given to a Rule Induction engine (Table 7.3). The Rule Induction engine will identify patterns by which sets, subsets, and permutations of independent variables have any positive correlation with the dependent variable. These correlated patterns are the Rules.[18] A Rule Induction engine will identify many Rules, some useful and some useless. Each Rule is accompanied by two measures: Coverage and Accuracy.

Coverage measures the portion of the input records for which the Rule applies. Accuracy measures the strength of the prediction provided by the Rule. A Rule may have an accuracy of 95 percent for 0.01 percent of the input records, or a Rule may have an accuracy of 75 percent for 95 percent of the input records. Coverage and Accuracy, therefore, are the measures by which a BI analyst can determine whether or not a Rule should be used by the enterprise to predict the dependent variable.

Genetic Algorithm

A Genetic Algorithm applies the concept of mutation to Rules or Patterns, which have already been identified (Figure 7.9). The focus of Genetic Algorithm is the Rules, not the input data. Input data is used to test mutated Rules. The output of a Genetic Algorithm is not a predicted dependent variable. Rather, the output of a Genetic Algorithm is a Rule that can predict a dependent variable.

In one form of Genetic Algorithm, two Rules are combined (i.e., crossbred), yielding a new Rule that shares characteristics of its parent Rules. The new rule is then tested for its ability to predict the dependent variable.[19]

Table 7.3 Rule Induction

Independent Variable #1	Independent Variable #2	Independent Variable #3	Independent Variable #4	Independent Variable #5	Independent Variable #6	Dependent Variable
0.436378326	2.1	0.301712432	28	0.431759141	14	0.486287577
0.193267369	0.5	0.41215494	32	0.243513294	59	0.760652421
0.131211436	0.1	0.387898013	0	0.219540639	7	0.620490496
0.754526083	2.7	0.067556225	36	0.211306938	153	0.538406397
0.211595866	1.9	0.100185321	3	0.541210063	181	0.762989838
0.315825229	1.3	0.189470411	5	0.149141519	101	0.677718158
0.914341876	2.8	0.939135939	21	0.97084797	430	0.112577913
0.948186861	2.2	0.1983475	29	0.763762177	377	0.561912731
0.265790178	2.3	0.562533077	33	0.35837477	282	0.211817047
0.654756934	2.4	0.014014485	37	0.46110425	411	0.813301519
0.080283594	0.2	0.53087372	25	0.045511724	352	0.479450001
0.89293365	2.8	0.498041273	36	0.930839628	380	0.7179979
0.526538626	1.1	0.565357121	28	0.936552183	353	0.960082906
0.552062596	1.2	0.603052894	4	0.067425636	42	0.538515975
0.787415442	2.4	0.423917664	8	0.553729297	281	0.205675167
0.544833745	0.2	0.778987413	3	0.921877819	405	0.124263152
0.974367877	1.1	0.030276999	13	0.213102347	270	0.83361743
0.117215381	2.6	0.695766069	17	0.460062286	76	0.75917827
0.256906542	0.1	0.521972832	13	0.976999191	1	0.354609343

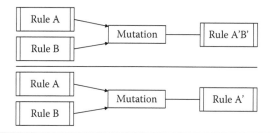

Figure 7.9 Genetic Algorithm.

In another form of Genetic Algorithm, two Rules are juxtaposed against each other. The weaker Rule is discarded and the stronger Rule is allowed to continue with a slight random modification. The Rule resulting from this method is then tested for its ability to predict the dependent variable.[20]

Rule Validation and Testing

Every Rule, regardless of the algorithm that generated it, must be validated and tested using a significantly large set of data. That set of data cannot be the set of data that was used to derive the Rule. Tempting as it may be, a Rule should not be accepted based on its ability to predict one set of data. Without validation in another set of data, the risk that the Rule may not apply to data "in the field," has not been mitigated.

Overfitting

If something is too good to be true, it probably is. A pitfall common to all Data Mining efforts is the desire to find the perfect Rule. No Rule is perfect. If a Rule predicts 100 percent of the dependent variables with 100 percent accuracy, that Rule is useless. Why? Because a Rule that can predict 100 percent of the dependent variables with 100 percent accuracy in a set of data can predict dependent variables only in that set of data. The natural variations and randomness that exist in the world will not allow a Rule to predict 100 percent of the dependent variables with 100 percent accuracy. Therefore, when a Rule begins to compensate for natural randomness, the Rule is overfitting the test data and will not be able to predict dependent variables in real data.

Closing Remarks

Business Intelligence (BI) Reporting has come a long way from the carbon-printed reports on green bar paper that were distributed on employees' desks during the night. The product offerings of static, dynamic, push, pull, ad hoc, and OLAP BI applications are varied and plentiful. An enterprise can now generate and distribute its data and information from a data warehouse, ODS, or operational information system. Data Mining is still maturing and available for those on the leading edge. With these technologies and methods available, an enterprise only need ask, "What do I want to see?" and "How do I want to see it?"

References

1. Dorian Pyle, *Business Modeling and Data Mining* (Amsterdam, Boston: Morgan Kaufmann Publishers, 2003).
2. Louis Agosta, *The Essential Guide to Data Warehousing* (Upper Saddle River, NJ: Prentice Hall PTR, 2000).
3, Ken Bisconti, Integrating BI tools into the enterprise portal, *DM Review* (2005).
4. Philip Russom, TDWI: BI search and text analytics: Best practices in search, *DM Review* (2007).
5. Wayne W. Eckerson, The real value of BI search," *TDWI* (2007).
6. Brandon Lucado, Aligning your BI Environment with SOX internal controls," *DM Review* (2007).
7. Kamran Parsaye, Datamines for data warehouses, *DM Review* (1999).
8. Information Discovery, Inc. A characterization of data mining technologies and processes by Information Discovery, Inc., *DM Review* (2004).
9. William H. Inmon, R. H. Terdeman, and Claudia Imhoff, *Exploration Warehousing: Turning Business Information into Business Opportunity* (New York: John Wiley & Sons, 2000).
10. W. Edwards Deming, *Out of the Crisis* (Cambridge, MA: Massachusetts Institute of Technology Center for Advanced Engineering Study, 1986).
11. John F. Elder and Dean W. Abbott, A comparison of leading data mining tools, *Fourth International Conference on Knowledge Discovery and Data Mining*, New York, August 1998, http://www.datamininglab.com/pubs/kdd98_elder_abbott_nopics_bw.pdf.
12. Pyle, *Business Modeling and Data Mining*.
13. Ibid.
14. StatSoft, Inc., Data mining techniques, http://www.statsoft.com/textbook/stdatmin.html.
15. Janine Okell, Neural networks versus CHAID, *DM Review* (1999).
16. StatSoft, Inc., CHAID analysis, StatSoft, Inc., http://www.statsoft.com/textbook/stchaid.html.

17. Alex Berson and Stephen J. Smith, *Data Warehousing, Data Mining, and OLAP*, McGraw-Hill Series on Data Warehousing and Data Management (New York: McGraw-Hill, 1997).

18. Ibid.

19. Ibid.

20. Information Discovery, Inc., A characterization of data mining technologies and processes by Information Discovery, Inc., *DM Review*, 2004.

Chapter 8

Data Quality

Introduction

The quality of the data in a data warehouse determines the reputation and value of that data warehouse. If customers perceive the data in a data warehouse to be misleading or just plain wrong, they won't use the data warehouse. If customers can find or create a superior source of data elsewhere, they will abandon a data warehouse altogether. Data Quality, the perceived reputation and value, of a data warehouse, therefore, is vital to the success of a data warehouse. Unfortunately, perceived reputation and perceived value are subjective qualifications and cannot be measured. Quantitative measurement, however, is the key to Data Quality (Figure 8.1). To understand how to apply quantitative measurement to data, we turn to the statistician who defined and quantified quality during the twentieth century—W. Edwards Deming.

Deming's Definition of Quality

Deming's definition of Quality begins with a distinction between Features and Quality.[1] Features are the buzzers and whistles included with a product that do not specifically address the core purpose of a product. Typically, people see Features first. For example, the following are features of a product.

- Leather seats in a car

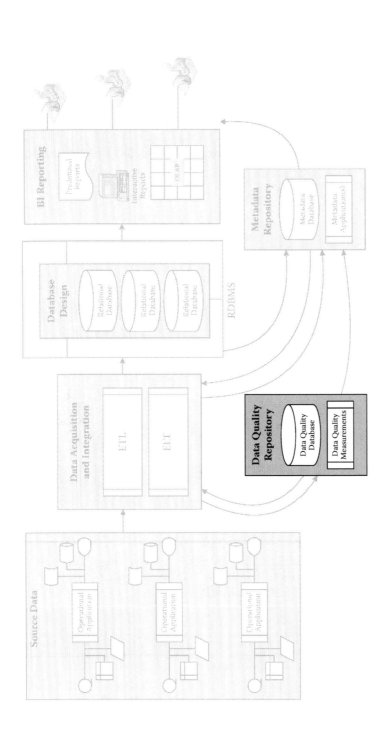

Figure 8.1 Data Quality.

- Graphical user interface (GUI) point-and-click buttons and scroll bars in a spreadsheet
- Mother of Pearl inlays in a guitar

Deming's point is not that Features have no value. Of course, the leather seats, GUI screen, and Mother of Pearl inlays all have value, but, they are features. They do not make the car move, make a spreadsheet calculate, or make the guitar play. Their value is subjective and, therefore, impossible to measure.

So, what is Quality? Deming's answer is based on expectations and whether or not those expectations are achieved. Deming defined Quality as the success or failure to achieve a customer's expectations.[2]

- **Quality in a car**
  - When I start the car, the car starts.
  - When I drive the car, the car moves.
  - When I stop the car, the car stops.
  - The speedometer indicates the speed of the car accurately.
  - The odometer indicates the mileage of the car accurately.
- **Quality in a spreadsheet**
  - When I turn on the spreadsheet, the spreadsheet starts.
  - When I turn off the spreadsheet, the spreadsheet stops.
  - When I sort data in a spreadsheet, the spreadsheet sorts correctly.
  - When I perform arithmetic calculations in a spreadsheet, the spreadsheet calculates the numbers correctly.
- **Quality in a guitar**
  - When I play a G chord on a guitar, the guitar sounds a G chord.
  - When I tune a guitar, the guitar stays in tune.
  - When I stop playing a guitar, the guitar stops making sounds.
  - When I play the guitar tomorrow, the guitar sounds as it did today.

These are the expectations of customers as they consume a car, spreadsheet, and guitar. Deming would measure the quality of a car, spreadsheet, and guitar against expectations such as these. For each of these products, their quality is their ability to meet these expectations.

Note that quality is not their ability to exceed these expectations. In the measurement of quality, the idea of exceeding an expectation is non sequitur. For instance, if the expectation of a manufacturing process is that a bolt will be two inches long, a bolt cannot exceed this expectation. A two inch bolt cannot be more than two inches. A car cannot start more than start. A spreadsheet cannot calculate 2×3 any better than the product of 2×3, which is 6. A guitar cannot play a G chord more than a G chord. Likewise, in a data warehouse, a complete dataset cannot be more complete than complete. And, the arrival of data in a data warehouse cannot be any more on time than on time. In all of these cases, Quality is the success or failure to meet customer expectations.

Data Quality Service Level Agreement (SLA)

In a data warehouse, Quality is the success or failure to deliver data that meets the expectations of its customers. Back in the bolt manufacturing plant, the quality of bolts can be measured with a two-inch measuring tape. Bolts are compared to the measuring tape. If a series of bolts measure to consistently be between 1.995 and 2.005 inches, then the bolt manufacturing process is deemed to be working correctly. Quality in a data warehouse also requires measurement. Customer expectations of a data warehouse, therefore, must be expressed in well-defined and quantifiable terms. For example:

- **Completeness**
  - Not Quantifiable: Most of the warehouses should be present in the data warehouse.
  - Quantifiable: 95 percent of the warehouses should be present in the data warehouse.
- **Latency**
  - Not Quantifiable: The warehouse data should be in before the staff arrives.
  - Quantifiable: The warehouse data should be in by 6:30 a.m.
- **Accuracy**
  - Not Quantifiable: The warehouse data should equal what actually happens in the warehouse.
  - Quantifiable: The total inventory movement of each product in a warehouse reported by the data warehouse should be within 2 percent (+/–) the total movement of each product as reported by the warehouse end-of-day process.
- **Reasonable**
  - Not Quantifiable: Total inventory movement in a warehouse should be similar to the average inventory movement.
  - Quantifiable: Total inventory movement in a warehouse should be within 5 percent (+/–) the seasonal average.

You cannot use a measuring tape, scale, or measuring cup to quantitatively measure data and, therefore, Data Quality. But, in a dataset with millions of rows, you can measure the frequency with which binary conditions occur and you can validate data warehouse data against other information systems with similar data. The first step toward achieving a quality data warehouse is the creation of Quality expectations. Those expectations are captured and documented in a Data Quality Service Level Agreement (SLA).

A Data Quality SLA is a repository of the quantifiable expectations of data warehouse customers. A Data Quality SLA is also an agreement and includes these provisions:

- The expectations in the Data Quality SLA are defined precisely and clearly.
- The expectations in the Data Quality SLA are quantitative and can be measured.
- The data warehouse team will perform the measurements in each expectation.
- The data warehouse team will use the results of the Data Quality measurements to improve the data warehouse.
- The data warehouse team will publish the results of Data Quality measurements.

These provisions of a Data Quality SLA provide a set of expectations against which a data warehouse can be measured. Data Quality measurements can be performed, the results documented, published, and compared to previous and subsequent periods.

Deming's Statistical Process Control

In manufacturing, Deming defined Quality as the consistency with which manufactured product matches expectations.[3] If a bolt is expected to be one-half inch wide by two inches long, then that bolt and every other bolt from that manufacturing process should be one-half inch wide by two inches long. By measuring bolts as they come from the manufacturing process, Deming asserted the manufacturer can know whether or not the manufacturing process is in control or out of control. Deming did not propose measuring bolts to find good bolts, he instead proposed measuring bolts as a means of measuring the process. The manufacturing process was the focus of Deming's attention, not the bolts. If the manufacturing process is in control, it will generate bolts that are one-half inch wide by two inches long all day long.

A data warehouse has the same quality issues as a bolt manufacturer. A data warehouse process that is in control will generate data that meets expectations all day long. A data warehouse process that is not in control will generate nonsense data. The processes of the data warehouse are the focus of Deming's Process Control method, which measures the process by measuring the product—by measuring its data.[4]

Deming's focus on process rather than product ran counter to the quality enforcement methods of his contemporaries. Manufacturers had previously enforced quality by inspecting completed product as it left the assembly line. Defective product was returned to the assembly line for rework. Deming's focus on the individual processes removed the need for final inspection and the need for rework. By assuring each manufacturing process is in control, Deming asserted the final product, which is the cumulative sum of the processes that created it, will meet the customers' expectations.

If any manufacturing process is found to be out of control, that individual process is fixed. The problem could be a worn-down machine part, a new assembly line worker needing training, or a parts bin labeled incorrectly. The point is that the individual out-of-control process is identified before it is allowed to affect the finished product. The manufacturing process is stopped. Once the process is repaired, the manufacturing process resumes. The work interruption costs less than the rework that would happen had the process not been stopped.

Extract, Transform, and Load (ETL) processes have the same manufacturing properties. By measuring each individual ETL process, the data warehouse team can monitor the health of the ETL application. If a single process is out of control, the ETL process can stop, allowing time to adjust the errant ETL process. The time and effort spent to adjust an out-of-control ETL process costs less than the rework that would happen had the process not been stopped. When all ETL processes are back in control, the data in the data warehouse will meet the expectations of the customer.[5]

Process Measurement

The expectations of the source system are in the Source System Analysis. Yet, once again, this document is the map and lexicon of the source system. All the expectations of the data in the data warehouse come directly from the Source System Analysis. If the source system behaves contrary to the Source System Analysis, then the processes within the source system are probably out of control and need to be adjusted.

The expectations of the ETL applications are listed in the Target System Analysis. The ETL applications provide the behavior of the data in a data warehouse. Without the ETL to modify and move its data, a data warehouse would be static and have no behavior. If the data passing through an ETL application behaves contrary to the expectations identified in the Target System Analysis, then the processes within the ETL application are probably out of control, and need to be adjusted.

Listed below are the categories of expectations held by the data warehouse designer and data warehouse customers. Each of these focuses on a data warehouse process. By measuring the individual processes, a data warehouse team is able to identify those processes that are out of control and need help and those that are in control.

- **Data Model**: The Target System Analysis identified the data and data behavior expected to occur in a data warehouse. These data behaviors can be measured by identifying instances of data in the data warehouse that contradict the expectations identified in the Target System Analysis.
  - Relational Integrity: The primary key/foreign key relationships between tables in the data warehouse require a primary key in the parent table for every foreign key in a child table. Instances of orphan foreign keys without a primary key in a parent table can be recorded and counted as individual instances of failure to meet the expectations of the data model.
  - Domain: The universe of data values expected in a data element can be compared to the actual data values. Instances of actual data values that are not in the domain can be recorded and counted as individual instances of failure to meet the expectations of the data model.
  - Range: The boundaries within which all data values of a data element are expected to exist. Instances of actual data values outside the expected boundary can be recorded and counted as individual instances of failure to meet the expectations of the data model.
- **ETL (Extract):** The Data Mapping identified the source data that is expected to provide the data needed by the data warehouse.
  - Relational Integrity: The primary key/foreign key relationships between tables in the source system require a primary key in the parent table for every foreign key in a child table. Instances of orphan foreign keys without a primary key in a parent table can be recorded and counted as individual instances of failure to meet the expectations of the source system.
  - Domain: The universe of data values expected in a data element can be compared to the actual data values. Instances of actual data values that are not in the domain can be recorded and counted as individual instances of failure to meet the expectations of the source system.
  - Range: The boundaries within which all data values of a data element are expected to exist. Instances of actual data values outside the expected boundary can be recorded and counted as individual instances of failure to meet the expectations of the source system.
  - Completeness: The presence of the entire population of enterprise entities (e.g., manufacturing plants, warehouses, employees, etc.) in a set of data. Instances of gaps in the entities present in a set of data can be recorded and counted as individual instances of failure to meet the expectations of the source system.
  - Latency: Data from a source system should be available to the data warehouse within a time frame that allows the ETL application to process and load that data. Instances of unavailable source system data can be recorded and counted as individual instances of failure to meet the expectations of the source system.

- – Business Rules: Data from a source system exists within the context of that source system. The business rules of the source system govern the data from the source system. Typically, these business rules govern content of data in three ways.
  - ■ Intrarecord Business Rules: Column A + Column B = Column C. The business rule exists entirely within each individual record.
  - ■ Intradataset Business Rules: Row 1.Column A + Row 2.Column A = Row 3.Column B. The business rule spans across records within a set of data, but still remains within the set of data.
  - ■ Cross-Dataset Business Rules: File 1.Column A = Table 2.Column B. The business rule spans across sets of data within a source system.
- – Instances of source system data that violates the source system business rules can be recorded and counted as individual instances of failure to meet the expectations of the source system.
- ■ **ETL (Transform):** The Data Mapping identified the transformations that are expected to synthesize raw data elements into information. These transformations can inadvertently create data values that do not conform to the business rules of the data in the data warehouse. Transformed data values can violate the business rules of a data warehouse six ways.
  - – Relational Integrity: The Transform process creates orphan foreign keys that do not relate to a primary key.
  - – Domain: The Transform process creates data values that are not in the expected set of output data values.
  - – Range: The Transform process creates data values that are outside the expected boundary of data values.
  - – Completeness: The Transform process creates a set of data with gaps in the data.
  - – Latency: The Transform process consumes so much time creating the data that the data arrives too late.
  - – Business Rules:
    - ■ Intrarecord Business Rules: Column A + Column B = Column C. The business rule exists entirely within each individual record.
    - ■ Intradataset Business Rules: Row 1.Column A + Row 2.Column A = Row 3.Column B. The business rule spans across records within a set of data, but still remains within the set of data.
    - ■ Cross-Dataset Business Rules: File 1.Column A = File 2.Column B. The business rule spans across sets of data within an iteration of transformed data.
  - – Instances of transformed data that violate the data warehouse business rules can be recorded and counted as individual instances of failure to meet the expectations of the ETL application.

■ **Business Intelligence (BI) Reporting**: The reporting tools provide the data that the customers expect to see. The data warehouse team cannot programmatically discern whether or not the data warehouse customers are seeing the data they want to see. The only way to know if data warehouse customers are seeing the data they want to see is to ask them. Anecdotal information is less objective than quantitative measurement. Instances of data warehouse customers receiving, and not receiving, the information they expect can still be recorded and counted as individual instances of the BI Reporting application.

■ **Customer Education**: Data warehouse customers must understand the meaning of the data in the data warehouse. This understanding sets the customer expectations of the data warehouse. Members of the business in the enterprise will come and go. Some will move from one business area to another business area. Each of these changes is another opportunity for a person to come into contact with the data warehouse for the first time. These are the people who will need to learn about what is, and is not, in the data warehouse. Although Customer Education cannot be counted as a success or failure of a data warehouse, Customer Education does contribute to the success of a data warehouse.

■ **Data Warehouse Education**: The data warehouse team must understand the meaning of the data in the business from the perspective of the customer. This understanding sets the customer expectations of the data warehouse team. The business side of the enterprise is always changing. The business changes in response to competitive, marketplace, and regulatory changes in the world that surround the enterprise. The data warehouse team should maintain visibility and awareness of these changes in the business. Some of these changes will require the data warehouse change to keep up with the business. Although Data Warehouse Education cannot be counted as a success or failure of a data warehouse, it does contribute to the success of a data warehouse.

■ **Return on Investment (ROI)**: Stability is a great asset in a data warehouse. A data warehouse that cannot absorb the intermittent changes in the business without significant rework or repair will be perceived as more of a cost component of the enterprise, rather than as an investment. By designing a data warehouse with sufficient flexibility, the ability to absorb intermittent changes in the business will increase the perceived ROI of the data warehouse.

The Data Model, ETL (Extract), and ETL (Transform) expectations should be measured programmatically. Data volumes and rapid throughput render manual inspection infeasible. Deming's third point (cease dependence on inspection) advocates a departure from manual inspection. So, rather than inspect data as it passes through the ETL application, or after it has arrived in the data warehouse, the data should be tested programmatically by processes that measure the data against business rules.[6] By linking measurement processes with data warehouse processes, the measurement processes will not be inadvertently forgotten.

ETL (Extract) business rules are used to measure the data extracted from the source system and, therefore, occur immediately after data has been extracted from the source system. ETL (Transform) business rules are used to measure the data derived by the ETL application and, therefore, occur immediately after data has been derived in the ETL application. The Data Model business rules are used to measure the data in the data warehouse and, therefore, occur after data has been loaded into the data warehouse.

Methods and Strategies

The Source System Analysis identifies the business rules that should reflect in the data received from the source system. The Target System Analysis identifies the business rules that should reflect in the data loaded into the data warehouse. Process measurement provides a means by which data is measured against business rules, identifying data that does not conform to its expectations. That's all well and good. But, what happens when you find one? How can a data warehouse respond to data that does not conform to its expectations?

The following methods and strategies are options, not mandates or best practices. Rather, the options listed below should be chosen based on the corporate management and culture surrounding the data warehouse. Data Quality methods that work well in one setting may fail in another setting. So, there is no one-size-fits-all in Data Quality. Rather, involve members of the business to gain their feedback, approval, and buy-in.

All the methods and strategies listed below include a reporting function. Every Data Quality methodology is a communication methodology. Errant data will never be addressed if no one knows about it. The business needs to know that the data warehouse team is aware of the errant data. It's one of those human psychology phenomena. By announcing the existence and presence of errant data, members of the business will perceive the quality of data in a data warehouse to be at least somewhat under control. But, if the existence and presence of errant data are not announced, business members who find errant data (and, yes, they will find it) will perceive that no one is communicating with them and wonder if the errant data that was discovered is the tip of the iceberg or the entire population of errant data. Invariably, business members will decide the errant data is the tip of an iceberg. Communication, therefore, can reduce the perceived (but not the real) volume and severity of errant data, and engender some level of cooperation in the treatment of errant data.

Data Stewardship

Applicable expectations:

- BI Reporting
- Customer Education
- Data Warehouse Education
- ROI

Data Stewardship is a strategy. A member of each business area included in the data warehouse is engaged to participate in the data warehouse as a Data Steward. This person must have a complete understanding of the business area, its data, processes, and people. A Data Steward must also be able to understand the concepts and philosophy of the data warehouse. Finally, a Data Steward must be able and willing to engage in the general oversight of the data warehouse. In general, a Data Steward is not only a liaison between the business and the data warehouse, but a champion of both the business area and the data warehouse.

A Data Steward participates in all communications between the business area and the data warehouse. Sensitive communications should go through the Data Steward before they are published to the business area. A Data Steward represents the data warehouse to the business area. By discussing the data warehouse with members of the business area, a Data Steward is able to bring the opinions and preferences of the business area to the data warehouse. A Data Steward represents the business to the data warehouse. By discussing the business with members of the data warehouse team, a Data Steward is able to bring the questions and concerns of the data warehouse team to the business area.[7]

When you find a Data Steward who is able and willing to champion the data warehouse to the business and the business to the data warehouse, treat that person with consideration and respect. Some suggest that Data Stewardship should include deliverables and responsibilities that are intended to keep a Data Steward accountable to the data warehouse. But, more often than not, a person who is willing to be a Data Steward will respond when treated as a friend—a friend of the data warehouse.

Post-Load Audit and Report Errant Data

Applicable expectations:

- Data Model

After data has been loaded into a data warehouse, programmatically query the data in the data warehouse. The SQL should test and validate that the data in a data warehouse conforms to the expectations of the data warehouse, which are outlined in the Target System Analysis.

Errant data should be reported to members of the business area who are interested in, or using, that subject area from which the errant data originated, and the data warehouse team. Reporting the errant data is intended to communicate the existence and presence of errant data. The process that created that data is the focus. By reporting data that contradicts the Target System Analysis, members of the subject area from which the errant data originated can help remediate the data, or at least just be aware of the errant data and its treatment. Remember, the individual data elements are not the focus. The focus is on the processes that populate the data warehouse—the processes not the data—, but we use the data to measure the process.

Plug in a Default Value and Report Errant Data

Applicable expectations:

- ETL (Extract)
- ETL (Transform)

When an errant data element is encountered, the portion of the data element that does not conform to its expectations can be replaced by a default value (Figure 8.2). The default value may have a specific meaning (e.g., no known value,

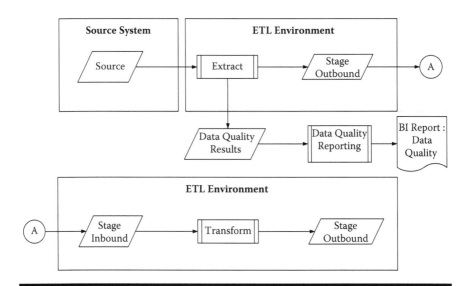

Figure 8.2 Default value.

rejected value, etc.). The data is allowed to proceed toward the data warehouse with the defaulted values in place of the errant values. This method is also known as a Soft Reject.

Errant data should be reported to members of the business area who are interested in, or using, that subject area from which the errant data originated, and the data warehouse team. Reporting the errant data is intended to communicate the existence and presence of errant data. The process that created that data is the focus. By reporting data that contradicts the Target System Analysis, members of the subject area from which the errant data originated can help remediate the data, or at least just be aware of the errant data and its treatment. Remember, the individual data elements are not the focus. The focus is on the processes that populate the data warehouse—the processes not the data—, but we use the data to measure the process.

Reject a Record and Report the Errant Record

Applicable expectations:

- ETL (Extract)
- ETL (Transform)

When an errant data element is encountered, the entire record or row may be discarded altogether. The remainder of the data is allowed to proceed toward the data warehouse, but without the rejected record or row. This method is also known as a Hard Reject.

Errant data should be reported to members of the business area who are interested in, or using, that subject area from which the errant data originated, and the data warehouse team. Reporting the errant data is intended to communicate the existence and presence of errant data. The process that created that data is the focus. By reporting data that contradicts the Target System Analysis, members of the subject area from which the errant data originated can be aware of the errant data and its Hard Rejection. Remember, the individual data elements are not the focus. The focus is on the processes that populate the data warehouse—the processes not the data—but we use the data to measure the process.

Reject a Dataset and Report the Errant Dataset

Applicable expectations:

- ETL (Extract)
- ETL (Transform)

When an errant data element is encountered, the entire set of data may be discarded altogether. No part of the data is allowed to proceed toward the data warehouse. This method is also known as a Hard Reject.

Errant data should be reported to members of the business area who are interested in, or using, that subject area from which the errant data originated, and the data warehouse team. Reporting the errant data is intended to communicate the existence and presence of errant data. The process that created that data is the focus. By reporting data that contradicts the Target System Analysis, members of the subject area from which the errant data originated can be aware of the errant data and its Hard Rejection. Remember, the individual data elements are not the focus. The focus is on the processes that populate the data warehouse—the processes not the data—but we use the data to measure the process.

Recycle the Data: In Place and Report Errant Data

Applicable expectations:

- ETL (Extract)
- ETL (Transform)

When management from the business area is committed to remediation of errant data in a data warehouse, this method facilitates that remediation (Figure 8.3). A data element that is subject to remediation can be recorded into two fields, rather than just one. The first field is the original errant data value. The second field is the defaulted data value. When a correct data value becomes available, that correct data value will overwrite the second defaulted data field. The first field, containing the original data value, is used only to find the correct data value. The second data field, containing the correct data value, is the data field that is visible to the data warehouse customers. The first data field that holds the incorrect data value is generally not available to data warehouse customers.

This strategy requires communication between the data warehouse team and the Data Stewards. The business person who is assigned the task of finding the correct data value must be included in the data warehouse team and its meetings and discussions. Contrary to Deming's focus on processes, rather than product inspection, a Recycle Wheel allows a data warehouse team to inspect, repair, and rework individual rows of data. A Recycle Wheel should only be used for data that merits the necessary overhead and involvement. If a Recycle Wheel is used indiscriminately for all Data Quality measurements, data that does not merit such treatment will taint the entire Recycle Wheel causing the Recycle Wheel to seem overdone and irrelevant. A Recycle Wheel, therefore, can be used to treat Data Quality measurements for only those data elements that merit such treatment, while all other

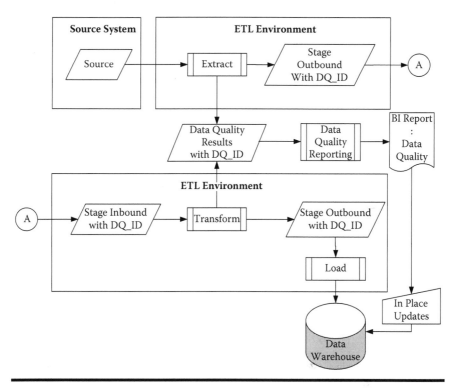

Figure 8.3 Recycle in Place.

data elements can be treated by another method. Such discriminate use of a Recycle Wheel will cast a connotation of relevance and value to those data elements that are treated by a Recycle Wheel method.

The cost of this method is the use of two data fields, regardless of whether or not any errant data is present. For every instance of that data element, twice the original data storage is consumed by this method. The benefit of this method is the fact that the nonerrant portion of the data is available, and remains available until or if a member of the business area provides the correct data value. In these situations, management (a member of the business area) may commit to participating in the treatment of errant data. The patience and priorities that make this participation possible often wane. When the business area management ceases to participate in the remediation of errant data, the remainder of the data is still allowed to add value to the data warehouse, and the default data values are not detracting from the value of the data warehouse.

Recycle the Data: Recycle Wheel and Report Errant Data

Applicable expectations:

- ETL (Extract)
- ETL (Transform)

When management from the business area is committed to remediation of errant data in a data warehouse, this method facilitates that remediation. A data element that is subject to remediation can be held in abeyance, away from the data warehouse, in a separate table. This separate table is often called a Recycle Wheel (Figure 8.4). When a correct data value becomes available, that correct data value will overwrite the errant data field in the Recycle Wheel. Then, the corrected record or row of data in the Recycle Wheel is forwarded to the ETL application to be included in the next iteration of data going to the data warehouse.

This strategy requires communication between the data warehouse team and the Data Stewards. The business person who is assigned the task of finding the correct data value must be included in the data warehouse team and its meetings and discussions.

The cost of a Recycle Wheel is the storage and maintenance cost of the table that functions as a Recycle Wheel. The benefit of a Recycle Wheel is the fact that data is allowed into a data warehouse only when that data is correct. Contrary

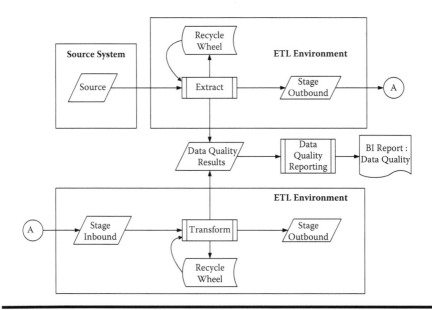

Figure 8.4   Recycle Wheel.

to Deming's focus on processes, rather than product inspection, a Recycle Wheel allows a data warehouse team to inspect, repair, and rework individual rows of data. A Recycle Wheel should only be used for data that merits the necessary overhead and involvement. If a Recycle Wheel is used indiscriminately for all Data Quality measurements, data that does not merit such treatment will taint the entire Recycle Wheel, causing the Recycle Wheel to seem overdone and irrelevant. A Recycle Wheel, therefore, can be used to treat Data Quality measurements for only those data elements that merit such treatment, while all other data elements can be treated by another method. Such discriminate use of a Recycle Wheel will cast a connotation of relevance and value to those data elements that are treated by a Recycle Wheel method.

The disadvantage of a Recycle Wheel is that management and, therefore, members of the business area quickly lose the commitment necessary to correct the data in the Recycle Wheel on a daily basis. When the management and members of the business area lose their commitment to the Recycle Wheel, the result is a Recycle Wheel that continues to grow larger as the data accumulates, and the data that is accumulating in the Recycle Wheel will probably never be loaded into the data warehouse, depriving the data warehouse of any value in that data.

Data Quality Repository

In the figures above, the boxes labeled Data Quality Results and Data Quality Reporting implicitly refer to a Data Quality Repository. A Data Quality Repository is a Fact table, or set of Fact tables, each documenting individual instances of data in the data warehouse that did not meet the expectations of a Data Quality measurement. The Data Quality function that performs a Data Quality measurement will record the results of errant data warehouse data in a Data Quality fact table.

Retention of Data Quality Fact rows requires two levels of planning. The first level of retention planning is true of all data in a data warehouse – How long should rows be retained? For a Data Quality Repository, the answer is usually based on the duration of time required to identify trends in the quality of the data in a data warehouse. How much data is required to identify and report individual processes that are out of control? The answer should be tailored to the individual process. A process that occurs annually will have different retention requirements from a real-time process. For each process, retention requirements are based on the data needed to monitor, triage, and treat the individual process. Retention requirements can be stated in the following:

- An absolute period of time (two months)
- A relative period of time (two months without a Data Quality incident)
- An absolute number of iterations (42 ETL cycles)

■ A relative number of iterations (42 ETL cycles without a Data Quality incident)

The second level of retention planning is specific to a Data Quality Repository – How many individual rows of data are required to cause someone to notice a Data Quality incident has occurred? When an ETL process completely breaks (e.g., files are out of sequence, a wrong file was used, a job was restarted incorrectly, etc.), do you really need 400,000 rows of Data Quality Fact table rows to know that something went dreadfully wrong? Probably not. In such situations, a Data Quality Repository needs only enough rows to triage the situation, and a summary row that is guaranteed to draw attention to the ETL process that broke. In other data warehouse Fact tables, the data warehouse team wants all of the rows. In a Data Quality Repository, however, when a single event causes an excessive number of rows to be inserted into a Data Quality Fact table, the data warehouse team may consider writing only enough rows to triage the process that is out of control.

Data Quality Fact Table: Dimensional Data Model

A Data Quality Repository should share Conformed Dimension tables with the Metadata Repository (Figure 8.5). This use of Conformed Dimension tables between the Data Quality and Metadata Repositories will enhance the ability of a data warehouse team to monitor individual instances of data warehouse processes and the quality of those processes. Therefore, if the Metadata Repository uses a

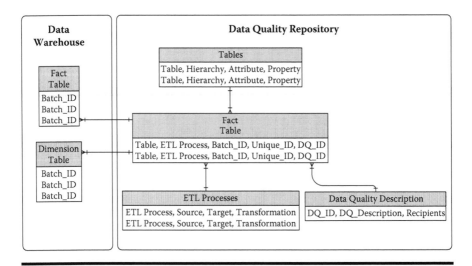

Figure 8.5 Dimensional Data Quality Repository.

Dimension Data Model, then the Data Quality Repository should also use the Dimension tables within the Metadata Repository's Dimensional Data Model.

By this approach, the tables unique to the Data Quality Repository should be the Data Quality Fact tables and any Data Quality Dimension tables that provide descriptions and look-up values to foreign keys in the Data Quality Fact tables. The remaining Dimension tables in the Data Quality Repository should be the Conformed Dimension tables that are shared by the Data Quality Repository and the Metadata Repository.

Data Quality Fact Table: Third Normal Form Data Model

The use of Conformed Dimension tables between the Data Quality and Metadata Repositories has a special significance for Third Normal Form Repositories (Figure 8.6). The data warehouse designer must design the Metadata and Data Quality Fact and Dimension tables so that they join at the same grains (Unit of Measurement and Hierarchy). The tables, ETL processes, Batch_ID, etc. referenced in the Data Quality Repository must match their corresponding references in the Metadata Repository. Otherwise, the data warehouse team's ability to monitor the data warehouse by joining the Data Quality and Metadata Repositories will be limited to the Dimensions that are Conformed Dimensions.

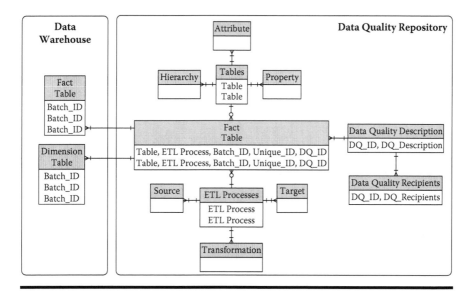

Figure 8.6   Third Normal Form Data Quality Repository.

Data Quality Reporting

Data Quality Reporting occurs by leveraging the BI Reporting infrastructures already present in a data warehouse. The list of recipients of a Data Quality Report is based on the DQ_ID. Those members of the enterprise and data warehouse team who have an interest in occurrences of a specific DQ_ID receive predefined reports, driven by a Data Quality Fact table, which are pushed to the DQ_ID Recipients.

Unlike conventional BI Reporting, Data Quality Reporting can have varying levels of repetition:

■ Following conventional BI Reporting design, a single Data Quality incident can be reported once with no follow up or repetition.

■ A single Data Quality incident that requires a follow-up action or resolution can continue to report until the follow-up action or resolution is complete.

■ A summary Data Quality report that measures the number of Data Quality incidents, responses to Data Quality incidents that require follow up or resolution can provide a high-level view of the quality of the data in a data warehouse.

Follow Through

Deming taught the real purpose behind process measurements was to identify processes that are out of control. The Data Quality Measurements discussed above are such process measurements. From the perspective of a data warehouse, there are two groups of processes that are measured: Source System and Data Warehouse processes.

The Data Quality measurements that measure the raw data from a source system are process measurements of the source system. The Subject Matter Experts (SMEs) of the source system will probably not believe or appreciate the measurements and results (when not favorable) of their source system. Regardless, the diplomatic mission of a data warehouse designer is to triage the Data Quality measurements.

On the one hand, the data warehouse designer may have misunderstood the data coming from the source system. The data coming from the source system may indeed be perfect and without error. The error may be in the data warehouse designer's understanding of the data coming from the source system. Such a misunderstanding could not be revealed until the ETL application began reporting Data Quality measurement results that were unfavorable. In such situations, the data warehouse designer must revise the Source System Analysis. The revision of the Source System Analysis ripples through the Data Model, ETL, Data Quality, and Metadata designs.

In another scenario, the source system has been modified. The Source System Analysis document, at the time of its writing, was correct. Since then, however, the source system has been modified, resulting in data that behaves differently than expected by the ETL application. In such situations, the data warehouse designer must revise the Source System Analysis. The revision of the Source System Analysis ripples through the Data Model, ETL, Data Quality, and Metadata designs.

In the last scenario, the source system has a bug. The Source System Analysis document is still correct and should not be updated. The SME of the Source System, however, has the task of fixing the source system. Data Quality measurements will continue to report results that indicate errors in the source system data. The challenges of this scenario are:

- Resist the temptation to ignore Data Quality measurement results from that source system. The identification and negotiation of a single Data Quality measurement does not mean that is the only error that can occur in a source system. Other source system errors can occur and be detected. Those additional Data Quality measurements should not be ignored.
- Communicate when the identified and negotiated source system bug is fixed. The source system SME may fix the bug and tell no one about it. The Data Quality measurements may continue to report the same bug manifestation. The data warehouse designer, unaware of the bug fix, thinks the Data Quality measurement results are still revealing the same source system bug, which apparently has not been fixed yet.

The second group of processes that are measured are the processes internal to the data warehouse. These processes, because they are internal to the data warehouse, are much easier for the data warehouse designer to triage and fix. All the processes are known and controlled by the data warehouse team. So, assessing the root cause and resolution of internal data warehouse processes can happen with much less negotiation.

In the life cycle of a data warehouse, the processes internal to a data warehouse must be addressed before any source system processes. Any flaws in data warehouse processes will be perceived (or at least accused) by source system SMEs to be the complete and total source of all data imperfections. In the case of a new data warehouse implementation, this is unfortunately usually more true than false. After the data warehouse internal processes have been fixed, so that data warehouse processes create no data flaws, the data warehouse designer is poised to address the source system. If after fixing the data warehouse processes, the source system is still creating data with flaws, the data warehouse designer can negotiate them with the source system SME. If the source system SME is willing to address the data flaws and fix the source system, then the data warehouse has realized an additional benefit to the enterprise beyond its purpose as a decision support system; the data warehouse has revealed errors in the operational applications of the enterprise. The fact that, at that point, the data flaws continued to occur, no one in the enterprise had known about or addressed the bug in the operational application that was creating the flawed data.

Closing Remarks

A data warehouse is intended to improve the decisions and processes of the enterprise. The data warehouse's contribution to the enterprise is muted by the presence of errant data. By focusing on a continuous improvement of the processes that create the data in a data warehouse, the data warehouse team and Data Stewards can mitigate the muting effect of errant data.

Errant processes in the ETL applications are the first processes to be improved. Once the ETL processes have been improved, the processes in the source systems can be addressed. As long as the data warehouse, through its ETL applications, continues to introduce errant data, the SME of the source system will point to the ETL applications as the sole source of errant data.

The first generation of Data Quality applications focused on mailing addresses and lists of names and addresses. Customer Relationship Management (CRM) continues to rely heavily on these first generation Data Quality applications to provide correct mailing addresses and consolidate duplicate names. These are difficult tasks. The Data Quality applications are available on the shelves of software stores and perform the CRM Data Quality functions very well.

The next generation, this generation, of Data Quality applications focuses on the data processes in a data warehouse. Following Deming's Fourteen Points, these Data Quality applications are intended to identify data warehouse processes that are out of control. Once identified, a data warehouse process that is out of control can be adjusted, and, once adjusted, that process will forward data to the data warehouse that meets the expectations of the designer and customers of the data warehouse.

References

1. W. Edwards Deming, *Out of the Crisis* (Cambridge, MA: Massachusetts Institute of Technology Center for Advanced Engineering Study, 1986).
2. Ibid.
3. Ibid.
4. Fon Silvers, Deming, data quality and ETL: Statistical process pontrol, *dataWarehouse.com* (2006).
5. Fon Silvers, Deming, data quality and ETL, Part 1: Point 3—Cease dependence on inspection, *DM Review* (2006).
6. Ibid.
7. Larry English, *Data Stewardship: Accountability for the Information Resource*, TDWI World Conference (The Data Warehousing Institute, Renton, WA, 2002).

Chapter 9

Metadata

Introduction

We all use Metadata daily (Figure 9.1). We may not be aware of it. But, we do use Metadata throughout the day. For example:

- The copyright date of this book tells us when this book was published.
- The timestamps on e-mail tell us when an e-mail was sent, received, and read.
- "Flammable" signs on the side of a truck tell us to be careful, and why.

Typically, Metadata is the weakest aspect of a data warehouse, not because Metadata itself is weak, but because we seldom associate metadata with, well, Metadata.

To understand Metadata, let's look at a few examples of the need for Metadata.

- On January 15, Fred ran a data warehouse profitability report, which showed the profitability of his business unit in the fourth quarter of the previous year was 12.7 percent. Fred's boss was thrilled by this profitability and asked Fred to drill down into the data to find the secret of their success. When Fred began to drill into the data, it was January 23, and, to Fred's shock and dismay, the profitability of his business unit in the fourth quarter of the previous year had changed to 3.1 percent. What changed? Why were the numbers different? If Fred's data warehouse had a metadata solution, Fred would know

259

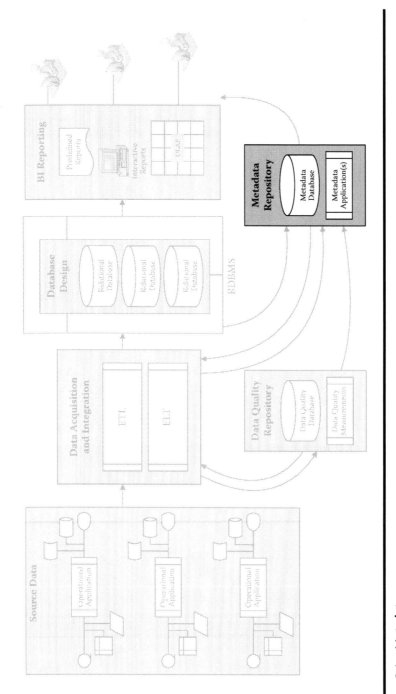

Figure 9.1 Metadata.

that fourth quarter labor payroll adjustments arrived in the data warehouse on January 16, drastically increasing the labor expense of his business unit.

■ Susan was a new internal auditor for a mid-size corporation. She had been assigned the task of auditing the Real Estate Department. The Real Estate Department had been getting their performance ratios from the corporate data warehouse. Susan, not knowing that she is expected to accept the data warehouse performance ratios at face value, asked how the performance ratios were derived. Without a metadata solution that explains this, the Real Estate Department had to find a programmer to explain the Extract, Transform, and Load (ETL) application and Business Intelligence (BI) Reporting application, which together derive the performance ratios.

■ Alice, the sales manager of a retail franchise, was alarmed when she ran the daily sales report from the data warehouse. The sales report showed a definite downward trend in sales in franchise outlets in southern California. If Alice's data warehouse had a metadata solution, Alice would have known that three of the franchise outlets in southern California were not able to send their sales data to the warehouse. Once these three stores were able to send their sales data, Alice was relieved. Had the data warehouse included a metadata solution, Alice would have been aware of the absence and arrival of the missing sales data.

Data about data. That's the textbook definition of Metadata. But, that doesn't really connote the ability to know what is and is not happening in a data warehouse, and when. The examples of Fred, Susan, and Alice demonstrate the need and application of insider knowledge of a data warehouse, of Metadata. Therefore, having understood the need to know what the numbers inside a data warehouse mean, when they didn't arrive and when they did arrive, the first question that must be answered is, "How?"

Types of Metadata

The answer to "how" begins by finding the answer to "what." What is Metadata and how can a data warehouse use it? The answer to what Metadata is begins with the two types of Metadata: Static and Dynamic.

Static Metadata

Static Metadata is information that does not change. Static Metadata provides the information about a data element that does not change. For all instances of a data element, the information in Static Metadata is always true. If a data element holds 400 rows, the information in Static Metadata is equally true for all 400 rows.

When a data element changes state (e.g., reviewed to approved to closed), the Static Metadata is specific to each state of a data element. The description of a Purchase Order in its Reviewed state is different from a Purchase Order in its Approved and Closed states. A single data element will have a Metadata description for each of its states. So, Static Metadata is more than a description of a column in a table or the table itself.

The audience of Static Metadata is the business side of the enterprise. Static Metadata provides the business meaning of a data element. That data element can be an entity in a Dimension table, an event in a Fact table, or a derived field in a BI Report. The information captured in Static Metadata should provide enough information about the business meaning and origin of a data element (i.e., entity, event, transaction, derived data, etc.) to equip the business side of the enterprise to use that data element. In the examples above, Fred, Susan, and Alice had data, but they were not equipped to use that data correctly. A Metadata solution frames its information in the language and context of the business, to equip members of the business to use the data from a data warehouse.

Static Metadata is everywhere. The nutrition information on food labels equips consumers with the information necessary to select and eat the food they want. The octane information on a fuel pump equips consumers with the information necessary to pump and burn the fuel they want. The table of contents of a book equips a reader with the information necessary to know whether or not that book might be of interest. Static Metadata equips data warehouse customers with the information necessary to select and use the data from a data warehouse that satisfies the business' data needs.

Dynamic Metadata

Dynamic Metadata describes each individual instance of a data element (Figure 9.2). A common form of Dynamic Metadata is a Load Timestamp field on each row of a table, which tells the moment, down to a subsecond, when each row was inserted into a table. Had Fred, in the example above, been querying data warehouse tables with Load Timestamp fields, he would have been able to isolate the rows that he had seen on January 15, and Fred would have been able to isolate the data that had arrived since that date. Without this simple Dynamic Metadata, Fred was unable to isolate what changed between January 15 and January 23.

For a time-variant data warehouse, Dynamic Metadata is extremely helpful. As entities change state, Dynamic Metadata includes:

- The moment the ETL application extracted the change of state from the source system.
- The moment the ETL application loaded the change of state into the data warehouse.

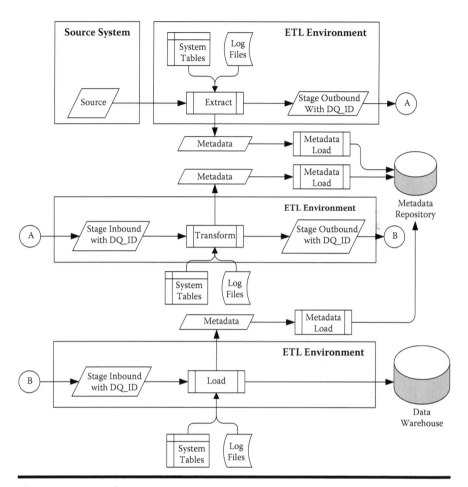

Figure 9.2 Metadata processes.

- The job number, start time, end time, and duration of the ETL job that extracted the change of state data.
- The job number, start time, end time, and duration of the ETL job that transformed the change of state data.
- The job number, start time, end time, and duration of the ETL job that loaded the change of state data.
- The name, timestamp, and version of the BI Report that Fred delivered to his boss.

As events occur, Dynamic Metadata captures:

- The moment the ETL application extracted the event from the source system.
- The moment the ETL application loaded the event into the data warehouse.
- The job number, start time, end time, and duration of the ETL job that extracted the event data.
- The job number, start time, end time, and duration of the ETL job that transformed the event data.
- The job number, start time, end time, and duration of the ETL job that loaded the event data.
- The name, timestamp, and version of the BI Report that Fred delivered to his boss.

These two sets of Dynamic Metadata look very similar for a good reason; both sets of Dynamic Metadata are describing the same thing—an update of a data warehouse. An update of a data warehouse is any action that changes any row in any table of a data warehouse. Thus, an entity-changing state is an update to a data warehouse, and an event record inserted into a data warehouse is also an update to a data warehouse. Both the entity change of state and the insertion of a new event row change the data warehouse. From the perspective of Dynamic Metadata, both are events that can be described by information specific to each data warehouse update event.

The dynamic part of a data warehouse is the ETL application because the ETL application creates and performs all the updates to a data warehouse. ETL applications, therefore, have the responsibility of gathering Dynamic Metadata and loading it into a Metadata Repository. The ETL application platform provides the source for some Dynamic Metadata in the form of a system clock, system tables, and log files. The ETL application will generate some Dynamic Metadata, probably the number of records inbound, rejected, and outbound, and others. Large data warehouse Relational Database Management System (RDBMS) platforms include system tables and log files that provide additional Dynamic Metadata. These system tables and log files are sources of Dynamic Metadata. So, there is no single source of Dynamic Metadata. The sources of Dynamic Metadata will change for every Source, ETL, and Target configuration. ETL application design should include functions necessary to retrieve Dynamic Metadata from available sources of Dynamic Metadata.

Metadata Service Level Agreement (SLA)

Metadata requirements are captured and documented in a Metadata Service Level Agreement (SLA). For Static Metadata, the Metadata SLA will indicate the features and layout of a data dictionary. The Metadata SLA will also document the methods by which data warehouse customers will be able to see the data in a data dictionary.

For Dynamic Metadata, the Metadata Repository will capture and hold metadata as it becomes available. The data warehouse team and Data Stewards will use the Metadata SLA as a place to document and agree on the Dynamic Metadata that will be loaded into the Metadata Repository; in other words, the Metadata SLA documents the metadata requirements. By including a Dynamic Metadata requirement in the Metadata SLA, the data warehouse team and Data Stewards agree:

- The Dynamic Metadata is available.
- An ETL application will retrieve the required Dynamic Metadata.
- Dynamic Metadata will be available to the business member, or application, that required the Dynamic Metadata in question.

Once the metadata requirements are identified and documented in a spreadsheet, the data warehouse team will know what metadata to load into the Metadata Repository.

Metadata Repository

Static Metadata describes each data element in a data warehouse and Dynamic Metadata describes each instance of each data element. In the language of Dimensional Data Modeling, Static Metadata is a Dimension and Dynamic Metadata is a Fact of a Metadata Warehouse. A Metadata Warehouse is a data warehouse that records the entities and events of a data warehouse, while the data warehouse records the entities and events of the enterprise. A Metadata Warehouse usually goes by the name Metadata Repository.[1]

Therefore, to go back to the original question, understanding the need to know what the numbers inside a data warehouse mean, when they didn't arrive and when they did arrive, the first question that must be answered is "how." The answer to "how" is a two-part answer. First, Static Metadata describes the meaning and being of data elements, and Dynamic Metadata describes the events (i.e., instances) wherein these data elements are updated. Second, Static Metadata is recorded as Dimensions and Dynamic Metadata as Facts in a Metadata Repository.

A Metadata Repository can exist in three forms. These three forms are not necessarily mutually exclusive. Elements of each can be used in conjunction with elements from the others. However, for purpose of discussion, the three forms will be presented as though they are mutually exclusive. When choosing a permutation of the three Metadata Repository forms, the form that is chosen should be instituted as a standard, to avoid confusion in subsequent and future data warehouse development efforts. Unlike the data warehouse, which experiences some design inertia force from the source system, a Metadata Repository does not experience any design inertia. Future data warehouse designers, who design using the Metadata Repository, will be tempted to interpret a Metadata Repository to their own preferences (even in the presence of design standards). Thus, a Metadata Repository, once established will benefit from the design inertia created by instituted design standards.

A Metadata Repository should include data elements, such as these listed here.

- Job number: The number assigned to a job by the application environment.
- Start date and time: The date and time at which the application environment began running the ETL application.
- End date and time: The date and time at which the application environment finished running the ETL application.
- Batch_ID: A sequential identification number assigned to a group of data by the ETL application.
- Rows/Records extracted: The number of rows or records retrieved from the source system by the Extract application.
- Rows/Records transform inbound: The number of rows or records passed from the Extract application to the Transform application.
- Rows/Records transform outbound: The number of rows or records that are allowed to leave the Transform application as load-ready data.
- Rows/Records transform rejected: The number of rows or records that are not allowed to leave the Transform application as load-ready data.
- Rows/Records loaded: The number of rows that were loaded by the Load application.
- Rows/Records load rejected: The number of rows that were rejected by the RDBMS during the Load application.

Central Metadata Repository: Dimensional Data Model

A centralized Metadata Repository can be designed as a Dimensional Data Model. The Static Metadata are the Dimensions. The Dynamic Metadata are the Facts, the events that update the data warehouse. The Dimensions in a Dimensional Metadata Repository are the:

- Tables: Source System table, Data Warehouse tables, Stage tables, and Lookup tables.
- Columns: The vertical fields in each of the tables.
- ETL Update Processes: Each individual process that updates a data warehouse.
- BI Report Processes: Each individual process that reads a data warehouse.

The Facts in a Dimensional Metadata Repository are the:

- Inserts: The instance of an event that inserts data into a data.
- Updates: The instance of an event that updates data in a data.
- Deletes: The instance of an event that deletes data from a data.
- BI Reports: The instance of a BI Report execution.

A data warehouse table is represented as a Metadata Dimension row. A data warehouse process is also represented as a Metadata Dimension row. A Metadata Fact row joins with the Metadata Dimension (table) and Metadata Dimension (process), and a Metadata Fact row joins with a data warehouse row by the methods discussed below (Figure 9.3).

A Central Metadata Repository uses a surrogate key (e.g., Batch_ID) to identify a group of rows. That surrogate key is placed as a foreign key in each row of a data warehouse table. The ETL application that transforms and loads the data warehouse, also calculates the next sequential surrogate key. That is the key that is placed in the data warehouse rows. The same ETL process also inserts a row into a Metadata Fact table. That Metadata Fact row should identify the data warehouse table, group of rows in that data warehouse table, and the ETL process that transformed and loaded them. A Batch_ID's only purpose and value is that of a primary key/foreign key, facilitating a join between a Metadata table and a data warehouse table. So, a Batch_ID can be physically stored in the most compressed format possible. Any data warehouse customer who queries a Batch_ID will find a sequential

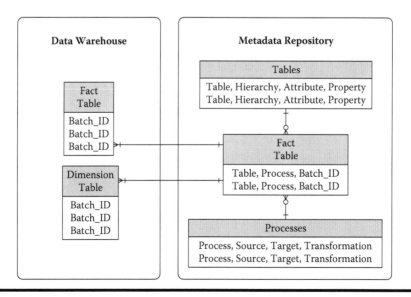

Figure 9.3   Dimensional Metadata.

number that has no meaning of its own. So, no concern should be given to the data value that will be seen by data warehouse customers querying the Batch_ID. Instead, the Batch_ID should be compressed to the smallest space possible, to reduce the overhead it creates on every row in a data warehouse.

A Metadata Dimension table identifies the source of data, target data warehouse table, and the transformation processes that created a batch of data. The identification of transformation processes varies in importance from one data warehouse to another. The formula by which financial figures (e.g., profitability, return on investment [ROI], net present value, etc.) are calculated may change over time. The identification of the exact formula that was used to calculate a number in the data warehouse may be valuable Metadata. Formulas for productivity, throughput, and customer queuing may also be valuable Metadata. The enterprise may need to know the exact formula that was used to derive a number can be important and valuable Metadata. For this reason, and other similar reasons, the identification of the exact transformation process that created a row in a data warehouse may be valuable enough to require its own Metadata. The identification of source data also enhances the data in a data warehouse. The inclusion of source data as a Metadata Dimension allows a data warehouse to directly associate data in a data warehouse with its source.

In all forms of Metadata Repository, the ETL application that writes data to a data warehouse table also writes data to Metadata Repository tables. An ETL application can identify itself and its attributes through hard-coded values, parameterized input variables, control tables, or any other mechanism by which self-defining data (e.g., program name and version number, job name and version number, etc.) can be fed into that ETL application. Once an ETL application knows its own identity (e.g., program name and version number, job name and version number, etc.), it can transform and load that information into a Metadata table.

An ETL application can also gather job statistics from generic platform tables. Typically, application and RDBMS platforms provide generic performance data (number of rows, central processing unit (CPU) cycles, inputs/outputs (I/Os), etc.). An ETL application can gather data from these generic performance tables and transform and load that data into a Metadata Repository. Job specific information can be derived by the ETL application as it transforms data. Information that an ETL application can gather or know about itself includes:

- **Self-identifying information**: Information that an ETL application can provide that defines and describes itself.
  - Program name: The name of the ETL application.
  - Program version: A sequence number that identifies a specific version of an ETL application.
  - Job name: The name of the ETL job.
  - Job version: A sequence number that identifies a specific version of an ETL job.

- Job Information: Information that an ETL application can derive from the application environment and the data passing through it. Job Information can be gathered and recorded at three different levels of granularity. At the most granular is every individual function or job. The second level is all the individual functions or jobs that comprise the Extract application grouped together as a collective Extract application (et al., for the Transform and Load applications). The least granular is the entire ETL application, with all its functions and jobs summed up into one statement of application activity.

Central Metadata Repository: Third Normal Form

A Third Normal Form Metadata Repository provides the same data as its Dimensional counterpart. At the center of a Third Normal Form Metadata Repository is a Fact table that captures the intersection of a data warehouse table, a group of rows in the table, and the ETL process that transformed and loaded the data.

A Third Normal Form Metadata Repository, like its Dimensional counterpart, is loaded in the same batch cycle that loads a data warehouse table. A Third Normal Form Metadata Repository, unlike its Dimensional counterpart, affords additional flexibility, which is the nature of Third Normal Form data models (Figure 9.4). A single ETL Process can be associated with multiple Transformations without losing its identity as a single ETL Process. A Dimensional Metadata Repository, by denormalizing the ETL Process and Transformation into a single row treats each permutation of ETL Process and Transformation as separate and distinct from other permutations of ETL Process and Transformation, even though both permutations may share the same ETL Process.

Both the Dimensional and Third Normal Form Metadata Repositories add value only as truly time-variant data models, specifically, Type II time-variant data models. The data in a Metadata Repository must provide the information necessary to see past iterations of data warehouse activity in their historical context. The data in a Metadata Repository references discreet events in a data warehouse.

Distributed Metadata Repository

A Distributed Metadata Repository (Figure 9.5) differs from a Centralized Metadata Repository by embedding the join between a data warehouse row and its Metadata Dimensions within each data warehouse row. Row-level Metadata using a Centralized Metadata Repository would effectively duplicate every data warehouse table as Metadata tables. Rather than double the capacity of a data warehouse, foreign keys that relate back to data warehouse Dimension tables are used in the Metadata Repository.

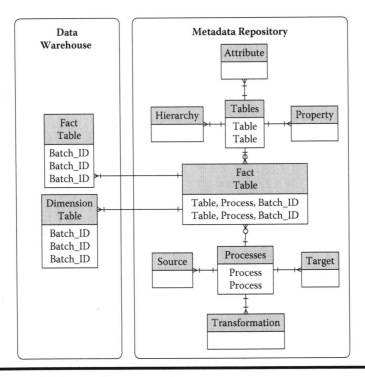

Figure 9.4   Third Normal Form Metadata.

A Distributed Metadata Repository based on a Third Normal Form data model typically includes associative (i.e., join) tables that consolidate each Metadata subject area. The primary key of those associative (i.e., join) tables is embedded in a data warehouse row. A data warehouse row could include foreign keys from each Dimensional entity; however, this approach tends to expand the storage capacity consumption of data warehouse tables. The primary key of associative (i.e., join) tables is often a sufficient compromise.

A Distributed Metadata Repository (Figure 9.6) can also include a Dimensional Metadata Repository. Each data warehouse row carries the primary key of a row from the Metadata Repository. A primary key/foreign key relation between Metadata Repository rows and data warehouse rows works best with surrogate keys.

Row-level Metadata tends to be most helpful when used in an Operational Data Store (ODS). The currency of the data in an ODS tends to make each row more immediate, focusing attention on the current activity of the enterprise. Row-level Metadata also works well if the volatility of rows in a table is relatively low, affording each individual row increased focus and attention.

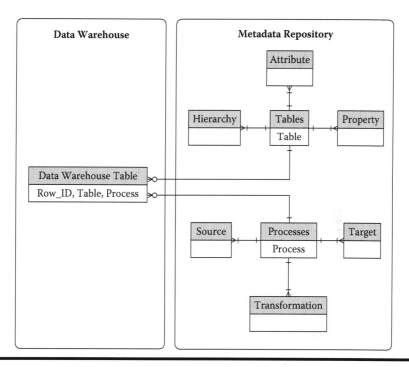

Figure 9.5   Distributed Metadata Repository.

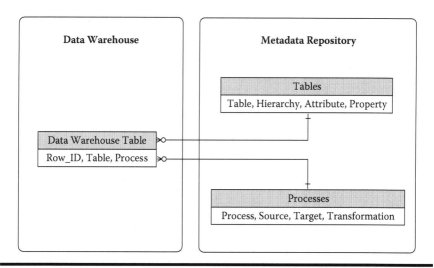

Figure 9.6   Distributed Dimensional Metadata Repository.

Real-Time Metadata

Real-Time ETL applications extract, transform, and load data into a data warehouse at the maximum throughput that can be reasonably maintained. The number of rows/records loaded at any one moment, therefore, is much lower than the number of rows/records loaded by a batch application that loads 24 hours of data in one job iteration. So, the challenge of capturing real-time Metadata is time.

If the true cycle of a real-time ETL application is six seconds (an iteration of ETL application every 6 seconds), then the Metadata might record 14,400 individual iterations of ETL application in a single day (10 6-second ETL iterations × 60 minutes in an hour × 24 hours in a day). Metadata requirements may indicate this level of granularity should indeed be recorded as Metadata.

The application environment may support continuous throughput without stopping and starting. ETL applications may use the continuous throughput infrastructure, which is real-time ETL. Metadata requirements must be very clear and precise in the presence of real-time ETL. Unless stipulated otherwise, data warehouse customers will expect real-time ETL to be recorded by real-time Metadata. If real-time Metadata is a true requirement such that the data warehouse customers can use real-time Metadata, the Metadata Repository and its applications can record the continuous throughput of ETL applications in real-time.

Data warehouse customers may not be able to use or leverage real-time Metadata. In that case, the Metadata Repository will superimpose a surrogate Batch_ID that will identify data warehouse rows received during a range of time (e.g., five seconds, five minutes, one hour) or other systemic event (e.g., Trade Cycle, Purchase Order, Activity Quota). The assignment of a surrogate Batch_ID must support the business in its needs to access data warehouse rows that were received via a real-time ETL application. Otherwise, data warehouse customers are left to search for a row of data like a needle in a haystack.

Data Quality as Metadata

The information derived by a Data Quality application is Metadata. Multiple Data Quality measurements can be applied to a single row/record of inbound data as it travels through an ETL application. Therefore, a one-to-one relationship cannot be implied for a row/record of data. Even more so, a one-to-one relationship cannot be implied for a batch of data. Thus, within the Metadata Repository, a Data Quality identifier (DQ_ID) can identify the permutation of Data Quality measurements and results that describes a batch of data.[2]

Data Quality Metadata can be captured in a Dimensional Data Model (Figure 9.7). Each individual row represents an individual permutation of Data Quality measurements, results, and meaning that should be interpreted by data warehouse

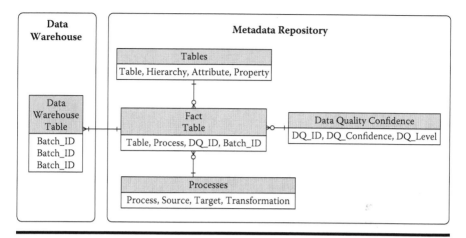

Figure 9.7   Data Quality Dimensional Metadata.

customers. The DQ_ID is embedded in the Metadata Fact table, which joins with the data warehouse table.

A data warehouse customer can find the level of Data Quality by joining the data warehouse table to the Metadata Fact table, and then joining to the Data Quality Confidence table. This level of information increases the data warehouse customer's ability to discern whether or not data from a data warehouse table should be trusted and, therefore, used to make decisions.

Data Quality Metadata that is captured in a Third Normal Form data model adds an additional level of granular flexibility (Figure 9.8). At its least granular, a Third Normal Form Data Quality table can be a normalization of the Dimensional Data Quality table. The tables that relate to the central Data Quality table can identify each individual Data Quality measurement and result, so that at its most granular a Third Normal Form Data Quality table resembles a Fact table chronicling every Data Quality measurement, result, and meaning that should be interpreted by data warehouse customers.

The end result of Data Quality Metadata is informed data warehouse customers. Not all data is perfect. Considering the volume of data passing through an ETL application into a data warehouse, inevitably some of that data will have imperfections. An ETL application cannot alter this reality. But, an ETL application can identify the instances when this reality occurs. In the examples at the beginning of this chapter, had Fred and Alice known the data in the data warehouse was incomplete, they might have calmed down and waited for the complete data to arrive. For them, and all data warehouse customers, Data Quality Metadata is a key component of the data warehouse.

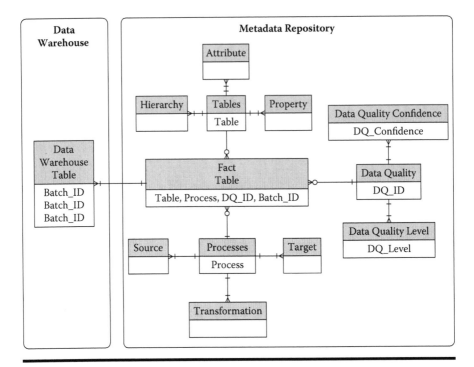

Figure 9.8 Data Quality Third Normal Form Metadata.

Make or Buy a Metadata Repository

The data warehousing marketplace includes a significant offering of Metadata Repositories. For new data warehouse development, these off-the-shelf applications deserve at least a review. These applications reflect years of experience, research, and development in Metadata Repositories. Since Metadata is usually the weakest element of a data warehouse, a review of Metadata Repository applications can only help.

On the one hand, a review of Metadata Repository applications can reveal the functions and features that have been deemed valuable enough to be included in a Metadata Repository. By understanding the meaning and purpose of these functions and features, a data warehouse designer can strengthen the Metadata design of the data warehouse under design. By taking this information back to the drawing board, a data warehouse designer can strengthen his or her own Metadata Repository design.

On the other hand, a review of Metadata Repository applications can reveal the scope and effort of a Metadata Repository. Considering the budgetary and timeline constraints of a data warehouse development effort, the purchase of a Metadata

Repository may be the optimal compromise. Delivering an off-the-shelf Metadata Repository is better than delivering no Metadata Repository, or a weak Metadata Repository.

Closing Remarks

Data about data. That is the textbook definition of Metadata. Yet, Metadata is so much more than that. Metadata is the information that provides the context and meaning of data. Metadata is also the least understood and most under-implemented aspect of data warehouses. By understanding the plight of Fred, Susan, and Alice, a data warehouse designer can understand how little information is available in the data of a data warehouse. For example:

- Sales = $54,234,293.23
- Manufactured Units = 43,524
- ROI = 14.4 percent

What do these numbers really mean? Can these numbers be trusted? When a data warehouse presents data such as this without a Data Dictionary to explain the numbers, without a context for these numbers, and without a confidence rating of the numbers, that data warehouse is not answering these questions.

Unfortunately, data warehouse designers and customers tend to think the meaning of the numbers corresponds to their personal interpretation of the name of the data field, and the context of the numbers is a perfect world where nothing goes wrong. These assumptions create risks for the data warehouse and the enterprise. These risks are significantly mitigated by a Metadata Repository solution.

References

1. Adrienne Tannenbaum, *Metadata Solutions: Using Metamodels, Repositories, XML, and Enterprise Portals to Generate Information on Demand* (Boston: Addison-Wesley, 2002).
2. David Marco, *Building and Managing the Meta Data Repository: A Full Lifecycle Guide* (New York: John Wiley & Sons, 2000).

Chapter 10

Data Warehouse Customers

Introduction

A data warehouse is like a highway. Both require significant investment. Both have a return on investment (ROI) that is so diverse as to prevent its quantification. Both have an almost infinite capacity to allow their cargo to pass through and yet a finite throughput. And, both will be used by a countless number of customers, most of who are currently unaware of the existence of either the highway or data warehouse. This is the challenge of a data warehouse, to meet the needs of myriad customers (Figure 10.1). Some do not yet know they need a data warehouse. Meanwhile, some have firm and concrete expectations of a data warehouse.

Back in the day, Decision Support Systems were small local databases with a single user interface. Joey from the second floor would bring a diskette up to the fourth floor to update the database. With that information and the ability to smell a shift in customer buying patterns, a manager would make the strategic and tactical decisions necessary to keep the business afloat. Since then, information has become a strategic weapon. The precision with which information is sliced and diced by all members of the enterprise has reached an art and science never seen by Joey from the second floor. The expansive use of information, shared with managers and workers on the line, has pervaded the enterprise to an extent not seen by Joey's manager. This new world of information was partially created by Decision

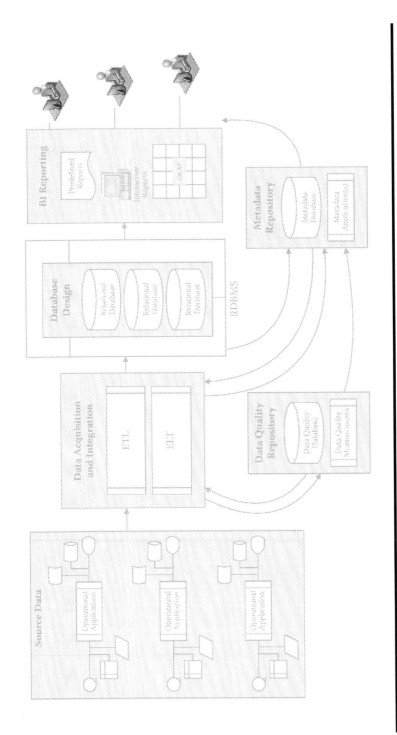

Figure 10.1   Data Warehouse Customers.

Support Systems, growing and integrating, growing and integrating, until some of them became a warehouse holding the data of the enterprise.

This growth of information from Decision Support Systems on the fourth floor to Data Warehouses used 24/7 around the globe is the context of Data Warehousing today. Today customers use a data warehouse through various interfaces, for multiple reasons, and all expect the same thing—subsecond response time. This expectation has been created by the information infrastructures that surround us today. Twenty years ago, everyone had to wait until the bank opened to find out whether or not a check had cleared; the delay was tolerated because it was expected. Ten years ago, a Web site without graphics required two minutes to load on a personal computer; the delay was tolerated because it was expected. Today, if an Internet-enabled cell phone experiences any delay downloading an online bank account, we feel unnecessarily inconvenienced. And then, we query a data warehouse and our expectations are framed in the twenty-first century. We expect subsecond response time, all 1,531 of us who just submitted a query.

For these reasons, a data warehouse team must profile the users of a data warehouse. The data warehouse team may never associate a name or face with a query. But, a data warehouse team can associate groups of people, groups of purposes, groups of usage patterns, and groups of expectations. A data warehouse team must at least try to profile the customers using the data warehouse. Like the highway, a data warehouse team may not know all the people using the data warehouse, but a highway engineer can estimate that 2.5 million cars and 1.4 million trucks and 500 military vehicles will use the highway in a year. Based on that sort of information—How many lanes? How wide will the lanes be? How much curvature and slope should the highway have? How steep can the highway incline? What speed limit? So, let's take a look at some of the customers of the data warehouse to see how they will use the data warehouse.

Strategic Decision Makers

These customers have the longest and strongest history with Decision Support Systems. Local Strategic Decision Makers want to see the trends and anomalies surrounding the enterprise. These customers have traditionally consumed historical data because all of history is leading to tomorrow, and they use historical data in their effort to be the first to see tomorrow.

To achieve this level of analysis, they need historical data using Type II Dimensions. They need to see historical data in its historical context. Their data warehouse, therefore, must be able to join Fact rows to their historical Type II Dimension rows. Since these customers are going to look for large and long-running trends, they will join the Fact tables with the data of greatest duration with the historical Type II Dimensions. In other words, they are going to join large Fact tables to large Dimension tables.

These customers will not use detailed granular data to see long-running trends. Instead, typically Fact data summarized to a less granular, less detailed form will provide the long-range information they need. This is fortunate because Summary tables perform better than Fact tables.

These customers are few, usually only the immediate subordinates of strategic-level executives. They understand their queries require a lot of churning. Therefore, fortunately these customers do not expect subsecond response time. They do, however, expect consistent response time within a tolerable (a few hours?) time frame. If they feel the data warehouse is not responding to their queries, these are the customers who can make their displeasure known.

These are not the customers who will sit and stare at an hourglass waiting for a query to return an answer set. Knowing their queries will churn a lot of data, these customers expect to submit a query, walk away, and come back after lunch (or maybe tomorrow) to the answer set. Given the toolset, strategic decision makers will submit their queries overnight so they don't have to watch an hourglass all day.

The bottom line is that these customers will join large Summary tables to Type II Dimension tables in large data volumes. But, they do not expect these queries to return a subsecond response time. In fact, these customers will wait until after lunch, or until tomorrow, to get their answer set back.

Tactical Decision Makers

Tactical Decision Makers have a history that rivals that of the Strategic Decision Makers. These customers began as the manager on the fourth floor with a single database with a single interface. They need the detailed data of their business area. They compile that detailed data into information. In the parable of "seeing the forest for the trees," data is the trees and information is the forest. These customers have always recognized the need for both data and information. They will do whatever is necessary to get the data and information they need. If the data warehouse does not provide the data and information they need, they will get it somewhere else.

Typically, these customers are not interested in the long-term trends of the Strategic Decision Makers. Also, they are not interested in the historical Type II Dimension or the entire enterprise. They are interested in the state of their business unit now. Their managers have given them tactical goals and objectives that will lead to achievement of a strategic plan. The tactical decisions these customers make require Type I Dimensions, which show the enterprise as it is now because that is where they operate—now.

Depending on each individual task, these customers may use detailed granular Fact tables or less-detailed and less-granular Summary tables. Fortunately, these customers will understand that Summary tables perform better and, therefore, will use Summary tables if detailed granular data is not required. But, when the task requires data sliced in a peculiar way (e.g., productivity by time of day, vendor delivery time minus scheduled time, throughput by machinist, etc.), these customers will not hesitate to use the large Fact tables to find what they need.

An enterprise will have many more Tactical Decision Makers. So, while their queries will have a relatively well-defined scope, more people will submit these queries. These customers need the data and information from the data warehouse within their business cycle. The window of opportunity to use the data and information from each query is short. So, their use of a data warehouse throughout the day consists of numerous focused queries in a rapid sequence, all within their business day.

The bottom line is that these customers will join large Fact and Summary tables to Type I Dimension tables in both large and small data volumes. They need these queries to return a subsecond response time, but will tolerate a subminute response time. These customers will submit numerous queries in a seemingly rapid sequence.

Knowledge Workers

Knowledge Workers are a relatively recent addition to the list of data warehouse customers. These customers have emerged as a logical progression in the world of Decision Support Systems, which began as a consolidated and consistent source of data. Data is the raw facts and figures of the business: How many, when, where? The raw facts and figures in Data provide a mostly objective view of the business, but only the business. Next, Decision Support Systems began to juxtapose and calculate Data to derive Information. Information is the set of observations and conclusions that can be drawn from the data. Today, Knowledge is the next frontier of Decision Support Systems. The search for Knowledge is the search for the science behind the Information. Science cannot always tell us why the universe works the way it does, but science can tell us how the universe works the way it does.

In the enterprise, Knowledge Workers are the explorers. They understand the enterprise and its business and they understand the data. Some would call them the Power Users. Within the business of the enterprise, these are the people to whom the business people turn for help understanding the data of their business. Knowledge Workers will use the data warehouse to maximize their ability to expand the knowledge base of the enterprise. Thus, these customers will use every feature and function within a data warehouse with no consistent pattern.

Knowledge Workers will occasionally need the data of the data warehouse reformatted to allow them to derive knowledge from the data warehouse. They may need data expressed in time intervals not included in the data warehouse. They may need data summarized by odd sets of attributes. They may need a Data Mart constructed specifically to answer a single question. Or, they may need a flat file of time series data for a Data Mining exercise.

Fortunately, Knowledge Workers understand that their potential to answer questions is directly linked to the data warehouse's ability to help them. The only way to make a symbiotic relationship succeed, such as this one, is by cooperation. For that reason, Knowledge Workers also understand how to cooperate with the data warehouse. These are the customers who know the members of the data warehouse team and their phone extensions. These are the customers who know which data warehouse team member to call in any given situation dealing with the data warehouse.

The bottom line is that Knowledge Workers will consume all aspects of a data warehouse with no consistent usage pattern. An enterprise usually has only a few Knowledge Workers. They expect a higher level of personal cooperation and they get it because Knowledge Workers are among the best allies for a data warehouse.

Operational Applications

The marriage of Data Warehouses and Operational Applications was driven more by politics and ROI than data. Considering that much of what happens in an enterprise is driven by politics and ROI, this marriage of Data Warehouses and Operational Applications is not surprising, and not all bad or all good.

The advantages of Operational Applications as customers are significant and real.

- A data warehouse team can point to their Operational Application customers as a real and tangible ROI for the enterprise.
- Leveraging the Extract, Transform, and Load (ETL) infrastructures of a data warehouse, the enterprise can increase the speed to market of new applications and decrease the infrastructure costs of new applications.
- A data warehouse team can point to its operational customers as a justification for continued and expanded investment in the data warehouse, which will benefit all the customers of the data warehouse.
- An Operational Application can cause a data warehouse team to increase the discipline and rigor of the data warehouse. By enforcing Data Quality Service Level Agreements (SLA), an operational customer can force a data warehouse team to achieve data quality service levels (e.g., latency, completeness, metadata, data quality, etc.) that had previously been lacking.

The disadvantage of an Operational customer is the syndrome of sitting with an elephant. Where does an elephant sit? Anywhere it wants. If an Operational Application has more clout, prestige, or ROI than the data warehouse, the members of the operational team will likely try to dictate how data will be stored in and reported from the data warehouse. At that point, the data warehouse is sitting with an elephant.

Unfortunately, this becomes a political discussion in the context of a Decision Support System. In these situations, the Data Warehousing Philosophy provides the guiding principles. A data warehouse is a nonvolatile, time-variant, long-term investment for the enterprise. The Operational Application will be replaced in five years (a normal application life cycle).

For these reasons, the marriage of Data Warehouses and Operational Applications best occurs in a Data Mart. The Operational Application can have their data in any form they want. The other data warehouse customers (Strategic, Tactical, and Knowledge) are buffered from the activity of the Operational Application. Without a buffer between Operational Applications and data warehouse customers, the Operational Applications will eventually gain the lion's share of design decisions and performance. When that happens, the value of the data warehouse to the enterprise has diminished.

The bottom line is that Operational Applications as customers can increase the ROI and visibility of a data warehouse causing a data warehouse to increase its rigor and discipline. Simultaneously, an Operational Application customer can be an elephant in the parlor. A data warehouse team must be careful not to allow an Operational Application to overwhelm the data warehouse.

External Partners

An enterprise will normally agree to share data with other enterprises or organizations. This data sharing can include marketing, productivity, or demographic data. Since a data warehouse has already gathered and integrated this data, a data warehouse is an obvious source of data for sharing with External Partners.

External Partners are the easiest of data warehouse customers. Their requirements are known and documented. The data they need can probably be generated by a batch job and distributed by another batch job. Any additional requests for data, because they come from outside the enterprise, must first be negotiated by enterprise management. This negotiation usually filters out frivolous requests.

Typically, External Partners are interested in the state of the enterprise as it is now. This means their queries will probably use the Type I Dimension tables, which consumes fewer resources than the Type II historical Dimensional tables. Also, External Partners are not given access to the detailed granular data of the enterprise. So, rather than querying the fine grain Fact tables, their queries will use Summary tables, which also consume fewer resources.

The bottom line is that External Partners are the easiest of customers. Their queries are predefined, optimized, and scheduled in batch jobs. This allows a data warehouse team to plan the queries for External Partners at a time and condition that has the least impact on other data warehouse customers.

Electronic Data Interchange (EDI) Partners

Electronic Data Interchange (EDI) Partners receive data from the enterprise on either a near real-time, or at least frequent batch, basis. Typically, EDI Partners are the suppliers and vendors in the critical path of a supply chain. EDI Partnerships streamline the speed to market and low overhead of Just In Time (JIT) manufacturing and distribution. Rather than wait until the enterprise needs 500,000 bolts, the enterprise periodically shares its consumption and balance on hand of bolts with an EDI Partner. On the other side of this data sharing, the EDI Partner agrees to monitor EDI data so the EDI Partner can deliver 500,000 bolts at the precise moment the 500,000[th] bolt has been consumed by the enterprise, rendering an empty bolt bin.

A data warehouse may be tasked with the responsibility of sharing data with EDI Partners. That assignment includes two functions. First, the data warehouse must be able to extract operational data from the source system at a frequency equal to, or faster than, the frequency of the EDI data sharing. If data is gathered every hour, sharing that data every 15 minutes makes no sense. Conversely, if the data is gathered every 5 minutes, then sharing that data every 15 minutes does make sense. Second, the data warehouse must be able to return an EDI query and distribute the result set at a frequency equal to, or faster than, the frequency of the EDI data sharing.

EDI Partners have precise and documented data requirements. Their queries are known, optimized, and scheduled. These render EDI Partners relatively easy customers. On the flip side, however, if a runaway query is allowed to consume the data warehouse Relational Database Management System (RDBMS), the EDI Partner will not receive the required data on schedule, which will defeat the whole JIT supply chain concept. That sort of visibility does not bode well for a data warehouse.

The bottom line is that EDI Partners can be a wonderful customer for a data warehouse. Their data needs are known, documented, and optimized. Their queries run on a schedule that is probably more frequent than any other customer. But, if a data warehouse is not able to support the required frequency then the data warehouse would be hindering, rather than helping, the enterprise achieve its business goals.

Data Warehouse Plan

A data warehouse does not exist for its own existence. A data warehouse exists to provide data information to the enterprise, its members, and partners. A data warehouse designer, therefore, must incorporate a plan to meet the data and information needs of the enterprise from the beginning of the data warehouse design, and carry that focus all the way through to the implementation of the data warehouse. A data warehouse comprised of 25 years of Type II time-variant Third Normal Form data is a truly magnificent testament to relational technology and design—and futile. In data warehousing, bigger is not better; rather, closer (to the customers' data needs) is better. Bigger is easier, but not better. In carpentry, this called "hitting a nail with a sledgehammer."

Strategic Decision Makers

These customers will join large Summary tables to Type II Dimension tables in large data volumes. But, they do not expect these queries to return a subsecond response time. In fact, these customers will wait until after lunch, or until tomorrow, to get their answer set back.

Strategic Decision Makers need Type II Dimension history data, going as far back in time as possible. They also need Fact and Summary tables that join well with the Type II Dimension history tables. The useful history goes only as far back as the shallowest table because the Strategic Decision Makers will switch back and forth between Summary and Fact tables as they investigate cause and nature of the trends and patterns they find.

For the Strategic Decision Makers, bigger is better because they are looking at the bigger picture. The ability to join Type II Dimension history tables will be key to their success.

Tactical Decision Makers

These customers will join large Fact and Summary tables to Type I Dimension tables in both large and small data volumes. They need these queries to return a subsecond response time, but will tolerate a subminute response time. These customers will submit numerous queries in a seemingly rapid sequence.

These customers don't need the overhead of a large Type II time-variant data warehouse. They need the speed and agility of a smaller Type I Dimensional Operational Data Store (ODS). By giving them a smaller, faster architecture, they will be able to answer the tactical questions they are asking. They are not asking strategic questions, and do not need strategic data to answer the strategic questions they are not asking. By segregating tactical data and tactical queries, they will not interfere with those who are asking the big strategic questions.

The ETL application feeding their Type I Dimensional ODS should operate in either real-time or near real-time (i.e., very frequent batch jobs). The smaller size of the ODS will make the frequent update cycle feasible. The frequent updates will provide the most current data possible.

Knowledge Workers

Knowledge Workers will consume all aspects of a data warehouse with no consistent usage pattern. An enterprise usually has only a few Knowledge Workers. They expect a higher level of personal cooperation and they get it because Knowledge Workers are among the best allies for a data warehouse.

Knowledge Workers need Type II Dimension history and granular detailed Fact tables. Knowledge Workers will use these tables directly for some of their analysis, but, for other analysis, they will use these tables to create Data Marts or datasets specifically for Data Mining efforts. This will allow them to create attributes and entities that don't yet exist from those that do exist. When helping them set up these Data Marts and Data Mining datasets, the important skill is listening, not so much to what they are saying they want, but the meaning of what they want. At that level of analysis, where few members of the enterprise are able to venture, even the Knowledge Workers can get one or two of the data elements wrong.

Operational Applications

Operational Applications as customers can increase the ROI and visibility of a data warehouse causing a data warehouse to increase its rigor and discipline. Simultaneously, an Operational Application customer can be an elephant in the parlor. A data warehouse team must be careful not to allow an Operational Application to overwhelm the data warehouse.

For Operational Applications, the keys to success are Data Quality and RDBMS performance. Unfortunately, an Operational Application is not going to respond to Data Quality confidence levels. So, the data warehouse team should diligently identify and repair any processes that are out of control. As processes are found to be out of control and repaired, the data warehouse team should communicate these developments with the operational team.

The required RDBMS performance is usually best achieved by an ODS or Data Mart. For each situation, the distinction is the data required by the Operational Application. If the ODS can meet the needs of the Operational Application, then a Data Mart is not required. If, however, the ODS cannot meet the needs of the Operational Application, then a Data Mart is required.

External Partners

External Partners are the easiest of customers. Their queries are predefined, optimized, and scheduled in batch jobs. This allows a data warehouse team to plan the queries for External Partners at a time and condition that has the least impact to other data warehouse customers.

Data for External Partners is usually provided via a batch job. The only challenge is to make sure the batch job that creates and delivers the data completes it by the required date and time.

Electronic Data Interchange (EDI) Partners

EDI Partners can be a wonderful customer for a data warehouse. Their data needs are known, documented, and optimized. Their queries run on a schedule that is probably more frequent than any other customer. But, if a data warehouse is not able to support the required frequency, then the data warehouse would be hindering, rather than helping, the enterprise achieve its business goals.

EDI Partners typically require the most current and up-to-the-minute data possible. The business cycles typically associated with EDI require that the data move very quickly. For these customers, the ODS is the only choice. An ODS has the current and up-to-the-minute data, and an ODS is able to return queries of simple to moderate complexity quickly.

Closing Remarks

All of these group profiles and data needs are based on a normal enterprise. Your enterprise may have some or none of these groups. Your enterprise may have all these groups, and more. The point is to plan for the groups of customers in your enterprise.

- What is their business function?
- What data and information do they need?
- How do they need that data and information delivered?
- What are the points of failure and success?
- How can the data warehouse avoid the points of failure while achieving the points of success?

Understanding the data warehouse customers in this way enables a data warehouse team to plan to meet the customers' needs and success points. All too often, data warehouse teams work diligently to build a data warehouse without accounting for the needs of the customers. In the twenty-first century, we can no longer get away with building a large database, expecting that if we build it, they will come. Instead, we have to build a Decision Support solution that is simultaneously close to the needs of the customers and close to the Data Warehousing Philosophy.

Chapter 11

Future of Data Warehousing: An Epilogue

Introduction

For years, Data Warehousing was the future of Decision Support. Now, as Data Warehousing enters its adolescence, we consider the future of Data Warehousing. Fortunately, Data Warehousing has proven itself scalable and flexible enough to have a future. Very few technologies pass their 10th birthday without rendering themselves obsolete. Data Warehousing has demonstrated the ability to maintain its core competence and support an ever-increasing Decision Support audience.

Scalability and Performance

The vendors who create Relational Database Management System (RDBMS) platforms for Data Warehousing continue to extend the possible data volumes, without a loss in query performance, in every budget range. Companies that can afford to invest multiple millions of dollars in RDBMS hardware will always be able to scale their data warehouse. But, for enterprises with lesser budgets, the ability to scale their data warehouse is more feasible every year. As scalability and performance improve annually, the feasibility of building and expanding a data warehouse in small- to mid-size companies continues to grow. As this trend continues, the information and knowledge available via Data Warehousing will become available to those same small- to mid-size companies.

Real-Time Data Warehousing

RDBMS and Asynchronous Transfer Mode (ATM) technologies now include the capacity to support a continuous stream of data for extended periods of time. With that capacity, RDBMS vendors give a lot of attention to Real-Time Data Warehousing. They advertise the ability to have up-to-the-moment real-time data in a data warehouse. For Real-Time Data Warehousing, the weak link is Extract, Transform, and Load (ETL). ETL applications are now catching up with RDBMS and ATM technologies. As the ETL applications catch up, the quality of real-time data will improve. For now, real-time ETL applications focus so much on the mechanics of moving a stream of data that they forget the basics and principles learned in batch ETL jobs. This gap is closing rapidly as real-time ETL incorporates more and more of the rigor and discipline of batch ETL.

When Real-Time Data Warehousing is seen as a peer among equal-yet-different Data Warehousing methodologies, data warehouse teams will be better equipped to weigh the cost, benefit, and return on investment (ROI) of Real-Time Data Warehousing. When that happens, data warehouse teams will be as confident assessing the need to not use real-time as they are assessing the need to use Real-Time Data Warehousing.

Increased Corporate Presence

Success begets success. Data Warehousing will become, to some extent, a victim of its own success. Data Warehousing has proven to be a stable and value-adding source of enterprise data. Thus, operational systems have begun, and will continue, to leverage the data in a data warehouse. This development saves the operational system from the overhead of gathering and integrating its own data. But, it foists onto the data warehouse the Service Level Agreements (SLA) promised by the operational system. And, it foists onto the operational system the gaps in data quality from the data warehouse.

Both environments, Operational and Data Warehousing, will realize this is not a short-term trend. Rather, this is the way of the future. They will learn how to mutually resolve their constraints. Data Warehousing will learn how to absorb the SLAs promised by the operational system. Operational systems will learn how to respond to Data Quality confidence levels and data remediation (e.g., delivery of missing data, repair of corrupted data, etc.). As they learn how to work together, Operational applications will be able to continue being operational, and Data Warehouses will be able to continue being informational.

Back to the Basics

While RDBMS vendors advertise their ability to scale a data warehouse ever larger, Data Warehouses continue to grow larger. The size and scale of Data Warehouses will continue to grow until they expand beyond their ability to meet the needs of the Tactical, Operational Application, and EDI customers. When that happens, data warehouse teams will go back to the basics, by reincorporating smaller Operational Data Store (ODS) and Data Mart solutions in their Data Warehouse. This will provide a solution to the Tactical, Operational Application, and EDI customers without impeding the improvements in Data Warehouse scale, size, and performance.

Data Quality

Data Quality is the next frontier in data warehousing. For the past decade, advances in technology have influenced the progression of data warehousing. Large data volumes, continuous throughput, complex application logic, and Web-based processes have expanded the scope and boundaries of data warehouses, which also increases the exposure to risks. The data warehousing community has done very well to assimilate technology changes.

In the coming years, the data warehousing community will strive to master the technology changes as they affect the quality of data in a data warehouse. When Structured COBOL and Customer Information Control System (CICS) screens were first introduced, they required an initial adjustment to assimilate their functions and features. Then, a subsequent adjustment occurred as programmers mastered Structured COBOL and CICS screens, which increased the quality and robustness of the resulting data. Likewise, the data warehousing community has begun to master the effects and impacts of recent technology changes. Soon, data warehouses will be able warranty the quality of all data, regardless of its source or the technology by which the source data arrived.

Bibliography

Agosta, Louis. *The Essential Guide to Data Warehousing.* Upper Saddle River, NJ: Prentice Hall PTR, 2000.

Barbusinski, Les, Chuck Kelley, and Joe Oates. What does granularity mean in the context of a data warehouse and what are the various levels of granularity? *DM Review* (2002).

Berson, Alex, and Stephen J. Smith. *Data Warehousing, Data Mining, and OLAP*, McGraw-Hill Series on Data Warehousing and Data Management. New York: McGraw-Hill, 1997.

Beyer, Mark. Personal communication, 2002.

Bisconti, Ken. "Integrating BI tools into the enterprise portal. *DM Review* (2005).

Deming, W. Edwards. *Out of the Crisis.* Cambridge, MA: Massachusetts Institute of Technology Center for Advanced Engineering Study, 1986.

Eckerson, Wayne W. The real value of BI search. *TDWI* (2007).

Elder, John F., and Dean W. Abbott. A comparison of leading data mining tools. *Fourth International Conference on Knowledge Discovery and Data Mining*, New York, August 1998, http://www.datamininglab.com/pubs/kdd98_elder_abbott_nopics_bw.pdf.

English, Larry. *Data Stewardship: Accountability for the Information Resource*, TDWI World Conference: The Data Warehousing Institute, Renton, WA, 2002.

English, Larry P. *Improving Data Warehouse and Business Information Quality: Methods for Reducing Costs and Increasing Profits.* New York: John Wiley & Sons, 1999.

Esteves, Bruno Miguel Craveiro, and Ricardo Miguel Bento Mateus. Data mining understand, model and learn—An approach to the management of data mining projects. *DM Review* (2004).

Harkins, Susan. Relational databases: The untold story. *ZDNet Australia* (2003).

Hay, David C. *Data Model Patterns: A Metadata Map*, Morgan Kaufmann Series in Data Management Systems. Amsterdam, Boston: Elsevier–Morgan Kaufmann, 2006.

Imhoff, Claudia, Nicholas Galemmo, and Jonathan G. Geiger. *Mastering Data Warehouse Design: Relational and Dimensional Techniques.* Indianapolis, IN: John Wiley & Sons, 2003.

Information Discovery, Inc. A characterization of data mining technologies and processes by Information Discovery, Inc. *DM Review* (2004).

Information Discovery, Inc. OLAP and data mining: Bridging the gap. *DM Review* (1999).

Information Discovery, Inc. The sandwich paradigm for data warehousing and mining. *DM Review* (1999).

Information Discovery, Inc. The top 10 data mining questions. *DM Review* (1999).

Inmon, William H. *Building the Data Warehouse*, 2nd ed. New York: John Wiley & Sons, 1996.

Inmon, William H. *Building the Operational Data Store*, 2nd ed. New York: John Wiley & Sons, 1999.

Inmon, William H., and Richard D. Hackathorn. *Using the Data Warehouse*. New York: John Wiley & Sons, 1994.

Inmon, William H., Claudia Imhoff, and Ryan Sousa. *Corporate Information Factory*. New York: John Wiley & Sons, 1998.

Inmon, William H., R. H. Terdeman, and Claudia Imhoff. *Exploration Warehousing: Turning Business Information into Business Opportunity*. New York: John Wiley & Sons, 2000.

Kimball, Ralph. *The Data Warehouse Lifecycle Toolkit: Expert Methods for Designing, Developing, and Deploying Data Warehouses*. New York: John Wiley & Sons, 1998.

Kimball, Ralph. A dimensional modeling manifesto—Drawing the line between dimensional modeling and ER modeling techniques. *DBMS* (1997).

Kimball, Ralph, and Joe Caserta. *The Data Warehouse ETL Toolkit: Practical Techniques for Extracting, Cleaning, Conforming, and Delivering Data*. Indianapolis, IN: John Wiley & Sons, 2004.

Lange, Kathy. Differences between statistics and data mining. *DM Review* (2006).

Lucado, Brandon. Aligning your BI environment with SOX internal controls. *DM Review* (2007).

Marco, David. *Building and Managing the Meta Data Repository: A Full Lifecycle Guide*. New York: John Wiley & Sons, 2000.

Marco, David. *Top 10 Questions to Ask/Mistakes to Avoid When Building a Data Warehouse or a Meta Data Repository*. Palos Hills, IL: Enterprise Warehousing Solutions, 2001.

Nisbet, Robert A. Data mining tools: Which one is best for CRM? Part 1. *DM Review* (2006).

Okell, Janine. Neural networks versus CHAID. *DM Review* (1999).

Olson, Jack E. *Data Quality: The Accuracy Dimension*. San Francisco: Morgan Kaufmann, 2003.

Parsaye, Kamran. Data mines for data warehouses. *DM Review* (1999).

Peco, Mark. *TDWI Data Warehousing Concepts and Principles: An Introduction to the Field of Data Warehousing*, TDWI World Conference: The Data Warehousing Institute, Renton, WA, 2004.

Pyle, Dorian. *Business Modeling and Data Mining*. Amsterdam, Boston: Morgan Kaufmann Publishers, 2003.

Reeves, Laura. *Dimensional Modeling Beyond the Basics: Intermediate and Advanced Techniques*, TDWI World Conference: The Data Warehousing Institute, Renton, WA, 2002.

Russom, Philip. TDWI: BI search and text analytics: Best practices in search. *DM Review* (2007).

Scofield, Michael. *Understanding and Reconciling Source Data for ETL and Data Warehousing Design*, TDWI World Conference: The Data Warehouse Institute, Renton, WA, 2002.

Silvers, Fon. Deming, data quality and ETL, Part 1: Point 3—Cease dependence on Inspection." *DM Review* (2006).

Silvers, Fon. Deming, data quality and ETL, Part 2: Point 5—Constant improvement. *DM Review* (2006).

Silvers, Fon. Deming, data quality and ETL: Statistical process control. *dataWarehouse.com* (2006).

Silverston, Len. *The Data Model Resource Book, Vol. 1.* Rev. ed. Vol. 1. New York: John Wiley & Sons, 2001.

Silverston, Len. *The Data Model Resource Book, Vol. 2.* Rev. ed. Vol. 2. New York: John Wiley & Sons, 2001.

StatSoft, Inc. CHAID analysis. StatSoft, Inc., http://www.statsoft.com/textbook/stchaid.html.

StatSoft, Inc. Data mining techniques. http://www.statsoft.com/textbook/stdatmin.html.

Tannenbaum, Adrienne. *Metadata Solutions: Using Metamodels, Repositories, Xml, and Enterprise Portals to Generate Information on Demand.* Boston: Addison-Wesley, 2002.

TDWI Data Acquisition: Techniques for Extracting, Transforming and Loading Data. The Data Warehouse Institute, Renton, WA, 2001.

Thousand, Cindy. Logical data modeling concepts. ed. Information Resource Management Unit of WisDOT: http://enterprise.state.wi.us, 2002.

Weik, Martin H. The ENIAC story—The world's first electronic digital computer was developed by army ordnance to compute World War II ballistic firing tables. (1961).

Index